THE NEW TESTAMENT CHURCH

Editorials of F.D. Srygley which appeared in the Gospel Advocate from 1889 to 1900.

Compiled and Edited by
F.B. SRYGLEY

GOSPEL ADVOCATE
A TRUSTED NAME SINCE 1855

Gospel Advocate Company
P.O. Box 150
Nashville, Tennessee 37202

The New Testament Church
Gospel Advocate Reprint Library Edition, 2001

© 1955, Gospel Advocate Co.
First Published 1910

Published by Gospel Advocate Co.
P.O. Box 150, Nashville, TN 37202
www.gospeladvocate.com

ISBN: 0-89225-478-5

PREFACE.

This book contains the editorials of F. D. Srygley on the New Testament church. These editorials appeared in the GOSPEL ADVOCATE from 1889 to 1900, and I give them in the following pages with but little change. The style is not, perhaps, what might be expected in a book of this character, as the editorials were hastily prepared and only intended for a weekly paper. So many calls have been made for some of these editorials in a more permanent form that I consented to make the effort to select and arrange them; and this volume is the result. There were but few more popular writers than F. D. Srygley, and few men had a clearer view of the New Testament church and undenominational Christianity than he. His position was assailed by a great many denominational papers and preachers. In this volume the reader will find almost every conceivable objection brought against his position, with the answer to the same in his own original way. And while the book might be improved in style as a literary production, it might lose in other ways; so I prefer to leave it just as he left those hastily written editorials and let it be what it claims to be in fact, the editorials of F. D. Srygley. True, there are many repetitions in the book; but it was by such that he impressed the truth on the minds of many people on this very important subject. "Precept upon precept; line upon line; . . . here a little, and there a little," is the way many were made to see the truth as it is taught in the New Testament.

The book will not be found as connected as it would have been had it been all prepared for one volume. But the reader should remember that it was prepared in paragraphs for the paper, and often the connecting links had to be omitted in the preparation of the book. While it may not read well as a book on account of this lack of connection, one can begin on almost any page and stop at any time and still find a complete thought.

The arranging of these articles has been a very pleasant and profitable task to me, and I pray that the reader may be as greatly pleased and benefited in reading the book as I have been in its preparation. The hand that prepared these editorials has been cold in death for more than nine years, and many of the readers who loved and admired F. D. Srygley have gone to their final reward; but it is to be hoped that others have taken their places in the church of the New Testament, and that they may be blessed and strengthened in undenominational Christianity by a careful reading of this book.

F. B. SRYGLEY.

Nashville, Tenn., March 17, 1910.

INTRODUCTION.

F. D. Srygley was a marvelous man. Notwithstanding he lived in this beautiful world scarcely forty-four years, he wrought a wonderful work for the salvation of the sons and daughters of men.

Some of his sterling characteristics were astonishingly strong. As a FRIEND, neither Damon nor Pythias, David nor Jonathan, was ever truer than he. Once, believing an innocent friend was about to be sent to jail, he sought permission to be sent with him and to stay with him as long as he might have to stay. The object of his last argument with a friend was to make that friend take money that each believed the other ought to have.

Though far from being a fanatic, he was an earnest, uncompromising Christian. He was neither stubborn, boastful, discourteous, nor unkind; but *nothing* could deter his defending what he believed it to be his duty to defend. He was a strong, fearless, gospel preacher —a stalwart man of God. He had convictions and the courage to defend them. It is scarcely necessary to say a man who has not is not much of a man; but F. D. Srygley was a MAN.

POWERFUL, because honest, earnest, intellectual, sincere, scriptural, and logical, *in the pulpit,* he was more and most potential *in wielding the pen.* He was a clear, concise, convincing writer. To say he was PEERLESS in his specific sphere is to speak the simple truth in disparagement of none.

The CHURCH QUESTION was his specific theme. He hoped to write a book on that theme—a theme that he studied as long as he lived. Death prevented his writing that book, however; hence we have, in its stead, only his *matchless editorials* on the subject.

From these editorials, his brother, Filo, has selected the contents of this book; hence, while I have neither read, examined, nor seen the collection he has compiled, I unhesitatingly commend the book, and bespeak for it an enormous sale and extensive circulation; for Filo himself is " a workman that needeth not to be ashamed," and, when selecting from Fletcher's editorials on the CHURCH question, he was selecting from a rich store of good things—and good things ONLY.

That this book may be a universal blessing is my earnest, sincere, fervent prayer.   T. B. LARIMORE.

THE
NEW TESTAMENT CHURCH.

THE CHURCH IN TWO SENSES.

The word " church " is used in two senses in the New Testament. Sometimes it means the congregation of disciples which comes together on the first day of the week to break bread and engage in other acts of public worship (Acts 20: 7; Rom. 16: 5; 1 Cor. 16: 19); sometimes it means the general spiritual body over which Jesus`is the head and in which every Christian is a member (Matt. 16: 18; Col. 1: 18, 24; Eph. 1: 22). In this general sense, the word is sometimes limited by a geographical term, as, "The church of God which is at Corinth" (1 Cor. 1: 2); "So the church throughout all Judea and Galilee and Samaria had peace" (Acts 9: 31, Revised Version). In this general sense, the church is not a denominational institution composed of a sisterhood of local churches " of the same faith and order," but a spiritual body composed of all Christians in the region defined by the geographical term of limitation, without any general denominational organization. In the sense of a congregation of disciples which comes together on the first day of the week to break bread and engage in other acts of public worship, there are several bodies of people " on earth now possessing the characteristics of churches of Christ as given in the New Testament." No one of these bodies perhaps possesses such characteristics in perfection. It is doubtful whether there is a church on earth which measures up to the divine standard in all of its members on every question of doctrine and practice so fully and faultlessly that there is no longer any room for improvement. The inspired measure of the stature of perfection is exceedingly difficult to fill, whether applied to a congregation of disciples or an individual Christian. There are many folks on earth now possessing the characteristics of Christians as laid down in the New Testament, but no one of them perhaps possesses those characteristics so fully and faultlessly that there is no longer any room for improvement. Christ is probably the only perfect specimen of Christianity this world has ever seen. For this reason the life of perfection which he lived in the flesh is the divine standard of individual Christian character toward which every disciple should strive, and the spiritual body of perfection over which he is the head and in which every Christian is a member is the divine model that every church should endeavor to reproduce in itself. In the one case, the sins and failures of the individual Christian do not enter into or mar the model set for us all in his life of perfection in the flesh; and in the other, the errors of congregations of fallible worshipers do not enter into or in any way affect the body of spiritual perfection set by inspiration and revelation in the New Testament for all churches to follow. Churches, like Christians, approximate the divine standard with different measures of success; but in no case, perhaps, has either a church or a Christian attained unto the absolute and faultless perfection set for us all in the divine model. In both cases the divine standard must be approached through many trials and tribulations by a tedious process of painstaking growth in grace and in the knowledge of the

Lord and Savior Jesus Christ. Owing to the difference
in degrees of earnestness and spiritual strivings with
which Christians and churches set about filling up the
measure of the divine standard, the progress in spiritual
attainments is by no means uniform. One star differ-
eth from another star in glory. So also does one Christian differ from another Christian in spiritual attainments. In like manner also one congregation of worshipers differs from another in the measure of its ex-
cellences when tested by the divine standard. It is difficult to find two Christians in exactly the same grade of
spiritual growth and developing at precisely the same
rate of spiritual progress. It is no less difficult to find
two churches equally near to the divine standard of spiritual perfection and approaching it at exactly the same
measure of growth in grace and in the knowledge of
the Lord and Savior Jesus Christ. Churches and Christians are continually outstripping and passing each other
in the race for heaven and immortal glory, and sometimes they meet each other going in opposite directions.
Churches have their backslidings and their fallings from
grace, as well as Christians. There is even an occa-
sional collision at the place where two churches or two
Christians meet on the road to heaven. God recognized
all these things in the arrangement of the Christian system, and left a wide margin for the free play of individ-
uality in both Christians and churches. On the New
Testament basis of individual activity and personal consecration in and through independent churches, the de-
velopment of individual Christian character and the
growth of an independent church are unhampered by
the restraints of general denominational institutions or
ecclesiastic organizations. But when local congrega-

tions are massed in denominational sisterhoods of
churches "of the same faith and order," the divine
standard and model are lost sight of, and the energies
of both churches and individual Christians are bent to
the attainments of the denominational standard. In
such cases the standard is erected and the model is set
for both the individual Christian and the congregation
of worshipers by the predominant sentiment of the denomination. The effect is the same, no matter whether
that sentiment is codified in a written creed, as in "the
method of the Methodists," or left unwritten, as in the
authoritative restraints of "Baptist usage" among the
Baptists, and the inviolate limitations of "our plea"
among the Disciples. In either case individual character and conduct, as well as congregational organization
and procedure, is measured by denominational standards. What it takes to constitute a Methodist is determined by one standard, and what it takes to make a
Disciple is determined by an entirely different standard.
In like manner, what constitutes a Methodist church
is ascertained by one test, and what makes a Disciple
church is determined by an entirely different standard.
A man can be a Christian without belonging to either
a Methodist church or a Disciple church, and a congregation of worshipers can be a church of Christ without going into the denominational organization of either
the Methodists or Disciples, or connecting itself in any
way with any kind of a denominational federation of a
sisterhood of churches "of the same faith and order."
Moreover, denominational institutions in religion are
hindrances to the spiritual growth of both the individual Christians and the congregations of worshipers
which constitute them, as well as wholly unwarranted

by the New Testament. This will appear from a careful examination of the practical workings of denominational institutions. When the character and conduct of an individual in such institutions measures up to the denominational standard, the person is passed as " in full fellowship and good standing." The holder of a denominational church letter is never rated any higher or any lower than that. When a denominational church measures up to the denominational standard, it is accepted as " of the same faith and order." A denominational church never gets a rating either higher or lower than that. The effect of this is to produce a soothing feeling of soporific religious contentment in both individuals and congregations on a plane of spiritual attainments that will pass the one as in " full fellowship and good standing," and grade the other as " of the same faith and order." There is no incentive for either individual Christians or congregations of worshipers to try to rise above the highest grade in the denominational institutions to which they belong. Hence, individuals under the soothing influence of denominational institutions slacken the restraints of their conduct to the lowest notch of " the rules of the church," and congregations of denominational worshipers broaden the gauge of their orthodoxy and dilute the strength of their spirituality to the last limit of their denominational standards of faith and practice. Moreover, the denominational standard itself, for both individual character and conduct and congregational faith and practice, being nothing else than the predominant sentiment of the denomination, is continually settling down to a lower and yet lower level of orthodoxy and morality as the denomination advances in age and increases in num-

bers. The predominant sentiment of a denomination
is the general average of the individual convictions of
its constituency. This gives all the errors in doctrine
and corruptions in conduct to be found in the constituency of the entire denomination their full force and effect in grading down the denominational standard of
doctrine and practice. Every denomination begins in
an outgush of individual consecration from some de-
cayed institution. In the beginning, therefore, every
member of the new denomination pitches his zeal on a
high key of spirituality. This necessarily gives each denomination a high standard of faith and practice to
begin with. The standard will never be elevated, for
the reason that no future converts to the party will be
lifted above the spiritual plane of those who take their
lives and their reputations in their hands to lead the
spiritual protest against the doctrinal errors and the
moral corruptions of the old institution. A stream
never rises above its fountain. On the contrary, future
converts will soon begin to fall below the high standard
of the new party in both doctrine and practice, and as
the general average of sentiment is graded from time to
time in the denomination, it will be found on a lower
plane each time than before. The predominant sentiment of the denomination each time the general average is struck will constitute a new denominational standard several degrees lower in doctrine and practice than
its predecessor. This gradual lowering of the denominational standards sets the whole drift of denominational institutionism toward the religious Dead Sea of
eternal spiritual stagnation. This is the logical cause
of the ever-recurring religious reformations, each of
which is but a protest against man's effort to maintain

the spirit of Christianity in unscriptural institutions. There is nothing of the kind in the New Testament. On the contrary, God, by inspiration and revelation in the New Testament, has set before each Christian and each congregation of worshipers a spiritual model of faultless perfection, and left no denominational standards or institutions to come, with soothing effect, between either the individual Christian or the congregation of worshipers and the standard of absolute spiritual perfection. New Testament churches, as well as individual Christians, were measured by the divine standard and graded according to their individual merits. See the first three chapters of Revelation.

TO BE A CHRISTIAN IS TO BE IN THE CHURCH.

The point has often been made in these columns that, according to the New Testament, one cannot be a Christian and not belong to the church, for the reason that the same process which makes one a Christian constitutes him a member of the church. The church is the household or family of God, and as such it includes and consists of all the children of God. (1 Tim. 3: 14; Eph. 2: 19-22; John 3: 5.) The church is the body of Christ, and every Christian is a member of it. (Col. 1: 18, 24; Eph. 1: 22, 23; Rom. 12: 1-5; 1 Cor. 12: 12-27; Eph. 4: 1-4; John 15: 1-10.) The *Baptist Helper* has compiled the following list of authorities in addition to the New Testament writers already cited in support of these propositions:

Alexander Campbell said: " We must live in the kingdom
or under the government of Jesus Christ if we would enjoy
the blessings of his reign." (*Millennial Harbinger*, Volume
II., page 53.) Moses E. Lard said: " There are two kingdoms on earth in which men exist—the kingdom of God and
the kingdom of Satan. The two kingdoms are separated by
one and the same line. All on this side are saints; all on
that side are sinners." (Cam. Ex., page 38.) J. A. Harding said: " Can a sinner be saved without entering the
church? I answer: There is no other way known." (Nashville Debate, page 38.) W. A. Inman said: " There is no
salvation outside of the church of Christ." (Sugar Creek
Debate.) Dr. J. R. Lucas said: " If I could go to heaven
without belonging to the church, I would go that way."
(Ash Grove Debate.) G. B. Hancock said: " There is no
other way under heaven to be saved except through the
church." (Verona Debate.) We might quote hundreds of
others; but, since they are all substantially agreed on this
point, it is unnecessary.

It may be remarked, in the light of this plain New
Testament teaching, that anything which a man can be
a Christian without belonging to is not the church of
the New Testament, and nobody ought to be a member
of it. Why should any one belong to anything which
he can be a Christian and go to heaven without being
a member of? Is it not enough for one to be a Christian while he lives and go to heaven when he dies?
Why should any one want to do more than this? God
has never required any one to be more than a Christian
while he lives or to try to do any better than go to heaven
when he dies.

THE PARTY THE NEW TESTAMENT APPROVES.

Some weeks ago the *Christian Preacher* challenged the statement made in these columns that "there is no religious party in the New Testament which does not include all Christians." The *Preacher* said that this statement "is incorrect." To avoid ambiguity, and if possible prevent a discussion where it was hoped that there is no real issue, the statement was "so amended" as to read: "The New Testament approves no religious party which does not include all Christians." In an editorial which will be found in another column of this paper the *Christian Preacher* declines to accept the amendment. What the *Preacher* engages to prove is that the New Testament approves a religious party which does not include all Christians. In that case the New Testament approves something besides the church, for the church confessedly includes all Christians. Then what is to be done with all those passages recently quoted from the New Testament in these columns to the effect that there is but one body, and every Christian is a member of it? The *Christian Preacher* fails to distinguish between approval of a party and indorsement of the truth. Wherever it finds people in the New Testament who contend for the truth against error on any subject, it calls them a party, and says that the New Testament approves the party because it indorses the truth they hold. Against that sort of a party I make no issue. Neither Paul nor any other writer in the New Testament condemned any man, or any number of men, for contending for the truth against error on any subject; nor do I. But those who hold the truth may, and often do, form themselves into a partisan brotherhood which does not include all Christians. Those who belong to that kind of a party speak of "our brethren" in a partisan sense, which they admit does not include all Christians. This is the kind of a party that I oppose and the New Testament condemns. If the *Christian Preacher* is disposed to defend that sort of a party, there is an issue between us; but the *Preacher* has no proof in the passages it has cited or anywhere else in the New Testament. If it declines to defend that kind of a party, the proof it cites may be pertinent, but there is no issue between us. In any case, there is no issue between me and the passages it has cited or anything else in the New Testament.

There was no "loyal party" in that church trouble at Jerusalem. There were Christians there who held the truth against error, but they did not form themselves into a partisan fraternity and speak of "our brethren" in a sense which did not include all Christians. The matter is not so clear as to "those Corinthians." Manifestly they did not go as far as "we as a people" have gone in forming themselves into a partisan fraternity or denominational brotherhood; but they went further in that direction than those who held the truth against error in that church trouble at Jerusalem, and probably far enough to come under Paul's condemnation as partisans. Paul's charge of carnality seems to apply to the whole church at Corinth; and if so, it covered those who held the name of Christ "as a party," for they were part of the church. If they were condemned at all, however, which is an open question, it was not because they held the truth against error, but because they corrupted and perverted the truth they held by forming themselves into a party and giving place to a partisan spirit. If they did this, they were condemned; otherwise, they were not. As to whether they were approved or condemned depends on whether they formed themselves into a partisan brotherhood. As to the next passage of scripture cited by the *Preacher*, those "who first trusted in Christ" did not form themselves into a religious party; neither did those who subsequently trusted in Christ, after they "heard the word of truth," form themselves into a religious party. Those who trusted first and those who trusted afterwards were all "one body in Christ, and every one members one of another." As to the next passage cited, those who were "not of them who draw back unto perdition" did not form themselves into a religious party; nor did those who drew back "unto perdition" form themselves into a religious party which did not include all Christians. The former constituted the church, which included and consisted of all Christians, and the latter drew back from the church, ceased to be Christians, and went to perdition. In the next passage that the *Preacher* cites, those who "went out from us because they were not of us." severed their connection from the church and ceased to be Christians. The "us" in that text was the body of Christ, the church, of which every Christian is a member. Does the *Christian Preacher* seriously think that the "us" in this text was a religious party which did not include all Christians, and that those who went out were Christians after they went out? The foregoing texts are the only passages the *Preacher* cites to prove that the New Testament indorses a religious party which does not include all Christians. So far as scripture proof is concerned, then, the case ends here; but it may

2

not be amiss to give some attention to a few other things in the *Preacher's* remarks.

Srygley admits that he cannot write on his favorite theme without using "we" and "us;" neither can he write on that theme without using such terms as "Methodist" and "Baptist." When he writes on any theme, he uses terms which designate the things he writes about. Why shouldn't he? He never uses quotation marks with "we" and "us" when those terms include himself; but when they stand for something he does not belong to, he knows no way to dispense with quotation marks without saying what is not true when he uses them. This whole business of "we," "us," "our brethren," "our people," "our movement," "our position," "our doctrine," "our cause," "our reformation," "our schools," "our papers," "our colleges," "our song books," "our Sunday schools," "our churches," "our preachers," "our publishing houses," "our books," "our tracts," "our Sunday-school supplies," etc., means simply a religious denomination, as clearly defined and as fully equipped with denominational machinery unknown in the New Testament as the Baptist denomination or any other religious sect. It dates its origin about the beginning of the present century under the labors of somebody somewhere, and traces its history and growth as a distinct religious party among all other religious denominations to the present time. In the way of denominational machinery, it has a foreign board, a home board, a woman's board, a negro board, a church building board, an old preachers' relief board, State boards, district boards, Sunday-school boards, and everything else that any other religious denomination has. A man can be a Christian, and a congregation of Christians can be a church of Christ, and as such can do everything that the New Testament requires without belonging to this or any other denomination in religion. No Christian and no congregation of Christians can belong to this or any other religious denomination without violating the plain teaching of the New Testament. Now this is the thing which has been masquerading as a religious denomination without a name in a land of dictionaries for more than fifty years under such vague terms as " we " and " us." Whenever I use such terms in a sense that by any reasonable construction can be understood to mean this thing, I resort to quotation marks in self-defense, because I do not belong to it. I do not object to " we " and " us " without quotation marks when they apply to myself and others who are laboring with me against sectarianism or anything else. I use " we " and " us " without quotation marks when they apply to myself and others in anything, even to the colored gentleman who works with me in the potato patch.

Those who propose to restore the New Testament order in religious work and worship should get a clear idea as to what that order is. There are in the New Testament three things—viz.: (1) Individual Christians. (2) Local congregations of Christians, called " churches of Christ." (3) The whole body of Christians, which is the church, or body, of Christ, and of which every Christian is a member. There is nothing else in the New Testament to restore. Whatsoever is more than this cometh of evil, and leads to something worse. The way to restore the New Testament order as to individual Christians is to preach and practice exactly what the New Testament teaches by precept and

example as to how a man is made a Christian and how
God requires him to live as a Christian. The way to
restore the New Testament order as to congregations of
Christians, called " churches of Christ," is to preach
and practice exactly what the New Testament teaches
by precept and example as to what it takes to constitute a worshiping assembly, called a " church of Christ,"
and how God requires such a congregation to conduct itself in all matters of religious work and worship. The
way to restore the New Testament order as to the body
of Christ, which is the church in a general sense, and
of which every Christian is a member, is to preach and
practice exactly what the New Testament teaches by
precept and example against all denominations or religious parties which do not include and consist of all
Christians. When individual Christians and congregations of Christians follow the plain teaching of the New
Testament, and withdraw themselves from all denominational federations and partisan brotherhoods and sisterhoods in religion, the whole denominational fabric
and institutional system will fall to pieces for the lack
of a sectarian constituency. This will restore the New
Testament order.

Of course we ought to differ from other disciples to
the full extent that they differ from the plain teaching
of the New Testament; but by what authority can we
or any other Christian belong to anything in religion
but the body of Christ, which is the church, and of
which every Christian is a member? To be sure, some
draw back now " unto perdition," and go " out from us
because they are not of us," and all that sort of thing;
but how can they get loose from us before they get out
of the body of Christ unless we are more particular than

God? Of course "they tear down what we build up;" but if we are working for God, they tear down what God builds up, too. As long as God can stand them we ought to "grin and endure" them. No man can have a brotherhood in religion which does not include and consist of all of God's children without acknowledging some other fatherhood than God. Every religious brotherhood which does not include and consist of all of God's children is the offspring of a purely denominational fatherhood, whether it traces its origin to John Wesley or Alexander Campbell

THE MASON AND DIXON'S LINE.

Several exchanges are using adjectives against "the effort by some to run a Mason and Dixon's line through the church of Christ." I am not worrying any on that point. I do not belong to anything larger than a local congregation in the way of a church organization, and it is entirely too far South to be struck by that historical old line. The idea to emphasize in this connection is that a man can believe on the Lord Jesus Christ, obey the commandments of God, and be a Christian without joining any *party, sect,* or *denomination,* in religion, and that the people of God—*Christians*—in any locality can form themselves into a church of Christ, keep all the commandments and ordinances of the Lord, and attend to their own business, *as a church of Christ,* without being a part of any general denominational organization or sectarian party in religion. And this principle applies on both sides of the Mason and Dixon's line and every other line in the United States and the rest of the world. Whenever "we as a people" begin to send men around over the country to "set in order" "*our churches,*" and "keep them set in order," *in the sense of a general denominational organization,* there will be trouble—I hope. All such efforts are unscriptural, and they ought to be opposed regardless of the Mason and Dixon's line or any other question extraneous to Christianity. I am not yet ready to assist in organizing "us as a people" into a religious denomination on the foundation of "our plea" for undenominational Christianity.

NO TIME TO WASTE EXPERIMENTING.

Do you think a man can be a member of the Baptist Church, or the Methodist Church, or the Presbyterian Church, or any other church of that sort, and go to heaven? Well, I have never thought much along that line. The Bible says nothing about such churches, and the preachers of all such churches tell me that a man can go to heaven without being a member of any of them. As the Bible and the preachers all teach me that I can go to heaven without joining any of these churches, I have never felt it necessary to inquire whether a man can be a member of such churches and still go to heaven. I'm not going to try it. I have no time to waste in trying such experiments.

IS IT NECESSARY TO JOIN A CHURCH?

Some.weeks ago I stated that "as the Bible and the preachers all teach me that I can go to heaven without joining the Baptist Church, or the Methodist Church, or the Presbyterian Church, or any other church of that sort, I have never thought it necessary to inquire whether or not a man can be a member of such churches and still go to heaven. I'm not going to try it. I have no time to waste in trying such experiments." The *Christian Advocate* (official organ of the Methodist Episcopal Church, South) says:

This is the coolest utterance that we have seen from any source. As there are many people, however, who think that it is possible for them to go to heaven from any of the churches, and as they may be mistaken on the subject, we suggest to the editor of the Advocate that he ought to look into it, so as to correct their views if they are in error.

I have not said " they are in error " in the sense that it is not " possible for them to go to heaven from any of the churches."

The Bible says not a word about such churches, and I am frank to say that I don't know whether " it is possible " for a man to go to heaven from any of them or not. But, as the *Christian Advocate* and all other religious papers, as well as the Bible and all the preachers, assure me that a man can go to heaven without joining any of them, I suggest that those " who think that it is possible for them to go to heaven from any of the churches " " ought to look into it, so as to correct their views if they are in error." The way that the Bible and the whole religious world assure me is perfectly safe, and which will lead to heaven, is good enough for me. If other people feel disposed to take the risk of an experiment along other routes, that is their business and their privilege. But I must say that, even if we

admit that " it is possible " to go to heaven from any of
such churches, I can't see why a man should strain himself to get to heaven by a route which the Bible says
nothing about. Can the *Christian Advocate* give any
good reason why a man should go to heaven by way of
the Methodist Church in preference to the route the
Bible clearly reveals? Or will it publish as much as a
column of plain statement of reasons why people *should
not* take the risk of trying to go to heaven by way of the
Methodist Church, if I can think of that many reasons
to state?

THE CURRENT REFORMATION NOT THE CHURCH.

Some weeks ago the *Christian Standard* said those
who are engaged in the current reformation and commonly known as " disciples of Christ," or " Christians,"
do not, in the aggregate, make up, or constitute, the
church of Christ. It is marvelous what a great com-
motion such an innocent-looking little statement has
produced. The usually clear-headed editor of the
"Texas Department" of the *Apostolic Guide* repudiates the *Standard,* and seriously asks what are we, anyhow, if not the church of Christ. The *Christian Leader*
rants over about all the ground between Campbell's
baptism and Gabriel's trumpet, pounding everything
that will make a fuss by way of opposing the *Standard*
on this question. True, the *Leader* does not, in so
many words, say we are the church of Christ; but it
says enough to show it has a small opinion of any man
who says we are not. Everybody seems to be either

hurling theological missiles of an argumentative character at random, or shying around logical corners, to dodge those thrown by somebody else. Would it not relieve the situation considerably if somebody would clearly explain: (1) Who are *we?* (2) What is the church of Christ? I have been thinking about the first of these questions, off and on, for years. I believe it was R. C. Cave who asked me, about six years ago, by what rules of measurement I located the lines and limitations around that *we.* I explained it to Brother Cave then—to my own satisfaction; but it is not so clear now. To get the exact "metes and bounds" of that *we* is a difficult problem. Suppose it is admitted that "*we as a people* constitute the church of Christ." What then? Am I one of the "*we as a people?*" Who is to decide that question? The *Leader* and the *Standard* could not settle it. They have never settled anything since I can remember. As to the second question, the *Standard* holds substantially that all who have been scripturally baptized and are living godly lives are members of the church of Christ. There are many who have been scripturally baptized and are living godly lives who are not counted with us. There are such persons in the Baptist Church, the Methodist Church, and in many other churches. Therefore, the *Standard* concludes we are not the church of Christ. The reasoning is good, the definitions seem correct, and the *Standard,* I think, is right. The question of apostasy enters into this problem. Men and churches apostatize. We do not know exactly the point at which God ceases to recognize a man as a Christian because of apostasy. We know Christians can apostatize, and we know God does not recognize apostates as Christians. The same is true of churches. What was the church of Christ while Paul lived ceased to be the church of Christ because of apostasy in the centuries after. But to determine the exact time when the Lord ceased to recognize it as the church of Christ because of apostasy would be impossible. God only knows that time. No church is at any time wholly free from apostasy. The mystery of iniquity is continually working in all churches. That God does bear with evil doers and continue to recognize a church as a church of Christ after it has committed some very grave errors, the Bible clearly teaches. That such errors, if persisted in and increased, will carry the church beyond the limit of God's forbearance and cause him to cease to recognize it as a church of Christ, is also clearly taught. But the exact point when it ceases to be a church of Christ because of apostasy no man can tell. From this point of view, therefore, it would be impossible to say "we as a people" compose the church of Christ. Many who yet remain among us as a people may have long since passed the limit of God's forbearance by apostasy. The safer plan, therefore, is for every man to "fear God, and keep his commandments."

WHICH DENOMINATION HAS THE LARGEST NUMBER?

"A sister asks" the *Baptist Gleaner* "which denomination of the two, Baptists and Methodists, has the larger number of members." The *Gleaner* says "the United States census is not yet in our reach," but according to the Baptist yearbooks the Methodists "will outnumber the Baptists a little." The Baptist yearbook is not in my reach. but the Bible is, and according to that book there were no such things as the Baptist and Methodist denominations in the world when the last New Testament writer went to his long home. (Acts 11: 26.) I don't see why they should be called either "Baptists" or "Methodists" nowadays.

THE KINGDOM.

The *Northwestern Congregationalist* has cut its denominational cables and launched out upon the open sea of undenominational religious journalism under the new name of *The Kingdom.* It has a good list of able editorial writers, and it proposes to "greatly enlarge its scope" and maintain a "correspondingly high order" of "literary and editorial" excellence. The most interesting thing about it, however, is its declared purpose to play the part of a harbinger of "a new movement" in religion. As an enterprising religious newspaper, the GOSPEL ADVOCATE proposes to comment from time to time on matters of interest in current religious literature, and to that end it quotes the following account of this alleged "new movement" from the columns of *The Kingdom:*

Times may have been in the last five hundred years when the best way to emphasize a forward movement in thought and life was to withdraw from the existing order of things and establish a form or organization or institution which would stand distinctively for the new movement. The Protestant reformation, the Puritan movement in England, the

Wesleyan movement, seem in the line of church history to have been of this nature. But clearly the time has now come when Protestantism must stop splitting itself to pieces. We have gone already beyond the limits of wise helpfulness. It is time for us to learn from abundant experience in the past four centuries the folly of more division. There is no surer way for any large spiritual movement to defeat itself than that it should repeat this tiresome process. It leaves things practically undisturbed, and narrows the field of its own mission. If there is any new movement in the time and the age that is worthy of any man's devotion to it, it is larger and profounder than that which should work its mission by the method of separation, withdrawal, or division. Let it, then, be clearly understood that any such notion is so foreign to any purpose of this paper and that for which this paper stands as to be fairly reckoned antagonistic to us. Anything of that kind is comparatively easy. A recent letter from a pastor says: "A thousand ministers are ready to follow the new movement whenever something definite in method is proposed." That is exactly the thing that will not be done.

Second, what is this new movement? There are those who believe that the voice of God is heard in this generation of Christendom, a divine call to those who bear the name of Christ, to justify the faith which they say is in them. It is not difficult to discover throughout the length and breadth of the churches of Christendom a magnificent discontent with that spiritual indolence and practical unbelief which none but the willfully blind can fail to see. The divine voice is nothing more than a call to "believe on the Lord Jesus Christ." It is nothing less.

In reply to the inquiry, "What is there new about this?" the answer is: It is hard to conceive of anything more startlingly and revolutionarily new than that Christendom should begin actually to believe on the Lord Jesus Christ and to obey him. Men are more ready to believe any conceivable number of things about him than to follow him even a little distance in the only way his feet ever took— the way of sacrifice. The cross is made an escape and a convenience instead of a call to follow. Theology is not blameless here. But the great fact with which we have to deal is the proud self-will and stubborn sin of men. It is against this self-will and sin, in the churches as well as outside, that the voice of this movement speaks.

From the foregoing general outlines of the "new movement" it is clear that one of the main features of it is to put the emphasis upon personal consecration and individual activity, rather than upon a new system of organization. In order to insure a personal following of the Lord in this new order of things, it is clearly announced beforehand that nothing "definite in method is proposed," or will be proposed. Those who "are ready to follow the new movement whenever something definite in method is proposed" are frankly notified that the movement itself is nothing less nor more than a protest against reliance upon things "definite in method," and a call to individuals to "begin actually to believe on the Lord Jesus Christ and to obey him." So far, so good. Along this line *The Kingdom* is not far from the first page of the GOSPEL ADVOCATE as a harbinger of a new movement. Howbeit, this sort of thing is not as new as *The Kingdom* seems to think. That movement is as old as the New Testament. It began with a "voice in the wilderness," went forward under the personal ministry of Jesus in Galilee, blazed out in full glory under the baptism of the Holy Ghost on Pentecost, and echoed down the ages to the close of the first century in the last expiring voice of New Testament inspiration. It is an old movement. The period of re-

liance upon things " definite in method " comes in between us and this movement led by inspired men over
eighteen hundred years ago. The " spiritual indolence
and practical unbelief " which characterize institutional
religion to-day have been accompaniments of dependence on things " definite in method " in religion in all
ages of the world. The individual zeal, personal consecration, and spiritual activity of the New Testament
period which the fires of persecution failed to quench
were effectually smothered by reliance on the definite
methods devised by " the proud self-will and stubborn
sin of men " in the ages of institutional religion which
come between us and the New Testament period. What
the religious world most needs to-day is a " new movement " to return to the old movement led by inspired
men in New Testament times. When religious people
cease to rely upon " things definite in method " unknown
in the New Testament, and set about believing on the
Lord Jesus Christ and obeying him in earnest as individuals after the manner of the early disciples in apostolic times, there will be throughout the world a re-
kindling of the flames of religious zeal and personal consecration which burned with such consuming fury in
apostolic times, but so hopelessly smoldered under the
rubbish of definite methods in the ages which followed
the period of New Testament inspiration.

The Kingdom correctly argues that a determination
on the part of each disciple to believe on and obey the
Lord Jesus Christ, if carried out, will solve all the religious problems of this age or any other age. The dis-
solution of religious denominations and the union of all
Christians in one spiritual body over which Christ is
the head and in which there is no schism are logical re-

sults of this personal following of the Lord. The kingdom of heaven will never come with observation or in outward manifestation till it rules by the Holy Spirit in the heart of every Christian to the subjugation of every proud self-will among the followers of the Lord. Partisans in religion may possess Christianity enough to go to heaven with a tight squeeze, but they will never have enough of the large-hearted love for God and mankind to inaugurate the millennium on earth, or do the will of God as the angels do it in heaven. No one who feels disposed to hang his harp on the willows and weep for the departed glory of Zion need look beyond his own heart for an explanation of the religious stagnation which continually rises as a stench in the nostrils of an insulted God. *The Kingdom* probes the right place when it throws definite methods to the winds and prods the individual conscience thus:

I am sure we Christian people, if we will be honest with ourselves, realize that there. is no adequate purpose in us absolutely to follow the Lord Jesus Christ. We know that we refuse to "fill up on (our) part that which is lacking of the afflictions of Christ." That is not a question to be argued. We know it. As for Protestantism, we know that we often worship our denomination more than we worship our God. We know that communities throughout the length and breadth of our land are rent asunder, and there is no proper communal life, because people prefer loyalty to their denomination to loyalty to the kingdom of God. If Protestantism will tell the truth about itself, it will acknowledge the charge brought against it when its jealousies and rivalries and prides are held up before it.

We are all ready to go to heaven, and we are all ready to pay any price for it, except one. We are ready to do anything to establish heaven on earth, except one thing.

We are ready to endeavor to go to heaven or establish heaven by means of enormous wealth, strong institutions, unceasing toil, countless edifices, all that can be done by increasing grandeur and wealth, social systems and laws, creeds and metaphysics, schools, richly endowed universities and seminaries that can command the service of the strongest minds—everything and anything but one, and that one is the only way that heaven can be won or the kingdom of heaven set up on earth—namely, the cross. When we are ready that all these things shall lose their life in order that their life may be the power of the cross of Christ, then a new social order may begin to be. It is to the establishment of that social order that the church of this age is called with a voice that can be neither purchased nor sneered nor frightened into silence. That one or more voices should become silent means nothing; a thousand would take their places.

Not much of a *new* movement that. It is a revolutionary movement only because of the wide departures of the whole religious world from the New Testament order of things. It remains to be seen whether even *The Kingdom* itself has the courage of its convictions. The man who follows Jesus must stray a long journey from the religionists of these modern times. It is much easier to promulgate principles than to follow them to their logical conclusion. Who shall be able to stand? Lord, help us all.

A denominational preacher, who seems to see a beauty of holiness in the new movement, writes to *The Kingdom* a suggestion that religious party leaders would do well to follow their convictions very leisurely and cautiously in this personal walk with God. His idea is that the wise course for those to take who hold favorable positions in institutional religion is to quench the spirit in themselves somewhat rather than surrender suddenly and completely to Christ, and walk off with God from their religious parties along the line of their honest convictions. Not to act thus prudently, he insists, is to lose a hearing in denominations and forfeit all opportunities to lead religious partisans into the light and liberty of undenominational Christianity. This is a very plausible obstacle in the way of many people who really feel inclined to believe on the Lord Jesus Christ and obey him along the line of their own convictions without regard to the doctrine or practice of religious denominations. *The Kingdom* editorially disposes of this difficulty in this way:

I should neither advise men to keep nor to abandon their pulpits. I do not think the preacher who really believes in God—that is, a God of the living and not merely of the dead—will be much troubled about this matter. We are all of us in certain positions in organized Christianity. So was Jesus in a position of organized religion, so was Paul, so was Luther, so was Savonarola, so was Wesley, so was Jonathan Edwards. But what you say about men always having been dependent upon some vantage ground of organized religion for a hearing is absolutely untrue to history. The men who have saved their hearing have always lost it. They have never been voices preparing the way of the Lord. They have never belonged to the party of the future. They have never laid the ax at the root of the trees of falsehood and wrong. I am astonished at your proposition that our first thought is to keep our vantage ground, when there is not a single instance in history—not a single movement for larger righteousness—in which the voices of the future have not gained their hearing through losing this very vantage ground of organized religion. There is not a single instance in which men have not had to lose their hearing in order to gain it. I suspect that the man whose first thought is to take care of his vantage ground may render service, but he will not be a prophet.

Our business is to preach the gospel of this "zeitgeist," to lay the ax at the root of the trees of social wrong, to prepare the way and declare the coming of the kingdom of Christ in a new social order. Whether we keep our pulpits or collegiate chairs or not is a matter with which we have absolutely nothing to do. It is simply none of our business. We are to preach wherever we are, without any consideration of whether the result will be our remaining in our positions or having them taken from us. I have no better vantage ground than you or my brethren. I have stood in jeopardy of my position every hour for the last three years. But it scarcely gives me a moment of concern. I say this because many of my brethren seem to feel, as you intimate, that I have some special vantage ground from which I may speak with impunity what others cannot speak. This is not so. We are to be altogether great enough to be unanxious about the morrow, and make ourselves of no reputation, if we are to be forerunners of the kingdom. We may, like Nicodemus, be borne along with the current of the kingdom's forces; but we will not prepare the way for the coming and work of those forces with the abandonment of self. If God is a living God, if his kingdom is coming to this and not some other world, if God is able to add two and two together and make four out of the result, then I think we need have no concern about what may become of us or how we shall get our hearing. I have repeatedly said within the past year that a thousand preachers of the gospel who were great enough to fail could regenerate the world.

Again, I have no method to offer, and I trust that God shall keep me strong enough to not yield to that temptation which is pressed upon me from every quarter of offering a modus. I offer only a spirit, an inspiration, a life. The fatality of the church is its unbelief in a living inspiration. The new social order, when it appears, will not come by what we call a "method." It will be a social regeneration.

It will be a unity, a communion of men in the Spirit of God. I think the very thing to be avoided as a delusion and temptation of the devil is this adoption of a method. We are not sent to organize, but to witness. There is but one organizing force, and that is the Spirit. We are not sent to construct, but to prepare the way of the order that has been constructed from the foundation of the world; to clear away the falsehoods, and the oppressions, and the traditions, for that eternally constructed social order, which is the holy city coming down out of heaven from God. Our work is not to construct, but to make way for God's construction, which is the government and union of men in the spirit of right. There is but one method—the method of the Spirit. Jesus gave no other method.

This effort to break the people away from reliance upon party organizations and institutional methods in religion unknown in the New Testament and encourage each one to put a personal trust in Christ and walk by an individual faith in God after the manner of the disciples in apostolic times is good, very good. But precaution should be taken to prevent the whole movement from exploding in zeal without knowledge. To this end the appeal should be constantly pressed upon the people to break camps and strike tents as religious partisans depending upon definite institutional methods unknown in the New Testament and march toward heaven and immortal glory as undenominational Christians; but at the same time every soul should be earnestly exhorted to walk with an open Bible in hand, and search the Scriptures daily, with an unceasing prayer for divine guidance and the wisdom that is from on high at every step along the way. In this way the people may be led out of the wilderness of partyism over the Dead Sea of dependence upon the definite methods of institutional religion unknown in the New Testament, and into the land flowing with the milk and honey of personal trust in Christ and individual activity in the work of the Lord. Let every soul sing: "I am bound for the promised land." "As for me and my house, we will serve the Lord." (Josh. 24 : 15.)

WHAT CAN WE LEARN FROM THE DENOMINATIONS?

The *Christian Standard* publishes a well-written article by John L. Brandt on "What Can We Learn from the Denominations?" Briefly put, his idea is that we can learn from the Catholic Church to respect the church, look after the poor, practice economy, and abound in charitable works of all kinds. From the Methodist Church he thinks we can learn zeal, business sagacity, revivalism, how to reawaken backsliders, how to care for new converts, and how to methodize missionary enterprises. From the Presbyterian Church his idea is that we can learn to properly appreciate law, conscience, duty, and an educated ministry. From the Congregational Church he thinks we can learn brotherly love and benevolence. The Episcopal Church, he says, can teach us dignity and propriety. The Baptists show us how to "cling with tenacity to our principles." The Christian Church teaches us sound doctrine, etc. After going over these items in detail and at considerable length, he puts the whole matter briefly in these words:

Thus it is that nearly every religious body presents some feature that is worth imitating; some idea that stands uppermost; some principle that guides, leads, and dominates her membership. This principle should stand out prominently as an inspiration to us, as an incentive to greater effort on our part—on the part of those who profess to *be right.*

If we could embody in one congregation the economy and charity of the Catholics, the zeal and business sagacity of the Methodists, the educated ministry and respect for law and conscience maintained by the Presbyterians, the brotherly love manifested by the Congregationalists, the tenacity of the Baptists, the dignity of the Episcopalians, a financial system as successful as that of the Mormons, the house-to-house visitation of the Adventists, the missionary zeal of the Moravians, and the doctrines of the Christian Church, we should have a model church—a church which would in a goodly degree be a reproduction of the ideal church of Christ.

This brings out with admirable clearness the theological scrap system of denominationalism in religion. No denomination embodies all religious truth, nor is any denomination without some truth mixed with a considerable quantity of error. The world looks almost entirely to denominations for religious instruction. Few people have yet grasped the idea that a man can be a Christian without being a partisan, or that he can learn the way of life without instruction from some denomination. The truth of God has been so widely scattered among the denominations and so adulterated with partisan error that the most painstaking student who undertakes to pick it out of the partisan tenets of modern times stands but a poor chance to get more than an insignificant portion of it, with almost a certainty of getting a vast quantity of denominational error mixed up with the little bit of genuine truth he is fortunate enough to discover. The chances are that the average seeker for truth among the denominations will swallow sectarian error enough with the first grain of good doctrine he gets from a denominational teacher to make him a religious partisan, and forever shut him up to the modicum of truth held by the denomination of his choice. Thenceforth he will chew the dry cud of partisan husks without finding truth enough in the sectarian straw which bigoted shepherds put into his denominational manger to keep his hungry soul from growing as lean as Pharaoh's famished cattle. Nor is there any remedy for this deplorable state of things so long as people seek only among the denominations for God's truth. It is manifest that all the truth which God has given to make souls fat cannot be found in any one denomination. It is impossible, therefore, for any soul to fully develop without grazing beyond the limits of any one denominational pasture. Nay, more: as each sect represents some truth, no man can find all the truth without familiarizing himself with all denominations, provided he seeks the truth only in denominational teaching. But there are few men who have time and opportunity to study the doctrines of all the denominations. Ordinarily, not more than three or four denominations out of the hundreds in existence are known in each neighborhood in the country, and probably not more than a score of them are usually found even in a whole city. The vast amount of truth that is represented by the denominations not known in a neighborhood or a city is inaccessible to the people of that neighborhood or city who seek truth only in denominational channels. But there are other obstacles in the way of the eclectic method of gathering truth from all denominations, even if every denomination could be made accessible to every soul. It is by no means certain that all the truth of God can be found even in all the denominations. Religious sects are still springing up all over the country every year, and each new party in religion seems to find and flourish some important truth not represented by any other sect heretofore. Who shall say, then, that there are not truths enough which cannot now be found in any party to make several new denominations yet? But even if all the truth has been divided among all the denominations, and each denomination could be made accessible to every soul, it would be very difficult, if not impossible, for a man to separate the truth from the error in each sect. The error in each denomination commended itself to the founders and supporters of the denomination. That is how it came to be mixed with the truth that is in the sect. Why, then, may it not commend itself to the honest seeker who undertakes to pick the truth out of all denominations, instead of seeking it at the fountain of inspiration, where it is uncorrupted by denominational error? If the world henceforth is to select the truth from each denomination and reject the errors of all denominations, the inevitable result will be the disintegration and collapse of all sects in religion without the loss of a single truth of inspiration, and the world might as well abandon all denominations at once and seek the truth of God in the Bible, where it can be found without any admixture of partisan error. No man çan hold the truth represented by all denominations and belong to any denomination. No denomination will allow its members to hold the truth represented by all the other sects in religion. The sum of it all is, therefore, that those who want all the truth of God and no error must keep out of all parties and hold fast the form of sound doctrine in religion as it is set forth in the Bible. The man who stands aloof from all sects and denominational doctrine and clings to the teaching of inspired men in religion has the whole truth of God unmixed with a single error. This has been aptly styled "the truth as it is in Jesus." The idea cannot be better put than Jesus himself put it when he said: "I am the way, the truth, and the life." "Thy word is truth." In the last paragraph of the article already quoted from, Brother Brandt hits the point exactly in these words:

While we are thankful for the many valuable lessons that we can learn from those not of our fold, yet let us study God's word, for we can learn all of these good things therein.

That is the idea exactly. No denomination can teach anything that is worth learning which the word of God does not teach, nor is there in all the Bible a single one of the blighting partisan errors each denomination mixes with the truth it holds. "I charge thee therefore before God, and the Lord Jesus Christ, who shall judge the quick and the dead at his appearing and his kingdom; preach the word." (2 Tim. 4: 1, 2.)

THE DOCTRINES OF MR. CAMPBELL AND THE DOCTRINES OF THE BAPTISTS.

The *Baptist and Reflector* proposes "soon" to publish "side by side the doctrines of Mr. Campbell and those held by us as Baptists." What difference does it make what doctrines were held by Mr. Campbell or "by us as Baptists?" While he is at it, why not publish side by side with the doctrines held by Mr. Campbell and "by us as Baptists" the doctrine held by the men who wrote the New Testament? Will people never learn to pass by all the doctrines held by all religious sects, parties, and denominations, and go to the New Testament, where God has stated his own doctrine?

WHAT THE CHURCH TEACHES.

By way of comment on a paragraph clipped from the *Cumberland Presbyterian* a few weeks ago, I said: " I am not specially concerned about what 'the so-called Christian Church, or church of the Disciples,' teaches, or Cumberland Presbyterians understand, on this or any other question. The main thing with me is to know what the men who wrote the New Testament understood and taught on all questions; and there is no 'so-called Christian Church, or church of the Disciples,' in the New Testament, nor are there any Campbellites or Cumberland Presbyterians in that book. When religious people begin to join each other and measure what they teach by what somebody else understands, I don't know what it means, unless it means that they have all lost the right way of the Lord." The *Cumberland Presbyterian* assumes that "Elder David Lipscomb" wrote what I said, and comments as follows:

Now we plead guilty to a degree of dullness which has always been a painful embarrassment, and doubtless it is due to this dullness that we can see absolutely no point in the foregoing paragraph. It was evidently designed to lead a troubled sister into the light, and we hope it has; but we are, nevertheless, sadly at a loss to comprehend what it means. Does it mean that Editor Lipscomb repudiates all churches, including his own? Does it mean that the organization of even his own church was an unscriptural proceeding? Or does it mean merely that nobody but the members of his church "knows what the men who wrote the New Testament understood and taught?" Really, what does it mean? Particularly, what does it mean as an answer to the question to which it purports to be a reply? Surely Editor Lipscomb is too old to learn the doubtful art of dodging.

It means that I repudiate all churches except the church of the New Testament, which includes and consists of all Christians. The organization of any other church is "an unscriptural proceeding," and to belong to any other church is in violation of the plain teaching of the New Testament. Does the editor of the *Cumberland Presbyterian* really think there is a Cumberland Presbyterian Church, a Christian Church, or church of the Disciples, etc., in the New Testament? Does he seriously believe Christians in New Testament times belonged to different sorts of churches after the manner of these modern times? Does he not know that all Christians in New Testament times belonged to the same church, and that it took all of them to constitute that church? When Christians organize or belong to denominational churches, they do something Christians in New Testament times did not do. There were no denominations in New Testament times, and there could be none now if nobody preached or practiced anything that was not preached or practiced in New Testament times. If Christians now will preach and practice nothing but what Christians preached and practiced in New Testament times, they will be nothing but Christians, and belong to nothing but the church, which is the body of Christ, and of which every Christian is a member because he is a Christian and as long as he remains a Christian. Is the editor of the *Cumberland Presbyterian* willing to do this? If not, why not?

NOT A MEMBER OF ANY DENOMINATION.

Some time ago I stated that "I am not a member of any *denomination* called 'Christians, or Disciples,'" and that "I have no more interest in, or connection with, any *party* in religion calling themselves 'Christians, or Disciples,' but not including *all* Christians, or disciples, than any other denomination in Christendom." And now the *Baptist Gleaner* says: "You say you are not a Methodist, nor Episcopalian, nor Presbyterian, nor Baptist, nor Campbellite, nor do you belong to any party in religion calling themselves 'Christians, or Disciples.' Where, in the name of sense, do you belong? Who are you, anyhow?" Well, I am Brother Srygley, a common sort of a Christian, or disciple of Christ, such as we read about in the New Testament, and I belong to the church of God, which includes "all Christians, or disciples of Christ," but which is not a denomination in any sense. How would it do, for instance, to say I belong where everybody else belongs who is simply a Christian such as we read about in the New Testament, and such as the *Baptist Gleaner* assures us any man can be without being a Baptist, or a Methodist, or a Presbyterian, or an Episcopalian, or a Campbellite, or anything else of that kind? If I rightly understand the matter, I "belong" where Paul, Peter, John, James, and all the rest of the Christians we read about in the New Testament belong—namely, to the church of God. I know it goes hard with the *Gleaner* to see a Christian keep out of sectarian pens and refuse to herd with denominational flocks, but it admits that the thing can be done, and my heart is fully set on doing it.

THERE WILL BE MANY BAPTISTS AND METHODISTS WHEN MR. SRYGLEY CEASES TO WRITE.

Brother Malone, the Baptist, so to speak, says, in a recent issue of the *Baptist and Reflector:* " There will be a great many Baptists and Methodists among us still preaching the gospel of Christ when Mr. Srygley ceases to write for the GOSPEL ADVOCATE." Possibly so, but there were no " Baptists and Methodists among us," as we might say, when inspired men ceased to write for the New Testament, and I don't see why there should be any now. The disciples were simply Christians in apostolic times if I rightly understand the Scriptures, and I don't see why they should be Methodists or Baptists now. Brother Malone and everybody else admits that a man can be a Christian and be saved without being a Methodist or a Baptist. Brother Malone can be a Baptist if he wants to, of course, but I think it will satisfy me to be a Christian while I live and go to heaven when I die.

WHAT WE TEACH.

The junior editor of the *Christian Messenger* thinks
"the worst thing of all" that has appeared in these
columns is the statement that "what we teach cuts
no figure in the case." He thinks the writer of these
paragraphs "has drawn some desultory conclusions
about what we teach and what the Scriptures teach,"
and says:

Brother Srygley does not seem to understand that it has
been our aim to speak where the Bible speaks and be silent
where the Bible is silent.

He also expresses the opinion that the editor of this
page "draws so heavily upon his imagination as to conclude that we teach one thing and the Bible a different
thing, and that it is a great sin to invite a man's attention to the doctrines we are contending for." The
brother further insists that "such great and good men
as Peter, Paul, James, John, Campbell, Lard, Fanning,
Lipscomb, Larimore, Wilmeth, Brents, Burnett, Creel,
Creath, and seven or nine thousand of others have taught
what we teach—the Bible, the whole Bible, and nothing
but the Bible." A little further on he says:

This loose-jointed, illogical, and sickly sentimentalism
is simply ruinous to every principle of right, and is in no
wise like the methods of the apostolic church. We will
have to call a halt, and cease to follow those fanatics who
are trying to lead the minds of the people away from the
pure teachings of the Scriptures; and if Brother Srygley
thinks that what we teach is of no more consequence than
what anybody else teaches, as he says, then he is in that
attitude that all lovers of Bible order envy not. This idea
that prevails in the minds of some that there is not much

of anything nor nothing in particular to be believed and advocated is entirely too indefinite for a basis of Christian union, or anything and everything that might perchance engage the speculative mind is by far of too much extent from side to side and from top to bottom to satisfy the lovers of Bible doctrines.

If the brother will read some in his Bible, he will discover that the Scriptures speak of the *doctrines* of men and the *doctrines* of devils, but the inspired writers never use the plural form of that word in referring to the *doctrine* which Christians should contend for. If " we speak where the Bible speaks," and in the way the Bible speaks, how does it come to pass that the junior editor talks about " Bible *doctrines* " and " the *doctrines* we are contending for?" This may not be " a great sin," but Brother Srygley declines " to follow those fanatics " who talk that way about it, no matter if there are " seven or nine thousand " of them.

" This idea that prevails in the mind of some that there is not much of anything nor nothing in particular to be believed and advocated " does not " prevail in the mind " of Brother Srygley. The idea that prevails in his mind is that everything " in particular " which is taught in the Bible is " to be believed and advocated," no matter if the junior editor of the *Messenger* does consider it " loose-jointed, illogical, and sickly sentimentalism." From the junior editor's list of " great and good men," Brother Srygley, therefore, very promptly selects Peter, Paul, James, and John as his leaders, and proposes to stand by all they (and the rest of the inspired men who wrote the Bible) teach, because they spoke as the Holy Ghost gave them utterance; but he declines to add " Campbell, Lard, Fanning, Lipscomb, Larimore, Wilmeth, Brents, Burnett, Creel, Creath, and seven or nine thousand of others " to the list of authoritative teachers, because they are not inspired. What inspired men taught may be, in the estimation of the junior editor of the *Messenger,* " of too much extent from side to side and from top to bottom," and " too indefinite for a basis of Christian union," but the editor of this page has no such objection to it. His idea is to unite on this basis himself, even if he can't get another soul in this wide world to accept it.

I agree with the junior editor that it is high time " to call a halt and cease to follow those fanatics who are trying to lead the minds of the people away from the pure teachings of the Scriptures," but the brother's idea that " *we* will have to call a halt " of that kind is impracticable. My idea is for every man to call his own halt. Why say " *we* will have to call a halt," as though one man had to call another fellow's halt? I have already called a halt myself, and the sooner the junior editor of the *Messenger* calls one, the better. The pity is that he didn't think to call that sort of a halt before he wrote that editorial against me because I halted and refused to meander all over creation after " doctrines we are contending for."

In the brother's list of " great and good men " who " have taught what we teach " are some advocates of what is commonly called " State work." If the " *doctrines* " taught by the brother's " great and good men " who are not inspired must be classed with the *doctrine* of Peter, Paul, James, John, and other inspired men, there is, therefore, no escape from " organized effort."

The senior editor of the *Christian Messenger* does not agree with the junior editor that " what we teach accords precisely with the Scriptures," so far as "State work" is concerned. In another column of the same paper in which the junior editor so sharply rebukes my "desultory conclusions about what we teach and what the Scriptures teach," the senior editor of that paper sets down a few "desultory conclusions" of his own concerning the "doctrines we are contending for" in the way of "State work." Speaking of the late State meeting at Dallas, he says, among other things:

It is no dishonor to be associated with these brethren in a social way, but it is damaging to a man's reputation for scriptural soundness to have connection with the ecclesiastical machine. . . . An ecclesiastical body like this State convention is wholly unauthorized by the word of God. But the Scriptures were very rarely mentioned in the proceedings of the convention. In fact, I believe it is the theory of the convention brethren that such assemblies as this State meeting belong in the list of necessary things not furnished by the Scriptures, but supplied by sanctified common sense. These brethren know that there was no such body in existence in the apostolic days. There was no convention of any kind for any purpose in that age. There was very little discussion in the convention. The old saints who used to call for chapter and verse were not in this meeting, and the brethren present were all of the same judgment in regard to those things they wished promulgated. The only friction in the convention was a little debate between Brother Bush and Brother McPherson on the subject of districts. Brother Bush thought this was the best way to reach the country churches that are opposed to State meetings, State boards, and State evangelists. Brother McPherson thought it looked too much like the Methodist system, and would bring down the thunders of the opposition, and he called it an ecclesiasticism. . . . Brother Bush was honest in his efforts to district the State. He was trying to make all things according to the pattern shown him in the Methodist Church, and the district conferences are part of the pattern. . . . My impressions of this convention are that it is traveling rapidly toward Babylon, and will, in a few years, have all the paraphernalia of a sectarian body. The brethren say and do things now that they would not have thought about doing ten years ago. They have permanent organization and permanent officers elected a year at a time, and the State convention is as specifically an ecclesiasticism as the Baptist denomination or Methodist Conference. The brethren are following Northern ideas and Northern men and patterning after sectarian plans and models, and have given up the Bible model. Those of us in Texas who advocate Bible order have only one course left, and that is to have no fellowship with this State machine, but go ahead in the course we have pursued in the past and do the Lord's work in the Lord's way, and let these erring brethren go to Babylon as soon as they can get there. They have already cut loose from our fellowship and the Guidebook of our direction and gone after strange gods.

It is easy to see from this that Brother Srygley has not " drawn so heavily upon his imagination as to conclude that we teach one thing and the Bible another," as the junior editor charges. Srygley has simply drawn on the *Christian Messenger,* and the *Christian Messenger* has drawn on the State meeting. Srygley's idea is that if " what we teach accords precisely with the Scriptures," as the brother declares, he will get it from the Bible without straining his imagination; and if the " doctrines we are contending for " are not in the Bible, he has no use for them. He, therefore, declines to drink from the branch when the spring is in such easy reach. He prefers to draw his religious faith from original sources of inspiration and seriously objects to " seven or

4

nine thousand " of " great and good men " getting between him and the Bible. If " Campbell, Lard, Fanning, Lipscomb, Larimore, Wilmeth, Brents, Burnett,
Creel, Creath, and seven or nine thousand of others have
taught . . . the Bible, the whole Bible and nothing but the Bible," as the junior editor so confidently
affirms, I don't see why Srygley should not be allowed
to teach it, too.

GET CHRISTIANS OUT OF THE DENOMINA-
TIONS.

I suggested some weeks ago that " the effort should
be to get Christians out of the denominations already
in existence, and not to build up another one of the
pestiferous thirîgs." Whereupon the *Baptist and Reflector* remarks:

" Get Christians out of the denominations already in existence " and into what? Why, into *the* Christian church,
of course, by which is simply meant the Campbellite denomination. That is breaking down denominationalism with a
vengeance.

The *Baptist and Reflector* is confused. I am making no effort to get Christians or anybody else " into
the Christian Church, . . . by which is simply
meant the Campbellite denomination." I am not
in it myself and I am doing all I can in my feeble
manner to get others out of it. My understanding of the New Testament is that all Christians are
in the church of God. The same things that make
one a Christian constitute him a member of the church.
When Christians get into sects, parties, or denomina-

tions, they are in something more than the church of
God. A Christian who belongs to the Baptist Church,
for instance, is in the church of God and the Baptist
Church both. The idea is to get him out of the Baptist
Church and leave him in the church of God. And if a
Christian is in "the Campbellite denomination," the
idea is to get him out of that denomination and leave
him in the church of God. The man who does what
God requires in the Bible, and nothing more, will be a
member of God's church and nothing else. Whenever
the Baptist denomination, or the Campbellite denomination, or any other sect, party, or denomination in religion undertakes to do anything not required by the
New Testament, the idea is for Christians who do not
wish to be partisans, sectarians, or denominationalists
to cut loose from it and stick to the Bible. That's the
way to get folks out of denominations without getting
them into anything else but the church of God. What
does the *Baptist and Reflector* think of it?

ALL CHRISTIANS ARE IN THE CHURCH.

To hammer constantly on one point is both tedious
and monotonous, but no man can drill a hole in a hard
substance without hitting many licks in the same place.
The point has been urged in these columns in season and
out of season for several years that the popular denominational idea that folks can be Christians without belonging to the church is contrary to the plain teaching
of the New Testament. The task has been hard and
laborious, but the results are beginning to appear in
many places. In a recent issue of the *Baptist Reaper*,

W. M. Rudolph, of Vienna, Ill., argues the point in the following words:

Now and then I meet one who says that he is not a church member, but that he is a child of God; and very often I hear expressions like this: "It does not matter whether you are a church member or not, just so you are a Christian." Not long ago I met a young lady who said that she was a Christian, but she never expected to join the church. Now, I am very far from believing or teaching the doctrine of church salvation, but I want to enter my protest against this Christ-dishonoring doctrine that "it does not matter whether you are a church member or not, just so you are a Christian." It does matter, and I will prove it. Jesus says: "If a man love me, he will keep my words;" "If ye love me, keep my commandments;" "Ye are my friends if ye do whatsoever I command you;" "Ye are my disciples if ye continue in my word;" "Let your light so shine," etc. No one will deny that baptism and the Lord's Supper are commanded. Christ's departing words were: "Go, . . . teach all nations, baptizing them," etc. As to the Lord's Supper, he said: "This do in remembrance of me." Again, it is admitted by all denominations, as well as plainly proven by the Scriptures, that baptism and the Lord's Supper are church ordinances. Hence, to properly obey these commandments, one must join the church. Jesus said: "Upon this rock I will build my church." Why did our Savior establish this church if there was no use for it? What is the church for? Did not Jesus make a mistake in setting up his kingdom? It is, indeed, useless if "it does not matter whether or not you are a church member, just so you are a Christian." It is an insult to the Lord Jesus Christ to treat his church in such a manner. It does matter, or Jesus would not have given it to his disciples and told them to go into all the world and baptize people into it. As a general thing, those who advocate this false doctrine are not very active workers in the cause. They usually boast of their self-righteousness, run the church down, when at the same time they know that it was at the church's expense, and in the church they heard the gospel salvation, the gospel that saved them (if they were saved). Is this treating the church right? I know of but one New Testament commandment that is obligatory on the nonchurch-member Christians, and that is: "Be baptized." All the other commandments are obligatory on the church member, and the command to be baptized is only obligatory on him when he has consented to be a church member. So let us not ignore a single one of our Lord's commandments, for it is by what we do that we show our love for him and his kingdom.

The brother does not yet see the point in the light of New Testament teaching, but he is thinking and arguing in the right direction. If he continues to study the New Testament along the lines of his present investigations, he will discover by and by that no one can be a Christian without belonging to the church. The church includes and consists of all Christians. The same process which makes a man a Christian constitutes him a member of the church. Those who are not members of the church are out of Christ, for the reason that the church is the body of Christ. (Col. 1: 18, 24; Eph. 1: 22, 23.) The church is the household or family of God. (1 Tim. 3: 14, 15; Eph. 2: 19.) No one can be a child of God without belonging to the household or family of God, which is the church. The same process which makes one a child of God constitutes him a member of the family of God, which is the church. A child does not have to join the family; it is born into the family. Just so a man does not have to join the church; he is born into the church. "Except a man be

born of water and of the Spirit, he cannot enter into
the kingdom of God." (John 3: 5.)

THE LOCAL CHURCH.

The *Church Register* takes up the mooted question
thus:

F. D. Srygley, first-page editor of the GOSPEL ADVOCATE,
says: "The New Testament approves no religious party
which does not include all Christians." The New Testament does not approve of any kind of "party," brother;
but the New Testament does approve of the local church,
which does not include all Christians.

F. D. Srygley recognizes and has often said that the
New Testament approves the local church, which does
not include all Christians; but he insists that it does not
approve a religious party larger than a local church, but
smaller than the whole body of Christ, which is the
church, and of which every Christian is a member because he is a Christian   What says the *Register* to this
proposition? The thing the New Testament does not
approve is a religious party made up of a sisterhood
of local churches "of the same faith and order," organized for religious work in a denominational brotherhood
which confessedly does not include all Christians after
the manner of "us as a people."

THE UNITED STATES CENSUS.

Several years ago I started out in all good faith to be
a Christian and obey all the commandments of God

without joining any denomination, championing any party, or becoming a sectarian in religion. It is a pretty hard thing to do, I admit; but I could get along reasonably well on that line if it were not for this everlasting United States census "round up" every ten years. These census fellows never can get the idea into their wooden heads that a man can be a Christian and yet not belong to any denomination. They seem determined to pen up the Lord's people in little denominational stalls, so that they may be counted, marked, branded, labeled, and waybilled for heaven and immortal glory in "original packages." They are after me now to get me into the pen with "us as a people," and they will put a party yoke on every man who will wear it. I am going to keep out of the party pen of "us as a people," if I can; but if they force me into it, by the blessings of God 1 will butt the cross fences all down if I can and get all those little denominational herds mixed so that there will be but one flock, with Jesus as the Shepherd.

BELONGING TO A DENOMINATION.

Baptist pastor John T. Oakley labors through more than three columns of the *Baptist Helper* trying to prove that "F. B. Srygley, Lipscomb, Sewell, and the rest of them belong to a denomination separate and distinct from other Christians," and rebukes the editor of this page for saying they do not belong to a denomination. Well, "F. B. Srygley, Lipscomb, Sewell, and the rest of them" say they do not "belong to a denomination" at all. They all say they are nothing but Christians, and that they belong to nothing but the body of Christ, or church of God, which includes all Christians. The editor of this page simply accepted their statement and took it for granted that they told the truth about it. But suppose Pastor Oakley succeeds in proving they have lied about it; what then? Does that prove that the Baptist denomination which Pastor Oakley belongs to is apostolic in origin, doctrine, and practice? Nay, verily. It only proves that " F. B. Srygley, Lipscomb, Sewell, and the rest of them " belong to an unscriptural and antiscriptural party in religion, and that they are no better than the Baptists in that respect. The fact still remains unchallenged that any religious party which does not include all Christians is unscriptural and anti-scriptural, no matter who belongs to it. This is the fact Pastor Oakley ought to tackle, or get out of the Baptist denomination. Putting the other fellow in the mud doesn't lift him out of the mire. Pastor Oakley admits that the Baptist denomination is a religious party which does not include all Christians. There is no such party in the New Testament. Indeed, all such parties are clearly and strongly condemned by the plain teaching of the New Testament. Suppose it be admitted, as Pastor Oakley argues, that " F. B. Srygley, Lipscomb, Sewell, and the rest of them belong to a denomination separate and distinct from other Christians; " what then? They are not the only men who belong to that sort of thing by any means. But Pastor Oakley will readily admit that a man can be a Christian and go to heaven without belonging to a denomination, and he evidently feels that he has scored a hard point against Srygley, Lipscomb, and Sewell in proving that they belong to a denomination. It is easy to see he thinks they

ought not to do it. But strange he can't see that his
gun kicks about as hard as it shoots on this point. He
himself is in a denomination, and every point he makes
against denominations pricks himself as severely as anybody else. But no matter who belongs to a denomination now, nobody belonged to one in New Testament
times. There was not a denomination in the world for
anybody to belong to when the New Testament was written. "F. B. Srygley, Lipscomb, Sewell, and the rest of
them" argue correctly in debating and preaching that
any religious party which does not include all Christians
is unscriptural and antiscriptural. They all say, also,
that they do not belong to any such party. Their arguments are unquestionably correct, whether their practice
is right or not. If they are not practicing what they
preach, they ought to stick to their doctrine and abandon
their denomination. But Pastor Oakley is wrong in
doctrine and practice both. He admits that he belongs
to "a denomination separate and distinct from other
Christians," and even tries to defend his position in
preaching and debating. However, his statement in the
article already referred to, that men like F. B. Srygley,
who decline to belong to or defend any denomination
in religion, "should be ignored in debate," indicates
that he is gradually coming to understand that denominationalism cannot be successfully defended against
undenominational New Testament Christianity. Of
course, those who belong to denominations can ignore
those who argue the teaching of the New Testament
against all denominations in debate if they want to.
No one can compel them to defend their position in debate or anywhere else. But in that case F. B. Srygley
and all other undenominational Christians will simply

continue to argue the question on its merits in preaching without an opponent. They can do it that way as well as in debate. They will divide time with denominationalists if any of them are willing to risk an issue in debate; but they will hardly get out a search warrant for an opponent, or abandon their ground and join a denomination to get opponents who have fled the field to come out of the woods and continue the debate.

ON GOSPEL GROUND.

"In our opinion," says the *Baptist Gleaner,* "Srygley makes out a pretty good case in his favor, because he seems to be on gospel grounds in what he says of himself, and it is probable that his principal mistake is in his religious identity at present. Instead of being content with his attainments as a Christian, he has united himself to the Campbellite Church, and is a Campbellite. In this relation he is directly opposed to his own experience; and his efforts to preach the simple story of the cross for the salvation of men are paralyzed by his Campbellite system of faith. It is his duty to leave the Campbellites at once; and if he wishes to secure a fellowship that will be the most scriptural, the most ancient, the most Christlike, the most congenial to a genuine Christian man, he should at once apply to the Baptists and receive gospel baptism at their hands, and enjoy the genuine freedom of a Christian indeed." All this is very well in its way; but what I am driving at is to be a Christian without being a Methodist, Baptist, Presbyterian, Episcopalian, Campbellite, or anything else in the way of a denominationalist. Everybody says the thing can be done, and my heart is fully set on doing it if I can. The *Gleaner* thinks I am probably a Christian and says I seem "to be on gospel grounds," but points out that instead of being content with my attainments as a Christian, I have united myself to the Campbellite Church, and am a Campbellite. The brother does not understand the situation. I have never united myself to the Campbellite Church. If I am in the thing at all, I didn't go to do it. I have no idea when or how I got in, and I would be under lasting obligation to any man to tell me how to get out of it without getting into something else just as bad. Now the *Gleaner* can tell me how to get out of the Campbellite Church and get into the Baptist Church; but what I want to know is how to get out of the Campbellite Church—provided I am in it—and be a Christian in the church of God without getting into the Baptist Church, or the Methodist Church, or any other church not mentioned in the Bible. What good would it do to get out of the Campbellite Church and get into the Baptist Church? One of them is as good as the other, if not better. Neither is mentioned in the Bible; and if I can be a Christian and stand "on gospel grounds," as the *Gleaner* says, without being in the Baptist Church, I don't see why I should strain myself trying to get into the thing.

MORE THAN CHRISTIANS.

A correspondent in the *Baptist and Reflector* quotes G. W. Yancey as saying: "If we should wear the name

' Campbellite,' we could not hope that others would unite with us under such a name." Upon this statement the correspondent makes the point that " to call this modern innovation ' Campbellism ' is an unpardonable offense, since it would prevent others from joining them." The editor of the same paper makes the point that Methodists, Baptists, Presbyterians, etc., are Christians, and to apply the name " Christian " to a single denomination is to reflect upon the members of all other denominations. I agree with the editor that it is wrong to use the name " Christian " in a denominational sense. It is wrong to belong to a denomination, for that matter. To build up denominations is but to promote divisions and perpetuate strife among the people of God. I do not doubt but there are many people in the denominations who are Christians. I would not use words so as to reflect doubt upon their Christianity. The trouble is that they are more than Christians. Some of them, for instance, are Christians and Baptists, too. Now, as we understand the matter, we can be Christians and not be Baptists; we could be Baptists and not be Christians; and, by a strong effort and a tight squeeze, we might be Christians and Baptists, too. But the thing is pretty hard to do, and we do not care to strain ourselves unless we could see some reason for it. We are not trying to be anything but Christians, and we are not willing to accept a name which would lead people to believe we are something which we have never made any effort to be. This is why we cling to such names as " Christians," " disciples of Christ," etc., etc. It is this effort to be more than a Christian that causes trouble. As long as Methodists and Presbyterians and Baptists work and worship as Christians only, they love each other and get on gloriously.

NOT A CAMPBELLITE, NOR YET A BAPTIST.

It is conceded by everybody that a man can be a Christian without being a Baptist, Methodist, Presbyterian, Campbellite, or anything else in the way of a denominationalist. Now that is what I want to do. I have been trying to do that ever since I started out to be a religious man. But the *Baptist Gleaner* thinks I have failed in the effort, and boldly declares that I am a Campbellite—a thing, by the way, which I have never tried to be and which I am exceedingly anxious not to be. So I asked the *Gleaner* to explain to me how a man can be a Christian without being a Baptist, Campbellite, Methodist, Presbyterian, or anything else in that line, and it says:

Most cheerfully will we direct you, poor erring brother; and if you accept our suggestions, you will be a Christian, nothing more.

1. We commend to you that you hear the gospel of Christ. Hear it from your heart; hear it with the Campbellite drums out of your ears. "He that HEARETH MY WORD . . . hath everlasting life." To have "everlasting life" is to be a Christian in the highest, truest sense of the word.

2. Repent of your sins. Repent heartily; repent with prayer, like the Ninevites; smiting your breast, like the publican; confessing your sins, like John's disciples; calling on the name of the Lord, like David; be afflicted, mourn and weep, as James directs. Such repentance is "unto life." When you thus repent, you will be a "Christian."

3. Trust Jesus. Give him your heart. Believe in his

work and his blood. Faith in Christ will save you—will make you a "Christian." "Look, and live." "Believe, and thou shalt be saved." If you will believe in Christ, you will be a Christian.

4. To be a Baptist, you must now, after having become a Christian, unite with a Baptist people, be baptized by a Baptist preacher, and enter the brotherhood of the Baptists, all of whom profess to have become Christians before uniting with the Baptists.

To become a Campbellite, you needn't become a Christian at all. All you have to do is to find some preacher who will dip you in the water, blood-raw sinner as you are, and unite yourself to the Campbellite brotherhood, and you are a first-class Campbellite.

If the *Gleaner* is good authority on this subject, it is safe to say I am not a Campbellite, nor yet a Baptist, whatever else I may or may not be. I have never united with " a Baptist people " nor have I been " baptized by a Baptist preacher." I have never united with " the Campbellite brotherhood," nor have I been dipped " in the water, blood-raw sinner as you are," if by " blood-raw sinner " is meant one who has not heard the gospel of Christ, repented of his sins, and trusted in Jesus, as the *Gleaner* describes. All these things did I do before I was baptized. At one point I am inclined to differ with the *Gleaner* as to what it takes to constitute a Christian. It occurs to me that a man who wants to be a Christian ought to be baptized, even though he may not want to be a Baptist, Methodist, Presbyterian, Campbellite, or anything else of that sort. The *Baptist and Reflector* expressed my understanding of the teaching of the Scriptures on this point when it said the man who refuses to be baptized after he is fully informed as to the teaching of the Scriptures touching this ordinance

cannot be a Christian while he lives or be saved when
he dies, "*because such refusal shows that his heart is
not right, his faith is not genuine.*" With this understanding, I was baptized after I had done those things
which the *Gleaner* sets forth as necessary to make one a
Christian. Now, the question is, did I "unchristianize" myself, as the preachers say, when I was baptized?
I should like to know what the *Gleaner* thinks on this
point. If I did not forfeit my Christianity in being
baptized, I feel encouraged to hope that I am still a
Christian, and certainly I am neither a Baptist nor a
Campbellite, according to what the *Gleaner* says. And
since I have never been accused of being a Methodist,
Presbyterian, or anything else in that line, it begins to
look as though I am simply a Christian without being a
Baptist, Campbellite, Methodist, Presbyterian, or such
like, after all. And if I am, the Lord be praised! I
am not in the humor to abuse those who want to be
Methodists, Baptists, Presbyterians, Campbellites, and
such like; but as for myself, I have no higher ambition
than to be a Christian while I live and go to heaven
when I die. I am a poor, weak, and fallible creature,
and don't want to overload myself in the race for heaven
and immortal glory. I would like to be a Baptist or a
Methodist—yes, I would glory in being a bishop—if I
thought it safe to try to take on any of these extra degrees. But I don't want to strain myself, lest that, in
trying to be something more than a Christian, I fall
behind the dead line and "come short of the glory of
God." "God forbid that I should glory, save in the
cross of our Lord Jesus Christ."

DOES THE BIBLE REQUIRE A CHRISTIAN TO JOIN A DENOMINATION?

The *Western Recorder* goes to record on the denomination question in these words:

> The GOSPEL ADVOCATE asks us to say whether the Bible requires a Christian to join a denomination. Yes, emphatically. The Bible requires every Christian to join a church, and every church is part of a denomination, and the denomination he should join is the one which "contends earnestly for the faith once for all delivered to the saints." A denomination is simply the aggregate of churches which agree in doctrine and polity. There was as truly a denomination in the days of the apostles as now, the difference being that all the churches then belonged to the same denomination. Any more questions?

Will you please tell in what chapter and verse "the Bible requires every Christian to join a church?" Does not the very act of becoming a Christian constitute one a member of God's church? Are there any Christians who are not members of the church of Christ? Of all the denominations now in existence, which one does the Bible require me to join, and where in the Bible can 1 find such requirement? It is too vague and indefinite to say I am required to join the denomination which "contends earnestly for the faith once for all delivered to the saints." Please name the denomination which does that. They all *claim* to be working along that line, and yet, according to my way of thinking, no one of them is succeeding to any great extent. My opinion is that when the *Recorder* begins to look for the chapter and verse where the Bible requires a Christian to join a denomination, it will discover its mistake and say nothing more about it. We shall see.

Some weeks ago I asked the *Western Recorder* whether or not the Bible requires a Christian to join a denomination. That paper very promptly answered that it did, and explained that the Scriptures require every Christian to join a church, and that every church is a part of a denomination. I asked it to please cite chapter and verse where the Scriptures require a Christian to join a church, stating at the same time that, as I understand the teaching of the Scriptures, Christians are all members of the church of God—that they became members of the church at the same time they became Christians. There being no such thing as a Christian out of the church of God, there is no such thing, of course, as a requirement in the Scriptures that a Christian join a church. I expressed the opinion at the time that when the *Western Recorder* began to look for chapter and verse requiring a Christian to join a church, it would discover its mistake and say nothing more about it. Just as I expected, the silence of the *Recorder* since then on this subject has been both dense and eloquent.

ARE CHRISTIANS IN ALL DENOMINATIONS?

The *Firm Foundation* says:

Any misunderstanding of the question propounded by me relative to the characteristics of the church of Christ, I take upon myself. The different figures used in the New Testament to illustrate the church do not, to my mind, sanction the loose idea, so current in religious circles, of a " general church " made up of the " true Christians " in all denominations. The church is a BODY—is *the* body of Christ on earth. As such, it has distinctive peculiarities

5

by which it can be readily known. These peculiarities might be classed as *inclusive* and *exclusive*. All who possess them are included in the term "the body;" all who lack them are excluded. These thoughts are simply suggested. There is a wall of separation—the law of Christ—between the world and the church. More than this, the law of Christ is a wall of separation between the church of Christ and all other religious bodies of whatever name or faith. Obedience to the law of Christ incorporates one into the body of Christ; obedience to the law of each denomination or church incorporates with that body. To win the battle for Christ, we must break down denominational walls or laws—supplant them with the gospel.

The *Firm Foundation* doubtless holds that the church of God, or body of Christ, includes all Christians, and that a man gets into the church at the same time and by the same process that he becomes a Christian. This much is clear from the most casual reading of the New Testament. But are the Christians who constitute the church of God, or body of Christ, " in all denominations? " This question suggests the idea at which the *Firm Foundation* probably aimed its protest. It is not the purpose of the GOSPEL ADVOCATE to spring an issue or begin a discussion with the *Firm Foundation* on this point at this writing, but simply to submit a few general remarks and random suggestions touching some practical difficulties along this line. It must be admitted that the Christians who constituted the church of God, or body of Christ, in New Testament times were not " in all denominations." There were no denominations to be in then. It is also clear that the Christians who closely adhere to New Testament teaching and precedents nowadays are not " in all denominations," or in *any* denomination, for that matter. It is still further

apparent that all denominations will be abolished if ever
the religious people of these modern times get back to
the teaching and practice of New Testament Christians
in all matters of religious work and worship. From
these plain statements of elementary and axiomatic principles this much is clear: If there are Christians " in all
denominations," or in any denomination, they ought not
to be there, and the sooner they get out, the better. A
determination to adhere to the teaching and practice of
New Testament Christians in all matters of religious
work and worship is a resolution to wage a war of extermination against " all denominations " in religion.
There may be, and there ought to be, in those who are
determined to closely follow the New Testament as a
religious guide the kindliest feelings for those who are
" in all denominations " and for everybody else; but the
denominations themselves are unscriptural institutions,
and the man of God has no alternative but to oppose
them. But still the question will not down: Are there
Christians " in all denominations? " Well, it seems to
be a weakness in Christians in all ages to get into things
they ought to keep out of. I have noticed evidences
of such weakness even in myself at times. In the very
days of the inspired writers of the New Testament
Christians were continually getting into all sorts of
things which the inspired men of God were eternally
pulling them out of and warning them not to go into
any more; and if there had been such a thing as a denomination for them to get into then, some of them
would have gone into it occasionally, or it would have
been the only thing they kept out of which they had
no business to enter. And, besides all this, a denomination is the easiest thing to fall into and the hardest

thing to climb out of that I ever came in contact with, anyhow. In the midst of all the denominations that beset this age and country, it would be absolutely miraculous if some Christians did not get into some of them occasionally. If there are no Christians in any denomination, it is the only place except hell they have all kept out of. When there are Christians—not the best variety of Christians, to be sure, but the same sort that lengthen the lists of members on all "our church books"—in saloons, on the race track, at the theater, in the ball-room, around the gambling tables, in the calaboose, behind the jail doors, in the penitentiary, and on the gallows, it should not create surprise or start a scandal if a few of the meanest specimens of them should occasionally be found temporarily in the most respectable and pious religious denominations of this degenerate age and God-forsaken country.

A DISTINCT RELIGIOUS SYSTEM.

Brother J. H. Spencer, a Baptist sort of a Christian, reasons thus in the *American Baptist Flag:*

Campbellism is as distinctly a system of religious doctrine as is Calvinism. Alexander Campbell was not the first to proclaim the doctrine, any more than Calvin was the first to advocate the system that bears his name. Robert Sandeman, of Scotland, was the originator of the system, or, at least, the predecessor of Mr. Campbell in its advocacy. But Campbell was the first to publish it in America; and hence while it is called "Sandemanianism" in Europe, it is designated by the term "Campbellism" in this country. Why its advocates should regard it a reproach to be called after the system of doctrine they profess is difficult to see, unless they deem the doctrine itself reproachful. A Presbyterian or Baptist takes no offense at being called a "Calvinist." A Methodist is not offended at being styled an "Arminian." Paul was not angered at being known as a "Pharisee." Why should an advocate of Campbell's system of doctrine feel insulted at being called a "Campbellist" or "Campbellite?"

The advocates of a distinct system of religious doctrine should not regard it a reproach to be called after the system of doctrine they profess, to be sure. If a man is a Baptist or a Presbyterian of the Calvinistic type, there is no good reason why he should not be called a "Calvinist;" or if he is a Methodist variety of the Arminians, he ought not to resent it when he is called an "Arminian" and a "Methodist." So, likewise, a man who advocates Campbellism ought not to object when he is called a "Campbellite." But everybody admits that a man can be a Christian and not be a Campbellite, a Baptist, a Methodist, a Presbyterian, a Calvinist, or an Arminian. There are folks who are determined to be simply Christians, without being any of these other things. What ought they to be called? Christianity itself is as distinctly a system of religious doctrine as is Calvinism or Campbellism. There were Christians in the world before Calvinism or Campbellism either one was ever heard of. What, for instance, would Brother Spencer call those Christians who lived before either Campbell or Calvin was born? The harm of the thing is not in being *called* a "Campbellite" or a "Calvinist," but in *being* either the one or the other. The man who consents to *be* a Calvinist or a Campbellite, and refuses to be *called what he is*, attempts to perpetrate a fraud. And the man who insists upon calling folks "Calvinists" or "Campbellites," when they refuse to be either, misrepresents his brethren in Christ and speaks against the facts in the case. The man who has a careful regard for accuracy of statement will hardly say people are "Campbellites" or "Calvinists," when they refuse to be either. It is eminently proper to call people "after the system of doctrine they profess," and in that way people who professed the system of religious doctrine preached by Christ and his apostles in New Testament times were called "disciples," "Christians," and such like, but never called "Methodists," "Baptists," "Calvinists," "Campbellites," or anything of the kind. "The disciples were called Christians first in Antioch." (Acts 11: 26.) They ought to be that and be called that, and nothing else, yet. It is manifestly wrong to call anything which the Bible teaches either "Campbellism" or "Sandemanianism," whether it be held in Europe or America; and it is equally wrong to hold to anything in religion which the Bible does not teach, no matter whether Robert Sandeman, John Calvin, Martin Luther, Alexander Campbell, John Wesley, or any other uninspired man was "the originator of the system," or "the first to publish it." What is in the Bible never made a Calvinist, a Methodist, a Sandemanian, a Campbellite, a Presbyterian, a Lutheran, an Arminian, or a Baptist, in the days when inspired men taught it, and it will not make any of these things now. It made Christians then, and it will make Christians now, and nothing else.

Further along in his article Brother Spencer remarks:

But I intended to speak only of the fundamental principles of Campbellism. It is at the base that it antagonizes all orthodox systems of religious doctrine. Unless all other systems of Christian doctrine are wholly false, Campbellism is utterly corrupt at its foundation.

About how many systems of orthodox religious doctrine, for instance, does Brother Spencer think the New Testament teaches on an average? He talks about "all other systems of Christian doctrine" against Campbellism as glibly as if he thought there are as many different varieties of Christian doctrine taught in the New Testament as there are different kinds of trees in the forest. Is it possible he has not yet learned there is but one system of religious doctrine and but one kind of Christians in the New Testament? Any system of religious doctrine not taught in the Bible is to be condemned, no matter whether it is Campbellism, Calvinism, Lutherism, Baptistism, Presbyterianism, Methodism, or Sandemanianism. It is a waste of time to compare all these isms with each other with a view to discovering their points of agreement or disagreement. No one of them is in the Bible. They are none the worse if they differ from each other, nor any the better if they agree with each other. They are all to be condemned alike because none of them can be found in the Bible.

The *Pennsylvania Disciple* speaks along the same line with Brother Spencer, touching the naming of things in religion. There seems to be a religious denomination of considerable proportions in its mind's eye that has no well-defined party name. The *Pennsylvania Disciple* numbers itself in that party, and urges the importance of general agreement upon a denominational name. It puts the point thus:

The general fact [lack of uniformity in party name] is very confusing and inconvenient, and betrays a weakness in us that we deeply regret. It has been commented upon by the authorities in the census bureau at Washington, very much to our disadvantage. There is no good reason why we should not agree on a name and make it uniform among us. There is every reason why we should. The whole difficulty is based on our extreme notions of church independency—notions as unscriptural, in our opinion, as they are detrimental to our progress. Each congregation claims the right to name itself, govern itself, live by itself, and die by itself; and though it is obviously unscriptural and unreasonable, in the extreme to which it is carried, it is the fact that explains the matter of diversity in name and the want of that coöperation which is essential to the highest success.

While our national missionary conventions are not delegated to any such work, we have often thought that they might safely, and should, recommend a name to our congregations. While it would have no force of authority, its moral force would, after a while, bring the desired result.

No congregation of New Testament Christians "claims the right to name itself." What it does claim is the right to accept such names as are applied to a congregation of Christians in the New Testament. Every congregation should assert this right against all efforts of "our national missionary conventions" or any other denominational authority to either impose upon it a name not found in the New Testament or limit it to the use of any one of several names that are found there. What the brother wants is a name that will distinguish "our" sort of Christians from other kinds of Christians. There is no such name in the New Testament. There was but one kind of Christians in apostolic times, and hence the only distinction that was made in those days was between Christians and sinners. All New Testament terms that apply to any Christians apply equally well to all Christians. The authorities in the census bureau at Washington ought to be taught that all efforts to divide Christians into partisan factions and to classify them according to sectarian dogmas and denominational doctrines are wrong, whether such efforts are made by religious party leaders or political statisticians. And when party leaders in religion and the authorities in the census bureau at Washington persist in assorting and classifying the children of God into sectarian squads and partisan statistical columns, Christian people ought to decline to be separated from each other and filed away in denominational pigeonholes to the division of the spiritual body of Christ.

THE NAME "CAMPBELLITE."

The *Baptist and Reflector* springs this question:

If the first-page editor of the GOSPEL ADVOCATE does not belong to the people called "Campbellites," why does he get so red in the face whenever he hears the name "Campbellite" used? What concern is it of his? We can hardly be persuaded that it is pure disinterested benevolence on his part which makes him object so strongly to the word.

The first-page editor of the GOSPEL ADVOCATE doesn't get red in the face whenever he hears the name "Campbellite" used. It has become so common for him to hear ill-bred preachers insult helpless ladies by spitting that offensive epithet into their faces that such clerical coarseness no longer surprises him. Nor does the first-page editor of the GOSPEL ADVOCATE object more strongly to the name "Campbellite" than to the name "Baptist," "Methodist," "Presbyterian," "Congregationalist," or "Catholic." He objects with equal strength to them all, and on the same grounds. They are not in the Bible in the sense they are now used in religion, nor is the thing either one of them now designates to be found anywhere in the Bible by any name. There is but one kind of Christians in the New Testament, and the editor of this page objects stoutly to any word or words which is used to distinguish one sort of Christians from other kinds of Christians. The church of the New Testament includes all Christians. In apostolic times there was no such thing as a Christian who did not belong to the church. The same process which made a man a Christian added him to the church. There is no such thing in the New Testament as a religious body of any kind larger than a local congregation of worshipers, but smaller than the whole body of Christ, which is the church of God, and includes all Christians.

The *Christian Standard* states wisely and well a timely point in these words:

If a group of disciples of Jesus band themselves into a local congregation, they do not thereby become a denomination or sect. They are simply Christians, who, after New Testament models, worship and work together in one place. Multiply this one by any number of local churches under the same conditions, and you have not changed the relationship. According to scripture, they are churches of Christ in particular localities. Spiritually, each is a member of the church of Christ because he is a Christian, because he has believed in and obeyed Christ. The Ethiopian officer whom Philip baptized was just such a man. He was a member of the church of Christ, but not of a local church. After he got home, he might have converted or found others who with him would meet together in one place. They would make the church of Christ at some point in Ethiopia.

But this banding together would in no way change their belief or their character. They were Christians before coming together; they are simply Christians afterwards. They
were members of the church of Christ before; they do not
differ from this afterwards. Universally and locally, they
acknowledge only the authority of Christ. Bringing Christians together into a congregation does not constitute a
sect or denomination. If human authority comes in—if
party names are chosen—the case is different. Then we
have a sect or denomination among Christians, the exalt-
ing of individual, local, sectional, or racial peculiarities in
the place of Christ.

In this local and limited sense the church of the New
Testament is merely the congregation of disciples who
come together on the first day of the week to break bread
and engage in other acts of congregational worship.
There was nothing larger than this in the way of a religious body in apostolic times except the general church,
which included all Christians. The teaching of inspired men set forth a perfect model of a church in this
local sense, just as it sets forth a perfect model of an
individual Christian. Churches then as now approached
this inspired and perfect model in different degrees of
excellence, just as individual Christians approximated
the perfect model set for them by inspired teaching with
different measures of success. Each local church differed from all other local churches in that it had its
own merits and demerits when measured by the perfect
model set forth in the teaching of inspired men, just as
each Christian differed from all other Christians in like
manner when measured by the same perfect standard.
This fact is made clear in the letters addressed to the
seven churches of Asia in the first three chapters of Revelation, as well as in all the epistles addressed to the

churches in the entire New Testament. But notwithstanding these differences between the churches, growing out of the imperfections of the members that constituted them, the churches of the New Testament were
never classified according to differences and family like-
nesses into different sisterhoods of churches " of the
same faith and order." All such work as that was left
to the formers of modern denominations and framers
of uninspired partisan creeds. In apostolic times each
church kept itself free from all entangling alliances
with denominational sisterhoods " of the same faith and
order," and endeavored to correct its own imperfections
by the help of inspired teachers, so that it might come
" unto the measure of the stature of the fullness of
Christ " as a church. In this view of the case, local
churches should be dealt with now on their merits the
same as individual Christians. There is in the New
Testament a perfect standard given by inspiration
whereby to measure both a local church and an individual Christian. In dealing with either the one or the
other, attention should be directed to the points of de-
ficiency as indicated by the perfect standard given by
inspiration, and all the efforts and admonitions should
be concentrated toward the correction of such defects.
If either an alleged church or a professed Christian is
defective when measured by the New Testament, or is
in error because a denominational model has been the
standard of measurement, the first thing to be done, of
course, is to secure the adoption of the perfect standard
given by inspiration as the rule by which all questions
as to what makes a perfect church or constitutes a faultless Christian must be settled. In this way local Methodist churches, Baptist churches, Disciple churches, and

all other sorts of churches may be dealt with on their individual merits, measured and corrected by the New Testament, the same as Methodist Christians, Baptist Christians, Disciple Christians, and all other kinds of Christians. The New Testament gives the standard for a local church and an individual Christian, and the claims of anything which professes to be either the one or the other can be settled by that standard. But the man who walks by the New Testament rule cannot deal with or correct the errors of anything larger than a local congregation of worshipers and smaller than the whole body of Christ, or church of God, which includes all Christians. There is no such religious body in the New Testament, and of course there can be no standard there by which to measure and correct such a body. The only thing that can be done with all such bodies, according to the New Testament, is to abolish them entirely.

Next, after the excerpt given in the foregoing paragraph, the *Christian Standard* proceeds to say, in the same article, the following words:

The work of the nineteenth-century reformation means simply the making of Christians. It does not aim to build up a sect. It has not established a new standard of authority. It claims that he who believes in Christ with the whole heart, and obeys him from the heart, is a Christian, a member of the church of Christ, and that a group of such men meeting together in one place to keep the ordinances is a church of Christ, or Christian church.

To speak of the "Disciples of Christ," or the "Christian Church," as a denomination or sect having ecclesiastical bonds other than that which joins individuals to Christ, forms local churches, or enlists its members in voluntary associations to spread the gospel, is entirely outside the facts. Yet such is the extent of denominational life, the medium of present-day Christianity, that both within and without it is difficult to maintain this catholic, this common Christian position. We make no doubt that even in our own pulpit there are good men who look upon the "Disciples of Christ," the "Disciples' Church," the "Christian Church," about as a Presbyterian or Methodist minister regards his own denomination. If this be true, we need to be patient under the misrepresentation of other good men whose whole Christian life has been influenced by sectarian or denominational ideals.

In the light of what has already been said, the following general statements will be understood: We strive to be peculiar in not being peculiar. We are that part of the Christian world which is trying to be simply Christian. We claim that the "local" congregations formed by the coming together of those who believe in and obey Jesus are churches of Christ, and that we, in common with all in every place who serve our Lord Jesus Christ, have been added to his church and are members of his body. Denominational names are discarded because denominational interests are condemned by the word of God. We do not wish to be distinguished from any of Christ's disciples. We do not plead with them to come to our church, but to repudiate everything which is not distinctively Christian. With human barriers taken away, we will be one in Christ, wearing the only name on earth or in heaven whereby men can be saved.

If "we do not wish to be distinguished from any of Christ's disciples," why do "we" use terms to designate "us" which will not apply to all of Christ's disciples? For instance, such terms as "the nineteenth-century reformation," "the Disciples of Christ," "the Christian Church," "our own pulpit," "the Disciples' Church," "we," "our," "us," etc., etc., as clearly and as effectively "distinguish us from" other disciples of Christ as the terms "Methodist," "Baptist," and "Presbyterian" distinguish those to whom they are applied from other religious people. Throughout the article from which the foregoing excerpts are taken the *Christian Standard* makes a clear distinction between disciples and Disciples. It indicates that distinction by the use of a small "d" in the one case and a capital "D" in the other case. The capital "D" is used to distinguish "us" from other disciples of Christ. If "we do not wish to be distinguished from any of Christ's disciples," why does the *Standard* use a capital "D" when speaking of "us" and a small "d" when speaking of the disciples in general? And if "we do not wish to be distinguished from" other disciples of Christ, why are "we" careful to count how many churches, preachers, communicants, meetinghouses, missionaries, missions, mission property, colleges, books, papers, etc., etc., "we" have, and set all this off in separate yearbooks and array it in the United States census in a column of "our own" over against Methodists, Baptists, Presbyterians, and other things? If all this does not distinguish "us" from other disciples of Christ, what further steps would the *Standard* take in that direction if it should undertake to so distinguish "us?" The exact truth of the matter is that "the nineteenth-century reformation" is a religious body larger than a local congregation of worshipers and smaller than the whole body of Christ, or church of God, which includes all Christians. There is no such religious body in the New Testament, and of course there is no name there for it. It is unscriptural and antiscriptural, and the sooner it and all other religious bodies like it are abolished, the better.

DISCIPLE CHURCH, DISCIPLE DOCTRINE.

The *Baptist and Reflector* puts it thus:

The GOSPEL ADVOCATE of late quotes President C. L. Loos, of Kentucky University, as saying recently, in discussing the terms "Disciple Church," "Disciple doctrine," "Disciple people," etc.:

"'Disciple,' in the singular as well as an adjective, is a most unmeaning abuse of this word, looking at it as it is used in the New Testament. 'The church of the Disciples,' 'the doctrine of the Disciples,' 'the school of the Disciples,' are expressions which have a meaning, in so far as merely the law of language is concerned; but what are we to understand by 'Disciple Church,' 'Disciple doctrine,' 'Disciple school?' It is a most unmeaning, illiterate, awkward expression, and not worthy of an enlightened people. It is both a misuse and an abuse of a most important New Testament appellation. Let us not make such a humiliating exhibition out of ourselves before an intelligent world."

The editor of the GOSPEL ADVOCATE agrees with President Loos, and so do we—only we should add that the term "Christian Church," in the sense in which our Campbellite friends use it, is just as "unmeaning, illiterate, awkward" an expression, "and not worthy of an enlightened people," as is the term "Disciple Church." The fact is, that there is only one name which describes our brethren of that faith, and that is the term "Campbellites." We do not mean to use it in an offensive sense, but simply to use an unambiguous term which at the same time is historically fitting. If, however, they object to that, what shall we call them? Here President Loos says that we ought not to call them the "Disciple Church." Alexander Campbell himself objected to the term "Christian Church" as of heathen origin; and what shall we do about it? Until these brethren settle upon a name themselves which will not by its very use be an insult to other denominations, we presume that the world will go on calling them what it does now—" Campbellites." If they don't name the baby themselves, other people will name him for them, as they have done.

If the *Baptist and Reflector* does not " mean to use it in an offensive sense," it will have to quit using it at all. The people to whom the term " Campbellite " is applied have plainly stated over and over, again and again, that the term cannot possibly be used in any other than an offensive sense. People who are too well bred to knowingly and needlessly insult a lady will not use that term after they are plainly, but kindly, told it is offensive. The GOSPEL ADVOCATE fully appreciates the *Reflector's* difficulty in trying to find words to designate the thing in question without using the offensive term " Campbellite." The ADVOCATE has the same difficulty itself, but it takes the trouble and pains to avoid giving offense by using awkward circumlocutions, and the *Reflector* must do the same or publicly write itself down either a bore in manners or something worse in religion. The ADVOCATE does not belong to the thing the *Reflector* is at such a loss to find a name for. It heartily accepts every Bible truth in teaching or practice held by this and every other religious party in Christendom. But in the very article from which the *Reflector* took the above excerpt the ADVOCATE clearly explains that it has no more interest in or sympathy for the nameless thing in question than for the Baptist denomination or any other unscriptural party in religion. The ADVOCATE wages a war of extermination against every religious party, sect, schism, faction, movement, reformation, restoration, denomination, or brotherhood in Christendom that is larger than a worshiping assembly and smaller than the

6

whole family or church of God on earth, which includes all Christians. It is willing to be called by any name and by all names by which the people of God are designated in the New Testament; but it never expects to "settle upon" or accept any name that will distinguish one sort of Christians from other varieties, or to apply to only a part of the family of God.

IS THE CAMPBELLITE DENOMINATION A SECT?

The *Baptist Gleaner* department of the *Western Recorder* remarks:

A very novel discussion is at this time agitating the ranks of Campbellite exchanges. It is as to whether the Campbellite denomination is a sect. It is conceded by all that other people possibly regard them as a sect, but some of them are inclined to deny it. The *Christian-Evangelist*, of St. Louis, puts itself on the side of common sense and truth, and says right out in meeting that they are a sect; but the *Christian Standard*, of Cincinnati, and the GOSPEL ADVOCATE, of Nashville, stoutly resist such a statement.

The brother speaks against the record when he says the GOSPEL ADVOCATE, of Nashville, stoutly resists the statement that "the Campbellite denomination is a sect." The ADVOCATE does not resist that statement at all, but, quite to the contrary, heartily indorses it. The Campbellite denomination and every other denomination in Christendom is a sect, and is severely condemned as such by the plain teaching of the New Testament. The point the ADVOCATE makes is that no Christian has any scriptural authority to belong to the Campbellite denomination or any other denomination in religion. Anything in the way of a religious party which does not include all Christians is unscriptural and antiscriptural, and ought to be dissolved. The church of the New Testament includes all Christians. The same process which makes Christians adds them to the church, according to the New Testament. The ADVOCATE opposes everything and belongs to nothing in religion which does not include all Christians. It has no more sympathy for the Campbellite denomination than for the Baptist denomination.

FREEDOM OF THOUGHT.

A few weeks ago I objected to Baptist doctrinal standards on the ground that no uninspired man or set of men had any right to stand between me and the Bible, or to circumscribe me by their convictions in the study of the Bible. I have as much right to study the Bible and formulate "Articles of Faith" or other doctrinal standards as the Baptist Church or anybody else. I very distinctly stated that "I claim all the room that the Bible allows me," regardless of Baptist "Articles of Faith" or other "doctrinal standards" in "which to operate my thinking apparatus." The Baptist Gleaner thinks I want entirely too much freedom of thought in matters of religion. Yes, I see how that is. That's the way all denominationalists talk. The man who will not be fenced in by "doctrinal standards" made by uninspired men is not very highly esteemed by those who herd with denominational flocks and graze in sectarian pastures. Still, I am content to be simply a Christian while I live and go to heaven when I die; and all denom-

inations admit that this can be done without joining the
Baptists, Methodists, Presbyterians, or any other party
or denomination in religion.

I do not ask Baptists, Methodists, Presbyterians, etc.,
to " surrender " their " claim " to the name " Christian."
What I would like to see them do is to " surrender "
their " claim " to such names as " Methodist," " Baptist," " Presbyterian," etc., and be simply Christians,
or disciples of Christ. Since the name " Christian " is
" already appropriated to all who accept Christ of all
denominations," it is as clear as a sunbeam that a man
can be a Christian without belonging to any denomination. I am as unwilling as the *Recorder* to see the name
" Christian " " appropriated to one denomination."
What I want to do is to get men and women to be
Christians without being " appropriated to one denomination," or any denomination. The *Recorder* is clearly
wrong when it says that to call folks " Christians " will
make them " a denomination." There is nothing denominational in Christianity. People must be something more than Christians in order to be a denomination.

IT IS DOUBTFUL IF YOU REMAIN AMONG
THE CAMPBELLITES.

The *Baptist Gleaner* speaks this word of fatherly advice to the editor of this page: " You can evidently get
to heaven without belonging to the Baptists, Methodists,
etc., but it is doubtful about you ever getting there if
you remain among the Campbellites." That begins to
sound like business. I have never been " among the
Campbellites," and now if the editor of the *Baptist*

Gleaner will get out from among the Baptists, we will love the Lord, obey God, and be Christians together while we live and together go to heaven when we die, without any Methodist, or Baptist, or Campbellite foolishness about it. By the way, what does the editor of the *Baptist Gleaner* want to be a Baptist for, if he can "evidently get to heaven without belonging to the Baptists?"

ARE WE, AS A PEOPLE, THE CHURCH OF CHRIST?

About a year ago, when the question was up as to whether "we, as a people, are the church of Christ," I ventured to say: "Suppose it is admitted that we, as a people, are the church of Christ, what then? Am I one of the 'we as a people?' Who is to decide this question?" My good Brother Stone, in the *Firm Foundation,* runs into italics to emphasize my heresy on this point. After quoting the words just given, he exclaims: "Is it possible that he does not know by what rule one may decide whether he is a Christian or not?" Certainly not. That is not my difficulty. I know well enough how to decide whether one is a Christian or not. I have never had any trouble about that. I explained all that in the paragraph Brother Stone so rabidly criticises, in these words: "All who have been scripturally baptized and are living godly lives are members of the church of Christ." That's all clear enough, and Brother Stone himself admits the correctness of it. The point that worries me is to determine whether I am one of the "we as a people." Brother Stone, as I understand him, thinks I am not. Very well. If Brother Stone will now point out anything God, in the Scriptures, requires me to do which I have not done or am not doing as hard as ever I can, I will thank him for it and set about the doing of it at once.

But nqw that he has decided I am not one of " us as a people," I am going to make an honest effort for heaven and immortal glory on my own hook, with the Bible for my guide. If Brother Stone sees any obstacles in my way, I hope he will call my attention to them. But don't bother me with this " we-as-a-people " business. I am beginning to think " we, as a people," are very much like other folks, as a people, anyhow. I know a man who has a way of saying some people have as much human nature in them as anybody, and I halfway believe it.

AN EXPLANATION.

The *Baptist Helper* calls for an explanation in these words:

The GOSPEL ADVOCATE frequently uses such language as this: "The church of God, which includes all Christians." We would like to know just what the ADVOCATE means by such language. Does it mean that the term "the church of God" is ever so used in the New Testament as to embrace all, of whatever name, who, putting their trust in Christ, walk in the light of Bible truth, and, according to the best light they have, so live as to be called "Christians," in distinction from those who make no pretensions to Christianity? If so, will it give us the scripture so teaching, or does it simply mean the Campbellite Church? We want to know.

The GOSPEL ADVOCATE never means the Campbellite Church when it says the "church of God." It always says what it means, and means exactly what it says. It has no more use for the Campbellite Church than for the Baptist Church, or any other church which is not known at all in the New Testament. When it says the church of God includes all Christians, it means that every man who becomes a Christian, at the same time and by the same process becomes a member of the church of God. There are no Christians outside of the church in the New Testament. No one "joined the church" after he became a Christian in New Testament times. The church is the spiritual body of Christ. (Col. 1: 18; Eph. 1: 22, 23.) Every Christian is a member of that body. (Rom. 12: 4, 5; 1 Cor. 12: 27; John 15: 1-8). No one has any more to do with joining the church of God than with joining heaven. God adds all who become Christians to the church while they live, just as he takes them to heaven when they die. (Acts 2: 47; 1 Cor. 12: 18.)

WERE NEW TESTAMENT WRITERS GENTLE-MEN?

The *Baptist and Reflector* makes another unsuccessful attempt to grasp an idea in these words:

Brother Srygley, of the GOSPEL ADVOCATE, objects violently to being called a "Campbellite." He says that it is a gratuitous insult to the people of his denomination to call them by that name, and that no gentleman would be guilty of it. In reply, we want to say that we object very violently to his people calling themselves "Christians" in the distinctive and exclusive sense in which they do. It is

a gratuitous insult to the rest of the Christian world for
them to do so, and no gentleman would be guilty of it, much
less a " Christian " in the true sense of the word.

Brother Srygley has no " people " but the children of
God. Every Christian in the wide, wide world is one of
" his people." He does not belong to any denomination.
Neither is he willing to be, or to be called, " Christian "
or anything else in any " distinctive and exclusive sense."
He is opposed to all distinctions and exclusiveness among
Christians, and he, therefore, " objects violently " to all
efforts to fasten on him any term which distinguishes one
sort of Christians from other kinds of them.   On this
ground he refuses either to be or to be called a " Baptist Christian," " Methodist Christian," " Presbyterian
Christian," " Campbellite Christian," " Disciple Christian," " Current Reformation Christian," " ' we-as-a-people ' Christian," or any other kind of a distinctive and
exclusive Christian that does not include all Christians.
Whenever the word " Christian " is used in a sense that
does not apply equally well to all Christians, Brother
Srygley agrees with the *Baptist and Reflector* that it is
" distinctive and exclusive," and joins it in condemning
such perversion of the word from the plain meaning it
always has in the New Testament.   The church of God
which is set forth in the New Testament, in any other
sense than a local congregation of worshipers, includes
all Christians, and Brother Srygley has stated time and
again, and now states once more, that any religious body
larger than a local congregation of worshipers, but
smaller than the whole family of God, which includes all
Christians, is unscriptural and antiscriptural.   As often
and as plainly as this has been stated in these columns
heretofore, the *Baptist and Reflector* seems not to have

grasped the meaning of it yet. The head which cannot chamber that little idea must have an interior cavity so small that it is practically solid. If the *Baptist and Reflector* really masters this idea, and still means to say that "no gentleman will refuse" thus to be, or to be called, anything "distinctive and exclusive" in religion, the plain meaning of the charge is that there was "no gentleman" among all the Christians we read about in the New Testament. No Christian in New Testament times was in fact or name anything distinctive or exclusive from other Christians by authority of inspiration. There was but one sort of Christians in those days, and they were the common kind which the plain and simple word "Christian" designated and distinguished without any qualifying or limiting term. There were no such things as Baptist Christians, Methodist Christians, Presbyterian Christians, Congregational Christians, Campbellite Christians, Disciple Christians, and such like in New Testament times, and there ought not to be now.

WHO WERE CALLED "CHRISTIANS?"

The *Arkansas Baptist* argues this way:

All who profess faith in Christ and espouse him as their Savior are called "Christians," and by this rule it is as reasonable to call the Methodist organization or the Episcopal organization "the *Christian Church*" as to thus designate the converts to the "Current Reformation." As long as there are diversions and disputes, resulting in separate sects, just so long will it be unjust to designate any particular faction, whose origin is dated since the Reformation, with the discriminating and untruthful title of "the Christian Church."

The foregoing excerpt does not speak in the language of the New Testament when it tells who "are called Christians." It would help wonderfully to clear away confusion in the public mind if writers and speakers would keep to the words which the Holy Ghost teaches in the Bible when they are talking on religious subjects. According to the Scriptures, "the disciples were called Christians first in Antioch." (Acts 11: 26.) As to who were disciples, and how they were made disciples, several passages are very clear. For instance: "Go ye therefore, and teach [make disciples of] all nations, baptizing them in the name of the Father, and of the Son, and of the Holy Ghost." (Matt. 28: 19.) "When therefore the Lord knew how that the Pharisees had heard that Jesus was making and baptizing more disciples than John." (John 4: 1, Revised Version.) The idea in the former of these texts is that the apostles were to make disciples by baptizing them. In New Testament times disciples, who were called "Christians," were never made any other way. There are no unbaptized disciples, or Christians, in the New Testament. "He that believeth and is baptized shall be saved; but he that believeth not shall be damned." (Mark 16: 16.) "Except a man be born of water and of the Spirit, he cannot enter into the kingdom of God." (John 3: 5.) "Repent, and be baptized every one of you in the name of Jesus Christ for the remission of sins, and ye shall receive the gift of the Holy Ghost." (Acts 2: 38.) "Arise, and be baptized, and wash away thy sins, calling on the name of the Lord." (Acts 22: 16.) "The Pharisees and lawyers rejected the counsel of God against themselves, being not baptized of him." (Luke 7: 30.) From all these and many other texts which might be cited to the same import, it is clear that in the New Testament those who believed and were baptized were called "Christians." No one was called a "Christian" who was not baptized. Those who were not baptized rejected the counsel of God against themselves, and that sort of folks were neither called "Christians" nor "disciples." But the *Arkansas Baptist* is right in holding that " as long as there are divisions and disputes, resulting in separate sects, just so long will it be unjust " and erroneous to consider or " designate any particular faction " of Christians the " Christian Church." There is but one church in the New Testament, and it includes all Christians. If it be proper to call anything the " Christian Church," that name should be applied to the thing that includes all Christians, and to nothing else. In fact, there is nothing else in the New Testament, in the way of a religious body, to apply that name or any other name to. The same process which made a man a Christian in apostolic times added him to the church, which was the only religious body then in existence. No one can, therefore, be a Christian and not be a member of the church. The church is the spiritual body of Christ. " He is the head of the body, the church." (Col. 1: 18.) " For his body's sake, which is the church." (Col. 1: 24.) " Gave him to be the head over all things to the church, which is his body." (Eph. 1: 22, 23.) There can no more be more than one church than there can be more than one body of Christ. There is one body, and every Christian is a member of it. " For as we have many members in one body, and all members have not the same office: so we, being many, are one body in Christ, and every one members one of another." (Rom. 12: 4, 5.) People were baptized into that one body in New Testament times. " Know ye not, that so many of us as were baptized into Jesus Christ were baptized into his death?" (Rom. 6: 3.) " For as many of you as have been baptized into Christ have put on Christ." (Gal. 3: 27.) Anything in the way of a religious body, in this general sense, which does not include all Christians, is not the church of the New Testament. It is a mere fragment of the body of Christ; and those who approve it, belong to it, or in any way encourage it are flying in the face of the plain teaching of the Holy Scriptures. The thing to do is to stand aloof from, and opposed to, everything in the way of a general religious body which does not include all Christians, and believe, preach, and practice simply what Christians and churches in New Testament times by inspired authority believed, preached, and practiced in all matters of religious work and worship.

THE CHURCH IS THE BODY.

The *American Baptist Flag,* of St. Louis, Mo., quotes from the GOSPEL ADVOCATE, and comments thus:

" These two parties were on the earth *before* the church was established, and they are here yet. The church of God, from its establishment to the present, includes all the saved, *for the same process which saves people adds them to the church of God, which is the spiritual body of Christ.*" (*Gospel Advocate,* December 14, 1893.)

Roman Catholics affirm that, outside of the " Holy Mother Church," there is no possibility of salvation in heaven. This

so-called "GOSPEL ADVOCATE," a radical Campbellite paper,
holds a similar doctrine. It affirms that there are none
saved except those who have membership in the "church of
God." Also, they claim that their self-styled "Christian
Church" is that "church of God." According to this, all
who are not members of the Campbellite Church are not
saved and are liable to eternal damnation. Such is the stu-
pid ignorance and miserable heresy of this fatal religion.

The GOSPEL ADVOCATE is not "a radical Campbellite
paper," nor any other sort of a Campbellite paper. Neither does the ADVOCATE claim that the "self-styled
Christian Church" is the "church of God." The AD-
VOCATE claims that the church of God is the spiritual
body of Christ, which includes all Christians. "Gave
him to be the head over all things to the church, which
is his body." (Eph. 1: 22, 23.) "He is the head of
the body, the church." (Col. 1: 18.) "For as we have
many members in one body, and all members have not
the same office: so we, being many, are one body in
Christ, and every one members one of another." (Rom.
12: 4, 5.) "For ye are all the children of God by faith
in Christ Jesus. For as many of you as have been baptized into Christ have put on Christ." (Gal. 3: 26, 27.)
"So many of us as were baptized into Jesus Christ were
baptized into his death." (Rom. 6: 3.) "Who hath
delivered us from the power of darkness, and hath translated us into the kingdom of his dear Son, in whom
we have redemption through his blood, even the forgiveness of sins." (Col. 1: 13, 14.)

The sum of it all is that the church of God is one
spiritual body in Christ, in which every Christian is
a member. No one can become a Christian without
also becoming, at the same time and by the same process,
a member of the spiritual body of Christ. The GOSPEL

ADVOCATE feels no interest in, and holds no fellowship with, any general religious party that does not include all Christians. Whenever the people of God form themselves into sects, factions, denominations, parties, and schisms, the GOSPEL ADVOCATE stands aloof from all such factions, whether "self-styled Christian Church" or self-styled Baptist Church.

CAMPBELLISM DEAD AGAIN.

The *Baptist and Reflector* has discovered that Acts 8: 37, on which it says "our Campbellist brethren base what is called the 'good confession,' is spurious." This one verse, it says, "constitutes the good confession, and is all that is required before baptism." And then, without even taking a few minutes of much-needed rest after such an effort, that journal exclaims: "A whole system of religion founded virtually upon one verse of scripture, and that a spurious one!" Dear me, Campbellism is dead again! But what has all this to do with those who propose to be simply Christians, or disciples of Christ, such as we read about in the New Testament, and to found their "system of religion" upon "every word that proceedeth out of the mouth of God," without being Campbellists, or Baptists, or Methodists, or Presbyterians, or Episcopalians, or anything else in that line? Does the fact that this verse "is spurious," if indeed it be a fact, prevent any man from being a Christian and being saved without being a Baptist, or Campbellists, or anything else in the way of a denominationalist? Must we all be Baptists, Methodists, Presbyterians, and such

like because Acts 8: 37 "is spurious?" This looks as
though not only the Campbellist, but every other sort of
an *ist* and a *tist* in the whole catalogue of sects, parties,
and denominations in religion was "founded virtually
on one verse of scripture, and that a spurious one!"

A CHALLENGE TO DEBATE THE CHURCH QUESTION.

The *Baptist Helper* says:

We are in receipt of a challenge to debate the church
question with F. B. Srygley at Dry Fork, Ky., this fall; and
if he has any brethren now living, and they will indorse
him as their representative, and he will identify himself
with them, we shall be pleased to accommodate them. We
have no time to waste on a fellow just floating around loose,
who belongs nowhere, who is not associated with anybody,
and denies his own brethren. If Srygley will not represent
them, we will take any other man among them that will
represent them and that they will indorse.

The GOSPEL ADVOCATE knows nothing about the challenge from Dry Fork, Ky., but it takes occasion to say
that F. B. Srygley, like all other undenominational
Christians in religion, has as many brethren as there are
children of God in the world. He claims to be nothing
but a child of God, and every other child of his Heavenly
Father in the wide, wide world is his brother or sister
in the Lord. As a member of the spiritual body of
Christ, he is identified with every other member of that
body which includes all Christians. It is to be hoped
he is not now, and never will be, identified with any
party, sect, denomination, or faction in religion smaller

than the church of God, or body of Christ, which includes all Christians. The GOSPEL ADVOCATE will engage to find thousands of brethren all over this broad
land who will indorse him or anybody else on the proposition that the Baptist Church, or any other church
which does not include all Christians, is not apostolic in
origin, doctrine, and practice. It will also engage to
find thousands of brethren who will indorse him or anybody else on the proposition that the church which is
apostolic in origin, doctrine, and practice includes all
Christians, and teaches and practices all that, and only
that, which New Testament churches taught and practiced with the approval of inspired men in all matters
of religious work and worship. And, finally, it will engage to show that any man who indorses and undertakes
to defend in debate the doctrine and practice of any
brethren that cannot be found in the New Testament
ought not to be indorsed by anybody.

THE CHURCH BEFORE ALEXANDER CAMP-
BELL.

Brother Malone, in the *Baptist and Reflector*, puts it
this way:

Where, Brother Srygley, was the organization you call
"the Christian Church" before the days of Alexander
Campbell? Do not history and biography accord to Mr.
Campbell the founding of the Christian Church?

It is not my manner of speech to call any organization the "Christian Church," but I read of the church
of God and churches of Christ in the New Testament

something like eighteen hundred years " before the days of Alexander Campbell." It is my understanding that the fragments of divine history and biography we have in the Bible accord to the inspired apostles the founding of the church of God. By the way, will Brother Malone tell us where was the organization he calls the " Baptist Church " when inspired men were writing the New Testament? I do not call to mind just now any mention of the Baptist Church in the Bible.

SADLY CONFUSED.

The *Baptist Gleaner* thinks I am " sadly confused " because I said " the Christians we read about in the New Testament were all church members." It says:

Jesus said to Nicodemus that a man must be born again, or he could not see the kingdom. The new birth is first; afterwards, addition to the kingdom. On the day of Pentecost the people " gladly " received the word of God, with glad hearts they believed, they became disciples of Christ, before either baptism or church membership.

I am not surprised that the *Gleaner* thinks I am " sadly confused." A man who belongs to a church which is not so much as mentioned once in the whole Bible naturally enough thinks everybody is " sadly confused " who sticks to the Scriptures. If the *Gleaner* man will read some in the New Testament, however, he will probably be surprised to discover that it talks about but two kinds of folks—viz., the saved and the unsaved. It speaks of but two ways—viz., a straight and narrow way in which the saved walk, and a broad way which the unsaved travel. It mentions but two places of final

7

destiny for the whole human race—viz., heaven for the
saved and hell for the unsaved.   The two ways are sometimes called the "kingdom of God" and the "kingdom
of the devil."   The *Gleaner's* idea is that a man can
get out of the kingdom of the devil and be saved without getting into the kingdom of God.   It would be interesting to hear the *Gleaner* explain what the fellow is
in during the time he is saved, but not a member of the
church of God or a citizen of the kingdom of heaven.
The *Gleaner* says "the new birth is first; afterwards,
addition to the kingdom."   About *how long afterwards*
would you suppose, at a rough guess?   And if I am
wrong in saying "the Christians we read about in the
New Testament were all church members," please give
the names and post-office address of six or seven Christians mentioned in the New Testament who were not
church members, and tell us why they did not "join
the church" or "put in their membership."   And while
you are at it, please tell us how a man can tell whether
he is one of the sort that ought to "join the church"
or one of the kind that ought to stay out.   The *Gleaner*
goes beyond the record when it says the people on the
day of Pentecost "became disciples of Christ before
baptism," unless it is prepared to say they became disciples of Christ before they received remission of sins,
for Peter told them to "repent, and be baptized every
one of you in the name of Jesus Christ for the remission
of sins."   Moreover, it is not left to the choice of Christians as to whether they join the church.   The Bible
says: "The Lord added to the church daily such as
should be saved." (Acts 2: 47.)   When people obey
God, the Lord adds them to the church without consulting them about it.   The only way to keep out of the

church, therefore, is to neglect or refuse to obey God, and that same thing keeps people from being Christians or being saved, for the *Baptist and Reflector* says that a man who refuses to be baptized after he is fully informed as to the teaching of the Scriptures concerning baptism can neither be a Christian nor be saved, " *because such refusal shows that his heart is not right, his faith is not genuine.*"

THE EARS AND THE VOICE.

The *Baptist Gleaner* puts it this way:

F. D. Srygley has been to Gadsden, Ala. He went there to represent undenominationalism. He succeeded in proselyting one poor Baptist to undenominationalism. Now, will Srygley tell us the real points of difference between his " ism " and the old-fashioned Campbellism we have been having in the country for so long a time? What real change in the *thing* does he secure by changing the *name?* The name is longer and less sensible and representative, but it is unscriptural, misleading, and deceptive. Srygley has too much sense to allow himself to suppose that the thin mask, the rotten and stale gauze he throws over his hideous religious deformities can succeed in hiding the genuine Campbellite stock. The size of your ears and the sound of your voice betray you, my friend.

The *Gleaner* is excited. F. D. Srygley has no ism but the Bible, and he cares nothing about Campbellism, or Baptistism, or any other kind of ism not authorized by the Bible, either old-fashioned or new-fashioned. The *Gleaner* admits that a man can be a Christian while he lives and go to heaven when he dies without being a Campbellite, a Methodist, a Baptist, or any other kind

of an ite, or an ist, or a tist. That is all F. D. Srygley
is trying to do. Anything wrong about that? Does the
Gleaner seriously object to folks being Christians while
they live and going to heaven when they die? Of course,
no one can keep the *Gleaner* man from being a Baptist
while he lives, or from going to the devil when he dies,
for that matter, if he is determined to do it that way;
but if it is all the same to him, the ladies would no
doubt be glad to see him observe the ordinary etiquette
of a gentleman along the road, no matter what he is or
where he is going. F. D. Srygley has not changed the
name of anything, nor is he at all concerned as to the
size of the ears or the sound of the voice by which the
Gleaner is so much disturbed. Srygley lays no claim
to either the ears or the voice. Both belong to Paul,
Peter, and other inspired men who wrote the Bible.

DISSATISFACTION WITH THE ESTABLISHED ORDER.

Close observers and careful thinkers in all religious
parties admit that there is widespread dissatisfaction
with the established order of things in institutional religion. People are not agreed as to what is the matter,
but they all seem to realize that something is wrong.
There is general unrest enough to justify the prediction
that existing religious organizations will soon fall to
pieces from gradual distintegration if public sentiment
does not undergo a radical change; but no man can fore-
see what the new order of things will be when the old
things pass away. The *Michigan Christian Advocate*

notes the changes that are going forward in the Methodist Episcopal Church, North, in these words:

There is a prophecy of change in the air. Men feel the advances of an approaching evolution. This is true socially; to Methodist Episcopalians it is true ecclesiastically. It is not strange it should be so, and there is no room for terror. Conditions have changed. Forms of work are altered. New institutions within the church have come and pushed to the front. It would be remarkable if some " old things " should not pass away.

A writer in the *New York Christian Advocate*, after attending " the three big conferences which were held in Greater New York," in which he " looked at things with two good eyes and listened with acute ears," puts his convictions that there is widespread dissatisfaction with the things that be, and states his prediction that radical changes may reasonably be expected in existing religious institutions in the near future, thus:

In view of some things that took place and of other things which are likely to take place, it is very evident that the good ship is laboring somewhat, and any man who listens can hear the creaking and straining of the timbers. Such seas as we are now in require careful seamanship. More is necessary than the shout through the trumpet of the man on the bridge. If the stokers should throw down their shovels, the engines would soon stop; and if the men before the mast should take it into their heads to mutiny, trumpets and uniforms would not be worth much. The next ten years have more possibilities of danger than many seem to imagine, and cool heads as well as warm hearts are very essential. A revolution is not only imminent, but inevitable; and its sweep and character will depend very considerably on what the next General Conference may do. Meantime the men on the bridge must be very careful.

The *Tennessee Methodist* also sees "the handwriting on the wall" of institutional religion, and acknowledges the trend of sentiment among advanced thinkers, thus:

Our larger sister church of the Methodist type seems to share the almost universal evidences of unrest and advancing changes. In the social, commercial, and political world everything seems to be in a most critical state. Some have denominated the times as being "out of joint." In religion, as well as society, there is unrest. There is, and should always be, that degree of restlessness which accompanies and evidences a healthful growth and improvement. But there seems a disposition of late to dig about the foundation of things. Men are inclined to scrutinize the basal elements of creeds and economics, and are evincing an unwonted fearlessness in expressing their convictions.

In line with all this the Savior's memorable words of prophecy will readily occur to every reader of the New Testament: "Every plant, which my heavenly Father hath not planted, shall be rooted up." (Matt. 15: 13.) Jesus applied these words immediately to Pharisaism, which was a form of institutional religion entirely without divine authority, but very popular at that time. There are no Pharisees in God's book of law and prophets. The people of God differentiated into Pharisees and Sadducees by adhering to the tradition of the elders and teaching for doctrines the commandments of men. (Matt. 15: 2, 9.) If Pharisaism was to be rooted up because it was a plant of institutional religion not planted by the Lord, it goes without saying that all other forms of institutional religion unauthorized by the word of God will share the same fate for the same reason. What the *Tennessee Methodist* calls "a disposition of late to dig about the foundation of things" is but another way of putting the Savior's declaration that " every plant, which my heavenly Father hath not planted, shall be rooted up." God never planted any Methodist, Baptist, Presbyterian, or Congregationalist plants. There is but one variety of Christians in the New Testament. The people of God have differentiated into Methodists, Baptists, Presbyterians, and ' such like by adhering to the traditions of the elders and teaching for doctrines the commandments of men. All these are sectarian plants from the hotbed of institutional religion. God never sowed a seed that would make anything but a Christian. The " disposition of late to dig about the foundation of things " is, therefore, no cause for alarm. It is the work of God to root up every plant of institutional religion which the heavenly Father hath not planted. The danger is, however, that the very men who root up these unauthorized plants of institutional religion will straightway set in their places other plants of the same kind, equally objectionable to God, which future generations will be forced by the Lord to uproot. The religious world has been running this way by a series of religious reformations which have followed each other in rapid succession since the first apostasy from New Testament order, and it will probably continue to the end of time on the same programme. Nothing is settled till God indorses it.

REPUDIATED.

Pastor John T. Oakley (Baptist) says in the *Baptist Helper:*

I heartily agree with J. N. Hall, W. H. Smith, and oth-

ers that as long as F. B. Srygley repudiates his denomination he should be repudiated by our brethren in public debate. During the Booneville debate I found him identified
with the Disciples of Tennessee, indorsed by D. L., E. G.
Sewell, Elam, Smith, McQuiddy, and others; but as he arose
and publicly withdrew from the Disciples of Tennessee by
giving me his hand, I think he should be allowed to rest
till he is willing to represent the people who call on him
to represent them in debate.

F. B. Srygley has no denomination to repudiate. He
belongs to nothing in religion but the church of God,
or body of Christ, which includes all Christians. For
fifteen years he has preached in almost every county in
Middle Tennessee, and extensively in West Tennessee,
Arkansas, Mississippi, Alabama, Georgia, North Caro-
lina, and Kentucky, saying that any church or denomination which does not include all Christians is not apostolic in origin, doctrine, and practice. He has held this
position in public debate more than a dozen times covering a period of several years. More than half of these
debates have been with Baptists. In all his preaching
and debating for fifteen years he has held the same position on this proposition, and sustained it by the same
scriptures and arguments. The decision of the Baptists
to let him "rest" from debates on this proposition is
no surprise to anybody who has heard him argue it.
Everybody who knows anything about the New Testament ought to see at a glance that the church of God,
or spiritual body of Christ, includes all Christians, and
that any church or religious party which does not include all Christians is not apostolic in origin, doctrine,
and practice. If Srygley ever was "identified with the
Disciples of Tennessee," the thing to do was to publicly

withdraw from them, of course. There are no Disciples of Tennessee in the New Testament. The disciples of Christ are the kind of disciples to be identified with in Tennessee and everywhere else. F. B. Srygley is still identified with them and "indorsed by D. L., E. G. Sewell, Elam, Smith, McQuiddy," and everybody else who is disposed to stand by the teaching of the New Testament for the church of God, which includes all Christians, against every unscriptural sect or party in religion which does not include all Christians. There are no "people who call on him to represent them in debate." The people who call on him to debate don't want to be represented. What they want is a man who will represent the teaching of the Bible in debate. F. B. Srygley is exactly that sort of a man, and he has done the work so thoroughly that the denominations he opposes have about reached a point where they can't get a man to represent them in debate. If they decline to debate with him because he does not represent nor stand identified with what they call the "Campbellites," of course they can no longer call him a "Campbellite" without stultifying themselves. And if he is not a Campbellite and is no longer to be so called, by the same token those who agree with him and stand with him for the church of God, which includes all Christians, against every sect, church, or denomination in religion which does not include all Christians, are not Campbellites, and cannot be so called. This is a point which the editor of this page has made over and over again during the last six years. The meaning of it is that people may be Christians and belong to the spiritual body of Christ, or church of God, which includes all Christians, and yet not be Campbellites, Baptists, Methodists, Presbyterians, Congregationalists, Catholics, or anything else in the way of a partisan in religion. A man can be a Christian while he lives and go to heaven when he dies, and yet not belong to any party, sect, faction, schism, or denomination in religion. This is the way all Christians are taught in the New Testament to be and to do, and F. B. Srygley, with all others who stand for that way in religion, should be commended for taking and maintaining that position in both preaching and debating.

A SUBSTITUTE.

The question was discussed on this page not long ago: "Are the Christians who constitute the church of God, or body of Christ, in all denominations?" The *Gospel Echo* quotes the paragraph from these columns, and remarks:

The above successfully answers the question it undertakes to answer; but that question is a wily substitute for another one that brings out the real point sought to be settled, and that is whether the process which makes sectarians, or members of a denomination, also makes them Christians. There is no question but that persons made Christians by the apostolic method may wander around and "fall into a denomination," or finally get "into hell;" but the process by which they get "into a denomination" no more makes Christians of them than the going into hell makes Christians. Christians are not made by entering into anything or body, save the church of Christ, and the same process that "adds them to the church" saves them.

It is in point now to inquire how the *Gospel Echo* knows the question discussed "is a wily substitute," or any other sort of a substitute, " for another one that brings out the real point sought to be settled." There is no question to settle with the editor of this page as to " whether the process which makes sectarians, or members of a denomination, also makes them Christians." That question has been settled with him these many years. To propound such a question and assign him a position he doesn't hold concerning it is a "wily" effort, or some other sort of an effort, to get him to argue a proposition he doesn't believe. It will not succeed. The only question there is to settle with me on this subject is, whether there are, in the various denominations, "persons made Christians by the apostolic method." It is clear enough that there is no way to make. persons Christians except "by the apostolic method." It is also clear that "the process which makes sectarians, or members of a denomination," does not make them Christians. The question is whether it is possible to work "the process which makes sectarians" and "the apostolic method" which makes Christians on the same man at the same time, so as to make him both a Christian and a sectarian without marring the mud in the potter's hands. Nearly everybody but the editor of this page seems to be trying to work this double process; and if the thing can't be done, it is high time to stop such fruitless efforts and save any further waste of raw material in experimenting.

HOW TO JUDGE OF THE TEACHINGS OF THE CHURCH.

The *Texas Baptist and Herald* has been commenting some upon the doings and sayings of Brother Martin, and Brother Poe gives notice in the *Firm Foundation* that "the *Herald* must not judge of the teachings and practices of the church of Christ by what" Brother Martin says. Correct you are, Brother Poe, whether you really intended to be or not. The right way to "judge of the teachings and practices of the church of Christ" is "by what" the New Testament says. What Brother Martin, Brother Poe, Brother Srygley, or any other uninspired man or set of men may say or do cuts no figure in the case.

WILL F. D. SRYGLEY TELL THE ORIGIN OF THE BAPTIST CHURCH?

The *Baptist Helper* wants to know whether "F. D. Srygley will tell us just *when, where,* and *how* the denomination now called 'Baptists' originated? We will allow him as much space on the origin of Baptists, in the *Baptist Helper,* as he will allow us in the GOSPEL ADVOCATE." F. D. Srygley begs to be excused. He draws his information on religious subjects entirely from the Bible, and there is no clue in that Book as to when, where, or how the Baptist denomination originated. No such denomination is so much as mentioned anywhere in the Bible; and when you get outside of that Book on religious subjects, Srygley loses all interest in the discussion.

"We will allow him as much space on the origin of the Baptists," in the GOSPEL ADVOCATE, as he can find on that subject in the Bible.

THE PROCESS WHICH MAKES ONE A CHRISTIAN ADDS HIM TO THE CHURCH.

Editor J. N. Hall, of the *Baptist Gleaner* department of the *Western Recorder,* quotes and comments as follows:

"No one can be a Christian and not be a member of the church. The same process which makes one a Christian adds him to the church." (*Gospel Advocate.*)

I don't believe such doctrine. It is Romanism, pure and simple, except it is somewhat aggravated. The idea that Christ and the church are the same, and getting into the church is the same thing as getting into Christ, is so exactly the reverse of the truth that it is hard to see how any one can advocate such a delusion. In the apostolic age men were "born again," and then entered the kingdom. The Lord "added to the church the saved." Men are saved by trusting in Christ. They are added to the church by taking membership with the saints after their trust in Christ. We are made Christians by faith in Christ; we are made church members by the act of associating ourselves with the church. Baptism and the consent of the church prepare us for church membership.

The church is the body of Christ. "And gave him to be the head over all things to the church, which is his body." (Eph. 1: 22, 23.) "And he is the head of the body, the church." (Col. 1: 18.) "And fill up that which is behind of the afflictions of Christ in my flesh for his body's sake, which is the church." (Col. 1: 24.) "Even as Christ is the head of the church: and he is the Savior of the body." (Eph. 5: 23.) Of course Editor Hall doesn't "believe such doctrine," but he can't get it out of the New Testament. If "getting into the church" is not the same as "getting into

Christ," people do not get into the church by baptism; for the New Testament plainly says folks are baptized into Christ: " So many of us as were baptized into Jesus Christ were baptized into his death." (Rom. 6: 3.) " For as many of you as have been baptized into Christ have put on Christ." (Gal. 3: 27.) If "men are saved by trusting in Christ" before they are baptized, they are saved before they get into Christ; if they " are made Christians by faith in Christ" before they are baptized, they are made Christians before they get into Christ. Of course men were " born again " in the apostolic age, but were they " born again " before they were baptized? That is the question. " Except a man be born of water and of the Spirit, he cannot enter into the kingdom of God." (John 3: 5.) That is the way it reads in the New Testament. " Born of water " means to be baptized. A man can't be " born of water " without any water to be born of. Suppose those who were " born again " did afterwards enter the kingdom, what then? They were born of water and raised up to " walk in newness of life." (Rom. 6: 4.) Certainly " the Lord added to the church the saved." He added all the saved, and as soon as they were saved. That is why " no one can be a Christian and not be a member of the church." God adds every one to the church who becomes a Christian at the same time and by the same process he becomes a Christian.

THE BAPTIST AND REFLECTOR ON NAMES.

The *Baptist and Reflector* remarks:

It seems necessary for us to remind the GOSPEL ADVOCATE again that every one who believes on Christ as his Savior is a Christian, and that all denominations—Baptist, Presbyterian, Methodist, Episcopalian, Catholic, and all—profess to be Christians. Does it deny that they are? But they differ in such principles as relate to the ordinances, church government, etc. These differences give them their individual names in some cases; in other cases the name is taken from the founder of the denomination. We do not believe in these different denominations. We wish we were all one, as Christ prayed that his followers might be. But they exist, and there is no use trying to blind your eyes to the fact. Even if you could induce everybody to call himself a "Christian" simply, without any other name to designate him, that would not wipe out the distinctions which now exist. If every man in the world should call himself "Mr. Smith," that would not do away with differences of eyes, hair, expression, color, character, etc. These would still remain. If you want them all to be one in fact, you must change the individual characteristics. As long as these remain, no amount of unanimity in name will make them one in reality. Or, suppose everybody were named "Smith," but all still have their different characteristics. How are you going to distinguish them? One would be called "John;" another, "Tom;" another, "Jim;" another, "Bill;" etc. As long as differences exist, there must be designations to indicate them. So in religion. All the followers of Christ were at first called "disciples," or, if you choose, "Christians." But soon they began to differ among themselves, and it was necessary that some terms be used to express these differences. In this way different designations arose. "Christian" is the surname, or general name, of all. But "Baptist," "Methodist," "Presbyterian,"

"Catholic," "Campbellite," etc., is the given name, accord-ing to individual peculiarities. The name "Baptist" is not one of our choice, as the ADVOCATE says. It was given to us. We are not ashamed of it, however. It means much, and at the same time it has a glorious history. We should prefer that all should be called "disciples," or "Christians," if all could see alike and aright—which, we think, would be to see as we do. As we have said before, we admit that the name "Baptist Church" is not in the Bible. But we claim that the *thing* is there, the principles in which we believe. And that is the great point. It matters little about the name so you have the thing. And claiming the name does not make the thing. A man's calling himself a "Christian" does not make him one. A leopard cannot change his spots by calling himself a "lion." Principles determine the name, not the name the principles. A "Campbellite" means a follower of Alexander Campbell in doctrine. So long as he remains such, no matter what name he may choose to apply to himself, he will be a sim-ple Campbellite still—unless he be a Campbell*ist.*

The *Baptist and Reflector* has a remarkably clear un-derstanding of the subject, considering the short time it has been under instruction. It is gratifying to hear it so frankly admit that "all the followers of Christ were first called 'disciples,' or, if you choose, 'Chris-tians.'" It is also encouraging to hear it say: "We do not believe in these different denominations. We wish we were all one, as Christ prayed that his followers might be." It is still further pleasing to hear it say: "The name 'Baptist' is not one of our choice, as the ADVOCATE says. It was given to us. . . . We should prefer that all should be called 'disciples,' or 'Christians,' if all could see alike and aright—which, we think, would be to see as we do." It seems clear from all this that the *Baptist and Reflector* is not at all pleased that those who do see as it sees persist in calling themselves by the unscriptural and party name, "Baptist." It is to be hoped, therefore, that the brother will now change his manner of speech, and in future use language in harmony with his convictions and preferences on this point. "To him that knoweth to do good, and doeth it not, to him it is sin." (James 4: 17.)

I agree with the *Baptist and Reflector* that denominations and denominational names originated in differences among Christians which sprang up after the New Testament was written. I also agree with it that the divisive principles always suggested the party names, whether those principles pertained to certain ordinances, or methods of work and worship, or theories of church policy, or mere personal preference as to distinguished leaders. He does not understand me, however, if he thinks I am in favor of a change which goes no further than the name. I favor an abandonment of all party organizations and divisive principles, as well as a surrender of all party names and unscriptural terms and phrases. I am opposed to any and all principles which are not sufficiently indicated by New Testament names and language. The point to emphasize here is that the dropping of all names but such as are found in the New Testament and a close adherence to the language of the Scriptures would logically compel the surrender of all principles and organizations not indicated by or essential to the undenominational names and nonpartisan language of the New Testament. On this point the brother states the truth in cogent English when he says: "Soon they began to differ among themselves, and it was nec-

8

essary that some terms be used to express these differences. In this way different designations arose." That is it exactly. It is impossible to keep up these divisions among themselves without some terms "to express these differences." They were, therefore, compelled either to give up these differences or select "some terms" not in the New Testament "to express" them. Unfortunately, they chose the latter. The brother's illustration is even stronger against him. "How are you going to distinguish" one Smith from another, he asks, without some kind of "given names to express these differences?" It seems never to have occurred to him at this point that we are not "going to distinguish" one Smith from another. That is the very thing we don't want to do. We want the Smiths all to be one. Christ prayed that all who believe on him might be one. For this reason we insist that all these "given names," which are not found in the New Testament at all, should be abandoned. One squad of Christians should not be distinguished from other squads of Christians by "given names," or in any other way. "As long as these differences exist," says the *Baptist and Reflector,* "there must be designations to indicate them." Just so; and as long as there are designations and party organizations in use to indicate "these differences" and perpetuate them, they will exist. But it is not at all necessary that "these differences" should be kept up, and hence all terms to indicate them and all party organizations to perpetuate them, and thus separate and distinguish one squad of Christians from another squad of Christians, should be abandoned. The thing to do is to keep one sect or party of Smiths from separating and distinguishing themselves from other sects or parties of

Smiths—one denomination of Christians from separating and distinguishing themselves from other denominations of Christians. What better way to do this than to abandon all partisan or denominational "given names" and phraseology and use only the undenominational names and language of the New Testament, which is equally applicable to all Christians?

It is wrong for any number of Christians, or disciples of Christ, to separate themselves from other Christians, form a party or sect in religion, and make anything a test of fellowship in the party which God does not make essential to Christianity or a condition of salvation; and whenever any number of Christians, or disciples, form themselves into such a party and erect such partisan tests of fellowship, it is wrong for any other Christians, or disciples, to enter into such party. No Christian should connect himself with any party, sect, or denomination in religion, no matter whether such party, sect, or denomination is led by Campbell, Wesley, Luther, Calvin, or any other uninspired man. Nor should one squad of Christians desire to distinguish themselves from other squads of Christians, or under any circumstances accept a name which will not apply to every child of God on earth or in heaven, as well as to themselves.

I agree with the *Baptist and Reflector* that these parties or denominations exist, and I am not trying to blind my eyes to the fact. I also agree with it that such parties or denominations did not exist in New Testament times, and that a man can be a Christian, obey every command God has ever given, and be saved without joining any of them. The point I am trying to make the brother see is that many Christians, or disciples of

Christ—myself among them—are unwilling to go into any of these parties or denominations in religion.   The *Baptist and Reflector,* therefore, is wasting time, showing bad manners, and needlessly giving offense and insult to those humble disciples of Christ, or Christians, when it tries to get them into any party ·or denomination in religion or force them to wear any party name which would distinguish them from other Christians, or disciples.

The brother has said before, and he now states again, that "the name 'Baptist Church' is not in the Bible; but we claim that the thing is there, the principles in which we believe." Then why call it the "Baptist Church," and how do you account for the fact that the principles did not give rise to the name in the New Testament? You say, correctly, I think, "principles determine the name." If the principles in which you believe are in the New Testament, how, then, does it happen that those principles did not "determine the name" in New Testament times? A man who cannot stay on the same side of a question any longer than that ought to write shorter articles.

"All the followers of Christ," says the *Baptist and Reflector,* "were at first called 'disciples,' or, if you choose, 'Christians.' But soon they began to differ among themselves, and it was necessary that some terms be used to express these differences. In this way different designations arose. 'Christian' is the surname or general name; but 'Baptist,' 'Methodist,' 'Presbyterian,' 'Catholic,' 'Campbellite,' etc., etc., is the given name." It seems clear enough from this that the Baptist Church is not in the New Testament at all—neither the name nor "the thing." It is merely a "given name" for a small squad, sect, party, or denomination of Christians to distinguish them from other squads, sects, parties, or denominations of Christians. There are no such things as Baptist Christians, Methodist Christians, Presbyterian Christians, or Campbellite Christians in the New Testament.

"'Christian' is the general name of all." This is in the New Testament, and it and other New Testament terms clearly indicate all the peculiarities of New Testament Christians. "But 'Baptist,' 'Methodist,' 'Presbyterian,' 'Catholic,' 'Campbellite,' etc., etc., are given names, according to individual peculiarities," says the *Baptist and Reflector.* These "given names" are not in the New Testament, and of course the "individual peculiarities" which they represent are not there, either. If the "individual peculiarities" were there, the "given names" would be there "to express" them. It follows, therefore, with the certainty of a mathematical demonstration, that there are some "individual peculiarities" about a Baptist Christian which make it necessary to call him a "Baptist" in order to distinguish him from the common sort of Christians which we read about in the New Testament. The word "Baptist" represents nothing but the "individual peculiarities," which are not in the New Testament. The names and terms that are in the New Testament clearly indicate all the peculiarities of the New Testament variety of Christians. The Baptist Church is simply an ecclesiastical organization of "individual peculiarities" which are not in the New Testament. This is why it is necessary to use a name not found in the New Testament to "designate" it. New Testament names will not "designate" anything but New Testament things. The "church of

God," " churches of Christ," etc., are the words which
" designate " the New Testament institutions. All
Christians in New Testament times were members of
the New Testament churches. A large proportion of the
Christians in these days are not members of Baptist
churches, according to the admission of the *Baptist and
Reflector.* If this does not clearly mark a wide difference between " the thing " now called the " Baptist
Church " and " the thing " we read about in the New
Testament, it would be interesting to hear the *Baptist
and Reflector* explain how it can be done. If " the
thing " we now call the " Baptist Church " is in the
New Testament, how does it happen that " the thing "
in the New Testament includes all Christians and is
called the " church of God," and in these days the same
" thing " includes but a small proportion of Christians
and is called the " Baptist Church ? " The fact is that
the Baptist Church is too short at both ends and too
narrow in the middle to be " the thing " which is called
the " church of God " in the New Testament. That is
why it is called the " Baptist Church."

CAN ONE BE A CHRISTIAN AND NOT BE IN A DENOMINATION?

Referring to the point recently made on this page to
the effect that a man can be a Christian without being
a Baptist, Methodist, Presbyterian, Campbellite, or anything of the kind, the *Baptist Gleaner* admits that if a
man should hear the gospel, trust in the Lord Jesus
Christ with all his heart, and truly repent of his sins,
he would be a Christian even if he should be baptized

along with other things God has commanded. Brother
Hall thinks it would not "unchristianize" a man, as
the preachers say, or jeopardize his salvation to obey
the command of God to be baptized. But as to my
own case he says:

There is one fact that he names which makes the case
suspicious. He says he really thinks that baptism is necessary to make a man a Christian. If this idea prevailed
in his mind sufficiently to cause him to trust to his baptism
for the remission of his sins, it is certain that he is not a
Christian. No man can be a Christian who places dependence upon baptism as a condition of his pardon. If Srygley
did this, he is deceived as to the confidence he thought he
placed in the Savior, and he is yet a sinner. We would ask
you, Brother Srygley, did you fully trust in Christ for the
pardon of your sins without depending on baptism to help
bring you the blessing? On your answer to this question
we may be able to say quite certainly if you are a Christian.

My mind is very clear on this point. I am sure I
"fully trusted in Christ for the pardon of" my sins
"without depending on baptism to help bring me the
blessing." It never occurred to me that baptism could
help bring me the blessing. In fact, I never would have
been baptized at all but for my unreserved trust in
Christ. To this day I cannot see any reason at all why
any man should be baptized save that Jesus and the inspired apostles taught it and required it. At that point
I most emphatically walked by faith and not by sight.
I was not baptized because I trusted in baptism to help
bring me the blessing, nor because it was popular, nor
because the preachers taught it, nor yet to get into the
Baptist Church. From my study of the New Testament, it seemed clear to me that Jesus and the apostles

ta:ught and required folks to be baptized. The places
in the Scriptures which impressed upon me the duty
of being baptized were many, such as the following:
" Go ye into all the world and preach the gospel to every creature. He that believeth and is baptized shall be
saved; but he that believeth not shall be damned."
(Mark 16: 15, 16.)   " Except a man be born of water
and of the Spirit, he cannot enter into the kingdom of
God." (John 3: 5.)   " Repent, and be baptized every
one of you in the name of Jesus Christ for the remission of sins, and ye shall receive the gift of the Holy
Ghost." (Acts 2: 38.)   "John did baptize in the wilderness, and preach the baptism of repentance for the
remission of sins." (Mark 1: 4.)   "And he commanded them to be baptized in the name of the Lord
Jesus." (Acts 10: 48.)   "And now why tarriest thou?
arise, and be baptized, and wash away thy sins, calling
on the name of the Lord." (Acts 22: 16.)   " While
the ark was a preparing, wherein few, that is, eight
souls were saved by water. The like figure whereunto
even baptism doth also now save us, (not the putting
away of the filth of the flesh, but the answer of a good
conscience toward God,) by the resurrection of Jesus
Christ." (1 Pet. 3: 20, 21,)   " So many of us as were
baptized into Jesus Christ were baptized into his death.
Therefore we were buried with him by baptism into
death; that like as Christ was raised up from the dead
by the glory of the Father, even so we also should walk
in newness of life." (Rom. 6: 3, 4.)   Now, from these
and many other passages of scripture it seemed clear
to me that Jesus and the apostles taught and required
folks to be baptized. As to whether I considered baptism "" a condition of pardon," as the *Gleaner* puts it,

I hardly think I can express my understanding on this point more clearly than these scriptures state it. I did not stop to inquire whether a man can be a Christian and go to heaven without being baptized. I have never seen the day since I believed on Christ and fully trusted him for salvation that I would have been willing to go to heaven without baptism, if I had felt confident the thing could be done. I loved God and wanted to keep his commandments. "If ye love me, keep my commandments." "He that hath my commandments, and keepeth them, he it is that loveth me." "If a man love me, he will keep my words." "He that loveth me not, keepeth not my sayings." (John 14: 15, 21, 23, 24.) "For this is the love of God, that we keep his commandments." (1 John 5: 3.) "But whoso keepeth his word, in him verily is the love of God perfected." (1 John 2: 5.) In view of these and other passages of scripture of similar import, I am rather disposed to agree with the *Baptist and Reflector* that the man who refuses to be baptized after he is fully informed as to the teaching of the Scriptures touching that ordinance cannot be a Christian or be saved, "*because such refusal shows that his heart is not right, his faith is not genuine.*" What does the *Gleaner* say about it?

NOT MONOPOLIZE THE NAME "CHRISTIAN."

I had occasion some weeks ago to say:

I have no earthly desire to monopolize the name "Christian." I have spent some of the best years of my life trying to persuade Baptists, Methodists, Presbyterians, and such like to quit the denominational business and be simply Christians.

Whereupon the *Baptist Gleaner* talks back at me in these words:

> The point in your whole argument was to make your proselytes simply Campbellites, and the name " Christian " was the sugar coating on the pill. The name " Christian " in your use of it embraces just what the word " Campbellite " embraces, and the man who identifies himself with your faith under the name " Christian " is no more nor less than a Campbellite. Your statement that you are simply a Christian, nothing more, nothing less, and that you are not a Campbellite, with all due respect to you, is contradicted by the facts. You are identified with Mr. Campbell's church in the same way and to the same extent that any Baptist or Methodist can be to these churches. Your relationship with your people makes you a brotherhood, and the brotherhood originated with A. Campbell; and from every standpoint of reason and justice the name of the brotherhood should honor the name of its founder.

I hardly think the *Gleaner* can tell me I have lied (and that is exactly what its language means) " with all due respect," but I accept its avowed intention to do this in all good faith and brotherly love. I suggest, however, that in future it need not waste words to say " with all due respect " when it is getting ready to tell a man he has lied. You can't tell a man anything of that kind " with all due respect," Brother Hall. The *Gleaner* is badly muddled when it says " the word ' Christian,' " as I use it, " embraces just what the name ' Campbellite ' embraces." As I use that word, it embraces Paul, Peter, John, and all the rest of the apostles, as well as all the disciples we read about in the New

Testament; for "the disciples were called Christians first in Antioch." (Acts 11: 26.) I also use the word to embrace all the disciples who lived on the earth from New Testament times to the preaching of Alexander Campbell. And, worst of all for the *Gleaner*, I use it to embrace all Christians, or disciples of Christ, who have erroneously, and, as I think, sinfully, connected themselves with the Methodists, Baptists, Presbyterians, and such like since the beginning of those denominations. I admit that it is a pretty hard job for a man to be a Christian and a Baptist, Methodist, Presbyterian, or Campbellite at the same time, especially under such teaching as the *Gleaner* delights to give; but I am inclined to think the thing can be done—with a hard strain and a tight squeeze!

But, after all, the *Gleaner* is confident I am a Campbellite. Well, I am sure I don't want to be one. I don't want to be anything but a Christian; and if the *Gleaner* will tell me how a man can be simply a Christian without being a Baptist, Methodist, Presbyterian, Campbellite, or anything else in the way of a partisan or denominationalist, I will be under lasting obligations. The *Gleaner* admits that the thing can be done. The problem now is to find out how to do it. Evidently it was done in New Testament times; for we don't read about any Baptist, Methodist, Presbyterian, or Campbellite churches in the New Testament. Surely the way to be a Christian, or a disciple of Christ, without being a Methodist, Baptist, Presbyterian, or Campbellite, is not a lost art.

And, finally, I should like to see Brother Hall, of the *Gleaner*, undertake to be simply a Christian without being a Baptist, Methodist, Presbyterian, or anything else in the way of a denominationalist. Quit the denominational business, Brother Hall, and be only a Christian. I have been trying to do that for several years, and you think I have made a mess of it all and ended by being a Campbellite, pure and simple. Well, "I didn't go to do it." Now, suppose you try your hand at the same job and see how you come out.

————

THAT GREATER REWARD.

The *Baptist Gleaner* says:

Because we have told . . . Brother Srygley, of the GOSPEL ADVOCATE, that he can go to heaven without being nominally a Baptist or Methodist or Campbellite, he says he is determined never to be either, but to simply be a Christian. That would be awfully nice; and if a man could meet the demands of his conscience by such a condition of affairs, he would certainly be pretty easy. But no man can do his duty as a Christian, nor secure for himself a proper Christian reward, unless he does what the Master commands all Christians to do. One of these commands is to receive gospel baptism, and this can only be had by becoming a Baptist. So that, while a man may become a Christian—simply a Christian—without becoming a nominal Baptist, he must become a Baptist in order to do the duties of a Christian and attain the greatest point of efficiency here and the greatest reward hereafter. If Brother Srygley is content to be simply a Christian, nothing more or less, he can do this by simply trusting Christ for salvation. But if he wants to be a Christian truly and secure for himself all that the Master has promised to a Christian, then he must leave the Campbellite Church, receive gospel baptism from the Baptists, and live to the honor of the Lord in all of his appointments. This can only be done by those who are genuine Baptists.

So that is it, is it? A man can be a Christian and go to heaven without being a Baptist, provided that will "meet the demands of his conscience;" but if he wants to satisfy "his conscience" and "attain the greatest point of efficiency here and the greatest reward hereafter," he must join the Baptist Church. Well, fortunately, I have my conscience under pretty good control, and to be a Christian and go to heaven will fully meet its demands. Of course, I would like to have that "greatest reward hereafter" which the *Gleaner* thinks the Lord has in reservation especially for the Baptists; but I am afraid to strain myself trying to get something better than heaven and immortal glory, lest I should overreach myself and fall short of that. So I think I shall try to restrain my ambition and be content to be a Christian and go to heaven. As to gospel baptism, I have already had that; and if the Master has required me to do anything else which I have not done or cannot do without joining the Baptist Church, I am perfectly willing to join it so soon as the *Gleaner* or anybody else points it out. But while this question is up, I will ask Brother *Gleaner* to refer me to some passage of scripture which requires me or anybody else to join the Baptist Church. And while he is about it, he may also refer me to a passage of scripture where the "Master, commands all Christians" to be baptized. All the *Gleaner* claims for the Baptist Church, as I understand it, is a monopoly of baptism, which it assures me is not at all essential to salvation, anyhow. This is hard on the Baptist Church. It puts it before the world as a veritable bull in the ecclesiastic stock market, trying to boost the price of a quantity of *watered* stock which really has no value at all, for the company has neither cash, credit, nor collaterals, and hasn't declared a dividend since it was organized! This, I think, is putting entirely too much stress on baptism.

GOOD MANNERS.

The *Baptist and Reflector* seeks to excuse bad manners in the copious use of the offensive term " Campbellite " by saying:

Our Campbellite brethren object to the term "Campbellite." They say it is offensive. They want to be called "Christians"—the "Christian Church." They do not stop to think that the term "Christian," in the exclusive sense in which they use it, as applying to themselves only, is offensive to others. It is selfish, arrogant, bigoted, insulting in the extreme. Other people claim to be Christians, as much as they are, if not a little more so. Before you try to teach us good manners, allow us to suggest that you learn a little yourselves. Meanwhile, allow us to say that we do not mean to use the term "Campbellite" in any offensive way. We do it simply to describe you. If you will agree upon any name by which to be called, the use of which will not stultify ourselves, we shall be glad to call you by that."

However much the *Reflector* may desire to use the term " Campbellite " without being offensive, the thing cannot be done. So far as I am concerned, it is offensive in any way he can possibly apply it to me. Now, the *Reflector* admits that a man can be a Christian and yet not be a Baptist, a Methodist, a Presbyterian, or a

Campbellite. Very well. If the thing can be done, why not allow folks to do it? Why try to compel people to form themselves into a denomination and to select some denominational name by which to be known, as a denomination, when they are fully resolved not to do anything of the kind? If Christ and his early disciples were on the earth to-day, would you undertake to compel them to organize themselves into a denomination and to select a denominational name by which to be known, or else join some of the denominations already in existence? And if they should refuse either to join any existing denomination or to organize themselves into another denomination and select some denominational name by which to be known, as a denomination, would you persist in calling them by some denominational name, to them offensive? Now, I have no earthly desire to monopolize the name " Christian." I have spent some of the best years of my life trying to persuade Baptists, Methodists, Presbyterians, and such like to quit the denominational business and be simply Christians. They all admit that folks can be Christians without being Baptists, Methodists, Presbyterians, or Campbellites, but they seem determined not to do such a thing themselves or let anybody else do it if they can prevent it. Why is this thus?

————

WHO SHOULD BE CALLED " CHRISTIANS?"

A writer in the *Texas Baptist Standard* complains because " Campbellism has actually about captured the exclusive right to be called ' Christian.' " The reason for this is that other people who claim to be Christians contend more earnestly for the right to be called other

things than for the right to be called "Christians."
Every Christian has the same right of any other Christian to be called "Christian;" but those who waive that
right, and call themselves, or consent for others to call
them, something else, have no one to blame but themselves. It should be observed, however, that the word
"Christian," in its New Testament sense, is not the
name of a religious party or denomination, but of a disciple. To speak of any religious party larger than a
worshiping assembly and smaller than the body of
Christ, which includes and consists of all Christians, as
the Christian Church, is an unscriptural use of the word.
If the word "Christian" can be scripturally applied to
a church at all, it cannot be so applied to a church that
is larger than a worshiping assembly and smaller than
the body of Christ, which includes and consists of all
Christians, for the reason there is no such church in
the New Testament. All this trouble about names and
churches and such like grows out of the efforts of different kinds of professed Christians to distinguish themselves from each other. The remedy is to return to New
Testament preaching and practice, and then there will
be but one kind of Christians, and they will all belong
to the same church, which is the body of Christ. No
one will want to be called anything but "Christian,"
because there will be no reason why any Christian should
distinguish himself from other Christians. So long as
it is necessary for different sorts of Christians to distinguish themselves from each other, it will be necessary to use unscriptural terms, or else use scriptural
terms in an unscriptural sense to do it. No one can
use the name "Christian" in a scriptural sense to distinguish himself from other Christians.

THE RIGHT NAME FOR THE DISCIPLES' CHURCH.

The *Cumberland Presbyterian* makes this point:

The *Herald and Presbyter* calls attention to an uncertainty, which we also have found sometimes puzzling, about the right name to apply to " the religious denomination that holds the views of Alexander Campbell." It is variously designated as the " Disciple Church," the " Church of Christ," and the " Christian Church." " Singularly enough," says our Cincinnati contemporary, " various sections of the denomination prefer each of the three names and object to the others. We should be very glad to have the *Christian Standard*, the *Christian Leader*, and the *Octographic Review* tell us in a few brief words which name each prefers, and why."

My idea about this thing is that the people of God ought now to follow the same rules of conduct and call each other by the same names that characterized the people of God in New Testament times. As to this dividing out into denominational squads and selecting some particular name to distinguish you from all other squads of the same kind, I don't want any of it. I want to be a Christian, but I do not intend to be a partisan or to join any denominational squad in Christendom. If there be such a thing as " a religious denomination that holds the views of Alexander Campbell," the *Cumberland Presbyterian* will please scratch my name off of that list. I want to be a Christian, and I am anxious to obey all the commands of God and to enjoy all the promises of the New Testament, but I don't want to be cooped up in any denomination so as to separate myself from all the people of God who are outside of that particular denomination. Call me any-

9

thing the people of God are called in the New Testament and I will not complain, but don't try to cage and brand me in a denomination. Don't.

NOT A COMMUNICANT IN THE DISCIPLES' CHURCH.

The *Baptist and Reflector* aims at the Gospel Advocate after this manner:

The Gospel Advocate, in its issue of January 11, said: "The Gospel Advocate claims nothing 'in behalf of the Disciples' Church.' It is not even a "communicant" in that church. In the way of general religious bodies it opposes everything smaller than the whole family of God as unscriptural and schismatic parties in the spiritual body of Christ. The church of God includes all Christians and constitutes the family of God into which souls are 'born of water and of the Spirit.' When souls thus born into the spiritual family of God divide themselves into parties, factions, sects, or denominations in religion, each claiming a doctrine of its own, the Advocate goes into none of the parties nor claims a partisan doctrine in behalf of any of the factions."

We should like to ask the Gospel Advocate a few questions, which we should be glad to have it answer in a plain, straightforward way, without any dodging. You say: "The church of God includes all Christians." Who are Christians? What does it take to make Christians? Is baptism one of the requirements? What is baptism? Is sprinkling baptism? Is pouring? Have any been baptized except those who have been immersed? Then if none have been baptized except those who have been immersed, if baptism is necessary to make Christians, the church of God includes only those who have been immersed, does it not? Well, would you invite to the Lord's table one who has not been baptized, and who, consequently, is not a Christian, and is not included in the church of God?

Again, would you fellowship, as belonging to the church of God, those who do not obey the teachings of Christ? Do you think it is obeying the teachings of Christ to have a pope? To have bishops? To practice infant baptism? To practice sprinkling or pouring for baptism? To teach the doctrine of unconditional election or of the final perseverance of the saints? Do not nearly all professed Christians, however, hold to one or the other of these practices and beliefs? But if they are disobeying the teachings of Christ in doing so, they are not included in the church of God, are they? No one who interprets the Bible differently from you, and so disobeys, as you believe, the teachings of Christ, *can* be a member of the church of God from your standpoint, can he?

Then there are very few who *are* included in the church of God, are there not? Who are included in the church of God? You? Who else? Brother Lipscomb? Who else? Brother Harding? Who else? Elder Brindle? Who else? "A few more?" Aren't you glad there are a few of you left? You are not a "party," or a "faction," or a "sect," or a "denomination," though, are you? You belong to the "church of God," don't you? In fact, you and a few others *are* the church of God, are you not? But we pause for a reply.

A child asks many questions which cannot be answered to its satisfaction and comprehension till it receives some instruction and enlightenment on general principles. But when it understands things in general a little better, the questions it once considered unanswerable are no longer worth the asking, and the age of innumerable interrogatories is forever past. The *Bap-*

tist and Reflector doesn't understand the elementary
principles of undenominational New Testament Christianity, else it would not ask such questions. The best
way to answer the questions, therefore, is to set forth
the teaching of inspired men on the general issues raised.

In matters of religion there are many things in the
way of doctrine, practice, and organization in the world
to-day which were never so much as heard of in New
Testament times. It is the purpose of the GOSPEL AD-
VOCATE to call attention from time to time to what existed in the days of inspired men, and to point out
the things which now are, but then were not, in religious doctrine, practice, and organization. Each soul
must, of course, determine for itself and answer to
God as to how far it will depart, if any at all, from the
things which then were in following after the things
that now are. What the GOSPEL ADVOCATE or any
other uninspired authority may or may not do or say in
the premises should not determine the course of others
on questions of such vital moment as these. One man
should not walk by another's convictions in religion or
try to go to heaven on another's faith. Folks are not
always in harmony with God when they are in concord
with each other, nor do people necessarily draw nigh to
God every time they huddle themselves together. The
effort of men to learn the mind of God by studying
the ways of each other has never been a bright and shining success in any age of the world, and the sooner people quit preaching and studying the doctrines, practices,
and organizations of religious sects, parties, schisms, denominations, and factions unknown in the New Testament, and devote themselves wholly to the study of the
Scriptures and the ministry of the word, the better it

will be for all parties concerned. The first mistake the *Baptist and Reflector* makes, therefore, is in aiming a long list of questions at the GOSPEL ADVOCATE, with the evident purpose to learn what it teaches and practices on the points at issue. The better way would be to point all these questions toward the New Testament in an effort to ascertain what the Scriptures teach, and what Christians under the guidance of inspired men practiced, on these subjects. By way of correcting this error, let it be inquired: What answers, if any, can be found for the brother's questions in the New Testament?

As to the question, " Who are Christians? " the New Testament answer seems to be: The disciples. " The disciples were called Christians first in Antioch." (Acts 11 : 26.) The disciples were the only ones called " Christians " anywhere. As to what it takes to make Christians, Jesus said: " Go ye therefore, and make disciples of all the nations, baptizing them into the name of the Father and of the Son and of the Holy Ghost." (Matt. 28: 19, Revised Version.) The idea in this seems to be that Jesus instructed the apostles to make Christians, or, rather, to make disciples, who " were called Christians," by baptizing them. To the same effect Jesus is quoted by another New Testament writer as saying: " Go ye into all the world, and preach the gospel to every creature. He that believeth and is baptized shall be saved; but he that believeth not shall be damned." (Mark 16 : 15, 16.) Other New Testament writers quote Jesus as directing the apostles to begin making Christians by this process in Jerusalem, but not till the Holy Ghost should come upon them. " Repentance and remission of sins should be preached in his name among all nations, beginning at Jerusalem."

(Luke 24: 47.) "But tarry ye in the city of Jerusalem, until ye be endued with power from on high."
(Luke 24: 49.) "Commanded them that they should not depart from Jerusalem, but wait for the promise of the Father, which, saith he, ye have heard of me. . . . But ye shall receive power, after that the Holy Ghost is come upon you." (Acts 1: 4-8.) Pursuant to these instructions, they tarried in Jerusalem. "They were all with one accord in one place. . . . And they were all filled with the Holy Ghost, and began to speak with other tongues, as the Spirit gave them utterance." (Acts 2: 1-4.) Thus equipped, they began to "make disciples," who "were called Christians," according to the process prescribed by Jesus in passages previously quoted; and this is the way they did it: "Then Peter said unto them, Repent, and be baptized every one of you in the name of Jesus Christ for the remission of sins, and ye shall receive the gift of the Holy Ghost. . . . Then they that gladly received his word were baptized, and the same day there were added unto them about three thousand souls." (Acts 2: 38-41.) "Then Philip went down to the city of Samaria, and preached Christ unto them. . . . But when they believed Philip preaching the things concerning the kingdom of God, and the name of Jesus Christ, they were baptized, both men and women." (Acts 8: 5-12.) "Then Philip opened his mouth, and began at the same scripture, and preached unto him Jesus. And as they went on their way, they came unto a certain water: and the eunuch said, See, here is water; what doth hinder me to be baptized? And Philip said, If thou believest with all thine heart, thou mayest. And he answered and said, I believe that Jesus Christ is the Son of God. And

he commanded the chariot to stand still: and they went down both into the water, both Philip and the eunuch; and he baptized him." (Acts 8: 35-38.) "And he commanded them to be baptized in the name of the Lord. (Acts 10: 48.) "And a certain woman named Lydia, a seller of purple, of the city of Thyatira, which worshiped God, heard us: whose heart the Lord opened, that she attended unto the things which were spoken of Paul. And when she was baptized, and her household, she besought us, saying, If ye have judged me to be faithful to the Lord, come into my house, and abide there." (Acts 16: 14, 15.) "And they spake unto him the word of the Lord, and to all that were in his house. And he took them the same hour of the night, and washed their stripes, and was baptized, he and all his, straightway." (Acts 16: 31, 32.) "And many of the Corinthians hearing believed, and were baptized." (Acts 18: 8.) "And now why tarriest thou? arise, and be baptized, and wash away thy sins, calling on the name of the Lord." (Acts 22: 16.)

The foregoing quotations are inspired statements of facts as to what it took "to make Christians" in New Testament times. Still further light is thrown on this subject by certain passages in the inspired letters to Christians in the New Testament, which refer to the way the Christians addressed in those letters were made: "So many of us as were baptized into Jesus Christ were baptized into his death." (Rom. 6: 3.) "For as many of you as have been baptized into Christ have put on Christ." (Gal. 3: 27.) "In whom also ye are circumcised with the circumcision made without hands, in putting off the body of the sins of the flesh by the circumcision of Christ; buried with him in baptism, wherein also ye are risen with him through the faith of the operation of God, who hath raised him from the dead." (Col. 2: 11, 12.) "According to his mercy he saved us, by the washing of regeneration, and renewing of the Holy Ghost." (Tit. 3: 5.) "The like figure whereunto even baptism doth also now save us, (not the putting away of the filth of the flesh, but the answer of a good conscience toward God,) by the resurrection of Jesus Christ." (1 Pet. 3: 21.)

And, finally, the New Testament teaches that what it takes to make Christians is to "be born again." "Whosoever believeth that Jesus is the Christ is born of God." (1 John 5: 1.) "Of his own will begat he us with the word of truth, that we should be a kind of firstfruits of his creatures." (James 1: 18.) "For in Christ Jesus I have begotten you through the gospel." (1 Cor. 4: 15.) "Being born again, not of corruptible seed, but of incorruptible, by the word of God, which liveth and abideth forever." (1 Pet. 1: 23.) "Except a man be born of water and of the Spirit, he cannot enter into the kingdom of God." (John 3: 5.)

The foregoing passages convey a very clear idea of what it took "to make Christians" according to the process prescribed by Jesus and practiced by the inspired men who established the New Testament churches.

But "is baptism one of the requirements" in making Christians? The answer to this question must be determined by what the New Testament says as to the doctrine and practice of the inspired men Jesus sent to make Christians and establish churches "among all nations, beginning at Jerusalem." As to doctrine, they taught: "He that believeth and is baptized shall be saved" (Mark 16: 16); "Baptism doth also now save us " (1 Pet. 3: 21) ; " He saved us by the washing of regeneration, and renewing of the Holy Ghost " (Tit. 3: 5) ; " Rejected the counsel of God against themselves, being not baptized of him " (Luke 7: 30) ; " Commanded them to be baptized in the name of the Lord " (Acts 10: 48) ; " Repent, and be baptized every one of you in the name of Jesus Christ for the remission of sins " (Acts 2: 38) ; "Arise, and be baptized, and wash away thy sins, calling on the name of the Lord " (Acts 22: 16) ; " Baptized into Jesus Christ " (Rom. 6: 3) ; " In whom ye have redemption through his blood, even the forgiveness of sins " (Col. 1: 14) ; " For as many of you as have been baptized into Christ have put on Christ " (Gal. 3: 27) ; " Therefore if any man be in Christ, he is a new creature " (2 Cor. 5: 17) ; " Except a man be born of water and of the Spirit, he cannot enter into the kingdom of God " (John 3: 5). As to the practice of inspired teachers in New Testament times, they baptized folks " when they believed " (Acts 8: 12) ; " forthwith " (Acts 9: 18) ; " as they went on their way " (Acts 8: 36) ; " straightway " (Acts 16: 33) ; " the same day " (Acts 2: 41) ; and " the same hour of the night " (Acts 16: 33). Another significant feature of their practice was that they baptized all who became disciples, or Christians. "Jesus made and baptized more disciples than John " (John 4: 1) ; " make disciples of all the nations, baptizing them " (Matt. 28: 19, Revised Version) ; " then went out to him Jerusalem, and all Judea, and all the region round about Jordan, and were baptized," etc. (Matt. 3: 6) ; " they that gladly received his word were baptized," and they that were not baptized " rejected the counsel of God against themselves " (Acts 2: 41; Luke 7: 30). All who became disciples, or Christians, under New Testament preaching were baptized immediately. Such is the material furnished by the New Testament, out of which must be constructed the answer to the brother's question: "Is baptism one of the requirements?" Out of this material each soul must build an answer for itself, on which it must meet God in judgment. In constructing an answer, every one should be careful not to strain any of the facts, put into the answer any material not found in the New Testament, or leave out of the answer any misfit New Testament statement. If the *Baptist and Reflector* and all other religious teachers will give the people all this New Testament material and let them form their own convictions as to whether baptism is one of the requirements, the GOSPEL ADVOCATE will not complain. No matter what conclusion the people reach as to whether baptism is one of the requirements, they will not fail to observe the difference between the doctrine and practice of New Testament preachers and Christians and the doctrine and practice of modern preachers and Christians on this point. The passages above cited from the New Testament, which were the utterances of inspired evangelists and revivalists in apostolic times, are rarely, if ever, heard in revivals now. Some of the most popular revivalists of modern times have refused to allow these passages and others of like import to be distributed in their meetings on circulars containing nothing but quotations from the Bible. The exact truth is that popular revivalists in these modern times do not baptize folks at all. Those who profess to becomes disciples, or Christians, in modern revivals are left unbaptized. Some of them are baptized on application to churches at regular meetings, usually weeks, and often months, and even years, after they profess to become Christians; but *many*, and probably *most*, of them are never baptized at all. There are no such cases of delay or of entire neglect and repudiation of baptism in all the New Testament history of the labors of the inspired men Jesus sent to make Christians and establish churches " among all nations, beginning at Jerusalem." Even if preachers should conclude that baptism is not " one of the requirements," would it not be well for them to follow the language of the New Testament in formulating their doctrine and shaping their practice? Or, to put it differently, ought not preachers and Christians now preach and practice what Christians and preachers in New Testament times preached and practiced on this subject and let folks determine for themselves, in the light of such preaching and practice, whether baptism is " one of the requirements? "

BEGINNING OF BAPTIST DENOMINATION.

The *Baptist and Reflector* says : " The Baptists began their denominational life under the ministry of Christ the Savior in the first century." Then how shall we account for the fact that the Baptist denomination is not mentioned at all in the New Testament? Was it because a man can be a Christian and go to heaven without joining the Baptist denomination, as the *Baptist and Reflector* and the *Baptist Gleaner* both admit, and the writers of the New Testament considered it unnecessary to pay any attention at all to it?

THE RATIO DECREASING.

The Baptist papers are worrying over the fact that "the ratio of Baptists to the population in New York has been long steadily decreasing." I see no cause for alarm in this. It is nothing more than John the Baptist—and, by the way, he is the only Baptist we read about in the Bible—predicted more than eighteen hundred years ago. Speaking of Christ, John said: "He must increase, but I must decrease." (John 3: 30.) The Baptists have a hard pull against the wickedness of New York and the prediction of the Scriptures, and it is no cause of surprise if they dwindle down to a mere handful in the struggle. The wonder is that they have not played out altogether these many years ago! But suppose they are decreasing; what then? A man can be a Christian, obey every command God has ever given, and go to heaven without being a Baptist, and even if there were not a Baptist in the world!

THE NAME "CHRISTIAN" IN THE MINUTES.

My Baptist brother, J. B. Moody, is greatly vexed in spirit because at the late General Baptist Association, at Owensboro, Ky., it was publicly announced "that a certain brother would preach at the Methodist Church, another at the Presbyterian Church, another at the Baptist Church, and still another at the Christian Church, thus locating the Baptist Church at one place and the Christian Church at another, and this announcement had gone into the minutes and no protest." Brother Moody says:

If I had ten thousand lives, I would lay them all down

before I would indorse the announcement by my personal
presence at that place and time. . . . If the Baptist
Church is not the church of Christ, then those who believe
it is not, and that so strongly as to say it under such adverse circumstances, ought to go out from it, and they ought
not to wait on the order of their going.

It is worthy of note that the church of Christ is never
called the "Baptist Church" in the New Testament.
There is no scriptural authority to call it the "Baptist
Church" now. If the Baptist Church is the church of
Christ, then those who believe it is ought by all means
to call it the " church of Christ." They have no right
to call it the "Baptist Church," and to do so is misleading as well as unscriptural. Brother Moody seems determined that the church of Christ shall not be called by its
right name if he can prevent it.

DISCIPLES BEFORE ALEXANDER CAMPBELL.

Some weeks ago I stated that " there were Christians,
or disciples of Christ, just such as we are trying to be,
who did not belong to the Baptist Church, or the Methodist Church, or the Presbyterian Church, or the Episcopal Church, or any other denomination, before Alexander Campbell was born." The *Baptist and Reflector*
says:

We are surprised at our brother for such a reckless denial of the facts of history. True, there were some in all
ages who held somewhat similar ideas to those expressed
by Mr. Campbell, but those ideas were cloudy and unsystematized. It remained for Mr. Campbell to lick them into
shape, and he it is who is recognized by the world and was

proclaimed by Henry Clay to be the organizer, the founder, and the father of the system of religion now known as Campbellism, which system Brother Srygley and his people now follow with slavish adherence.

As this is a matter of more than ordinary importance, I will make one more effort to set the *Baptist and Reflector* right. I read about Christians, or disciples of Christ, in the New Testament several hundred years before either Mr. Campbell or Mr. Clay was born. These ancient Christians, or disciples of Christ, were not members of the Baptist Church, or the Methodist Church, or the Presbyterian Church, or the Episcopal Church. There are no such churches mentioned in the New Testament. They are spoken of as members of the church of God, the churches of Christ, etc., etc. Their system of doctrine is fully set forth in the New Testament. It does not seem to me to be at all " cloudy and unsystematized; " but if it is, I am in favor of it remaining just that way. Mr. Campbell did not " lick it into shape," either, or, if he did, I decline to take it in the shape he *licked* it. I prefer to take it in precisely the shape it is given in the New Testament before Mr. Campbell or anybody else gets a *lick* at it. I do not belong to anything of which Mr. Campbell is " the organizer, the founder, and the father." I care no more about anything Mr. Campbell ever did or said than for what Mr. Wesley, Mr. Luther, or Mr. Calvin did and said. I dare say they were all great and good men, and that each of them held the truth of God on some points and believed and preached errors on other points, but not one of them ever held a correct idea in matters of religion which he did not get from the Bible. If people want to be partisans and factionists in religion and form themselves into sects and denominations by following these or other uninspired men instead of Christ and the apostles, that is their business, of course, but, "with charity for all and malice toward none," I prefer to stand aloof from all such parties and factions; be simply a Christian, or a disciple of Christ; "fear God, and keep his commandments;" and endeavor to keep "the unity of the Spirit in the bond of peace." Many others are of the same mind with me. The *Baptist and Reflector* can continue to misrepresent us and insult us by calling us "Campbellites" if it wants to, of course, but it can hardly misunderstand us. There is no law to compel a man to tell the truth and act the part of a gentleman in this State.

THAT GHOST OF A PONY.

The *American Baptist Flag,* J. N. Hall, editor, remarks:

The first-page editor of the GOSPEL ADVOCATE has ridden almost to death the ghost of a pony whose swayed backbone is made up of this sentence: "The same process that makes one a Christian adds him to the one body—the church." If that poor beast, that theological scrapegrace of a ghostly steed, could have the invigorating provender that can be gathered from the inspired writings, his leanness would not be so manifest; but one good grain of sound gospel food will kill the thing dead, for it can stand nothing of more substance than the thin gruel of editorial assertion and assumption from the advocates of Campbellism.

This proposition has been and will continue to be made prominent in these columns, because it makes a

clear issue between denominationalism and undenominational New Testament Christianity. If this proposition
is true, all denominations are wrong and ought to be
abolished. If Editor Hall will undertake to show that
this proposition is not according to the teaching of the
New Testament, I will publish his argument in the
ADVOCATE if he will publish my reply in the *Flag*.

DISCIPLES IN TENNESSEE.

Pastor John T. Oakley, of the Baptist denomination,
aims a point at his "friend Srygley" in the *Baptist
Helper* in the following words:

"There are no Disciples of Tennessee in the New Testament." (F. D. Srygley.)

On the same page, next column, but in another article,
the confused editor says: "There are over fifty thousand
Christians in Tennessee who object to everything but the
Bible as authority in religion." Here my friend Srygley
talks two ways. In one article he belongs to nothing in
religion smaller than all the Christians in Tennessee, but
in the next article, on the same page, he gives himself the
black eye by finding over fifty thousand certain kind of
Christians in Tennessee. This is Srygley's denomination.
He goes a little further in his sectarian views and says:
"In the city of Nashville there are over three thousand
such Christians." If F. D. Srygley is not a partisan in religion, not identified with any religious sect or party of
Christians, why does he find fifty thousand certain kind of
Christians in Tennessee? Why does he pick out three thousand in Nashville? The fact of the business is, the brother
is like a drunken man who charges that everybody else is

drunk but himself. Srygley is a sectarian of the deepest rank.

The fact that there are over fifty thousand Christians in Tennessee who object to everything but the Bible as authority in religion is no evidence that F. D. Srygley belongs to anything in religion smaller than the church, which is the body of Christ, and of which every Christian is a member. He doesn't belong to those fifty thousand Christians, except in the sense that they and all other Christians belong to the church, or body of Christ, of which he is a member. Any Christian, or any number of Christians, can object to everything but the Bible as authority in religion and still not belong to anything smaller than the church, which is the body of Christ, and of which every Christian is a member. In fact, no Christian can belong to anything smaller than that without accepting something besides the Bible as authority in religion. There is no authority in the Bible for any Christian to belong to anything smaller than that. There are no Disciples of Tennessee in the New Testament. For that reason Srygley declines to be a Disciple of Tennessee. All the Christians in the New Testament object to everything but the Bible as authority in religion. For that reason Srygley objects likewise. If those fifty thousand Christians who file that objection in Tennessee are Srygley's denomination, by the same token all the Christians in the New Testament are Srygley's denomination, too. Does Brother Oakley seriously think it makes one " a sectarian of the deepest rank " to " object to everything but the Bible as authority in religion? " If so, will he please explain how one can be a Christian and not be " a sectarian of the deepest rank? " According to his way of thinking, what must

10

one acknowledge besides the Bible as authority in religion in order to be a Christian and not be a sectarian?

MORE CONSISTENCY.

Our brother of the *Baptist and Reflector* dodges the issue again. I have taken pains to explain the situation to him several times, and, at the risk of being monotonous, I will quote the language again:

> We are not trying to be anything but Christians, and we are not willing to accept a name which would lead people to believe we are something which we have never made any effort to be. This is why we cling to such names as "Christians," "disciples of Christ," etc. It is this effort to be more than a Christian that causes trouble. As long as Methodists and Presbyterians and Baptists work and worship as Christians only, they love each other and get on gloriously; but when they begin to operate as Baptists, Methodists, and Presbyterians, they grow contentious and drift into very ugly divisions. And yet they all say it is not necessary to be Baptists, Methodists, or Presbyterians in order to be Christians and get to heaven. The point I make is simply this: No man has a right to be anything more than a Christian, and the man who causes strife and division in the family of God by introducing anything not essential to Christianity and eternal salvation is clearly condemned by the plain language of the New Testament. Will the *Baptist and Reflector* deny this?

And after all this the brother kicks against the pricks on this wise:

> Our Campbellite friends are continually crying out, "Unity, unity, Christian unity!" and yet they are not united among themselves. Be a little more united among your-

selves, gentlemen, before you insist so strongly upon Christian unity. It comes with bad grace, we must say, from you, to be urging unity when you yourselves are so divided into factions. By "Christian unity," of course, you mean that you want everybody to become Campbellites—that is, to think as you do. But before we all decide to go over to you, tell us which one we are to go to. A little more consistency may not hurt you, gentlemen, and may help along the Christian unity you so much desire.

The brother errs, not understanding our position. We are not asking anybody to come over to us. All we are trying to do is to obey the commands of God. We are perfectly willing to go over to him if such a thing is essential to obedience to God. I feel disinclined to do anything God has never required, just to gratify the Baptist brethren. I give it as my opinion that a man can do everything God requires, and yet not become a member of the Baptist Church. Will the *Baptist and Reflector* name a single thing God requires which cannot be done without joining the Baptist Church. I trow not. This is the whole thing in a nutshell. The Baptist Church is a very good sort of thing in its way; and if I had time, I would not be averse to taking a hand in it. But it keeps me busy to obey God. This doing something more than God has required—this trying to be something more than a Christian—is the point I make against him. Never mind about unity, dear brother. Do you just do what God requires and leave off those things he does not require and the unity business will take care of itself, so far as you are concerned. And whatever you do, please try to cultivate better manners than to use that offensive word "Campbellite." It does not speak well for your raising.

By the way, the *Baptist and Reflector* has not told us yet whether a man who deliberately and persistently refuses to be baptized after he is fully informed as to the teaching of the Scriptures concerning that ordinance can be a Christian and be finally saved in heaven. Please give attention to this question.

HOW TO BE OR BECOME A CHRISTIAN.

Some weeks ago I asked the *Baptist and Reflector* how a man can be a Christian without being a Campbellite, a Methodist, a Baptist, or a Presbyterian. The *Western Recorder* answers:

A man becomes a Christian by simply "repentance toward God and faith toward our Lord Jesus Christ." When he joins a church, he becomes a member of the denomination of which that church is a part. No denomination can claim to be simply Christians, since all the denominations claim to be Christians. So to call a man a "Christian" to mark his church or denomination is equivalent to saying that other churches or denominations are not Christians. Here in Louisville, not a great while ago, was organized the "Third Christian Church," and yet there were nearly a hundred churches in the city at the time, all claiming to be Christian. We have also what is called the "First Christian Church," though it was by no means the first Christian church organized in the city. So we see the Disciples adopt the name "Christian" as a denominational name, and to concede this name to them is to deny that other churches are Christian. The claim is, therefore, ridiculous.

I think the brother is in error as to how a man becomes a Christian, but for the present I waive any discussion of that point. When a man becomes a Christian, what more is required of him by the Bible than to keep the commandments of God, as a child of God, till he dies? In other words, does the *Recorder* defend this denomination business as a New Testament institution or simply a human expedient? Assuming that I am a Christian, by what authority am I required to join a denomination? I have never joined a denomination yet, and unless there is a Scripture requirement of that kind I feel disinclined to do anything of the sort. Will the *Recorder* please state whether or not it understands the Bible to require a *Christian* to join a *denomination?*

A NARROW CONCEPTION OF HEAVEN.

For several weeks I have been pressing the point that inasmuch as everybody admits that a man can be a Christian and go to heaven without being a Methodist, or a Baptist, or a Presbyterian, or an Episcopalian, or a Campbellite, or anything else of that kind, I see no reason why I should be anything but a common sort of a Christian, or disciple of Christ, such as we read about in the New Testament. It is enough for me to be a Christian and go to heaven. It is amusing to see those who belong to the various churches which are not mentioned at all in the Bible, and which they themselves admit a man need not join in order to be a Christian and be saved, try to explain why folks should join them. The latest effort of the *Baptist and Reflector* is to this effect:

The editor of the GOSPEL ADVOCATE has asserted a number

of times of late that just so he can be a Christian and go
to heaven when he dies, that is all he wants. Now, we
must say that is the lowest, narrowest conception of heaven
we have ever heard expressed. We confess that that is *not*
all we want. We believe in different degrees of reward in
heaven to a Christian, as Paul teaches in 1 Cor. 3: 14. For
our part, we shall not be satisfied just simply to get to
heaven and have all of our life work burned. We don't
want to be saved "yet so as by fire." We do not want just
to squeeze into the gates of heaven. We want to have what
Peter calls an *abundant* entrance into the everlasting kingdom of our Lord and Savior Jesus Christ.

I agree with the *Reflector* that it is not my desire
"just to squeeze into the gates of heaven," "yet so as
by fire," "and have all of our life work burned." I
want to save all my life work, as well as myself, and I
also want an *abundant* entrance into the everlasting
kingdom. That is why I decline to waste any time on
any kind of works not mentioned in the Bible. I am
putting in all my life work on things which he says the
Bible teaches and which I can read to anybody in the
Bible. If I suffer loss by fire in any of my life work,
the *Reflector* will not escape a singeing, too. But when it
comes to joining the Baptist Church, or the Methodist
Church, or the Presbyterian Church, or anything else
of that kind, which the Bible does not require, and which
everybody admits is not at all necessary to make a Christian or save a soul, I beg to be excused. It is difficult
to understand why the *Baptist and Reflector* so flippantly sets aside "some things which Jesus commands
to be done" as not being at all "essential to salvation,"
and so earnestly urges upon me some other things which
Jesus does not command to be done at all, and denounces
me as holding "the lowest and narrowest conception of

heaven we have ever heard expressed " because I decline
to engage in them. Now, on the hypothesis that there
are " different degrees of reward in heaven," about what
degree do you think the man ought to have who thus
irreverently slurs over and presumptuously sets aside
" some things which Christ commands to be done," and
defiantly wastes his time, and insists upon others doing
the same, in things which Christ does not command to
be done at all, and which he himself admits a man need
not do in order to be a Christian and be saved?

WHEN THE DENOMINATION BEGAN.

The *Baptist Gleaner* reminds " Brother Srygley: "

Your Brother Tyler is correct in saying the *denomination* to which you and he belong had its beginning in the
early part of the present century. Back of the days of the
Campbells it is not to be found anywhere on all the earth.
. . . To those who have observed your tantrums and ec-
centricities there is profound interest in·contemplating your
frantic efforts to be simply a Christian, when, in fact, you
began by being a Campbellite, and, while vainly imagining
yourself as independent of denominational affiliations as an
African Hottentot, you are bound hand and foot, heart and
life, voice and pen, to the ecclesiastical environments of
Alexander Campbell's movement, popularly known as the
Campbellite Church.

The *Gleaner* does not understand the situation. I do
not belong to the denomination which Brother Tyler
says " had its beginning in the early part of the present
century." It is a decidedly difficult matter to be a
Christian without being driven into a denominational

pen by such partisan herders as the *Baptist Gleaner,* I admit, but I think I will succeed along that line yet. And as to "tantrums" and "frantic efforts," I hardly think I am cutting any more of them trying to keep out of partisan pens than the *Gleaner* in trying to push me into a denominational corner. But if it takes "tantrums" and "frantic efforts" to be simply a Christian without being a Methodist, or a Baptist, or a Campbellite, or anything else in the way of a denominationalist, I rather think I will put in the rest of my days in "tantrums" and "frantic efforts."

THE ONE MAN AMONG US.

When the *Baptist and Reflector* complained about "the disposition which the ADVOCATE manifests in every issue to censure its own brethren in particular, as well as the rest of the world in general, including, of course, the Baptists," I explained that this part of the ADVOCATE "has no brethren in particular except those who fear God and keep his commandments. It contends earnestly for the faith once delivered to the saints, but serves no party in religion. . . . Those who depart from the truth of God in doctrine or practice will receive censure in every issue, no matter whose brethren they are."

Whereupon the *Christian-Evangelist* remarks:

What a blessed thing it is that we have *one* man among us who not only never departs from the truth of God in doctrine or practice himself, but who possesses a divine insight by which he is enabled to detect the slightest departures of all his brethren and to administer suitable censure for the same! Such things are too high for us. We cannot attain unto them. Still, we try not to envy one who has reached so exalted a height.

The *Christian-Evangelist* misses the point. In fact, it misses several points. (1) " We have *one* man among us." This is mistake number one. That one man is not " among us." The men " we " have " among us " in this denominational sense are very much like the men other people have among them; they work for the party and never do or say anything against " our brethren," lest they " damage the cause." (2) That " one man " has several times departed " from the truth of God in doctrine and practice himself," but as soon as he discovered the mistake he straightened himself up by the word of God without regard to the doctrine or practices of " all his brethren," or other people's brethren, either. His idea is to keep working along that line. (3) It does not require " a divine insight " to enable a man " to detect the slightest departures of all his brethren," and other people's brethren, too, " from the truth of God in doctrine or practice." The way to do it is to read the Bible carefully. If the *Christian-Evangelist* will read some in the Bible and abandon the old sectarian theory that it requires " a divine insight " to enable a man to understand " the truth of God " and to " detect " departures from it, I dare say it will soon begin to see a slight difference between truth and error touching the simpler matters of faith and practice. Will the *Evangelist* please try the experiment and report results?

CONCERNING INDEPENDENT THINKERS.

The *Christian-Evangelist* joins the *Christian Courier* against the proposition "to study the Bible carefully and give attention to what Christ and the apostles said when they first set themselves to work in the church of God, regardless of what Campbell and others said when they first set themselves to work in this reformation." It now seems that those who propose to "pass by Campbell, Wesley, Calvin, Luther, and all other uninspired men, and go straight to the Bible for information on all religious subjects," are not to receive any encouragement along that line from either the *Courier* or the *Evangelist*. The latter paper puts its veto in these words:

Alexander Campbell, Walter Scott, Dr. Richardson, Barton W. Stone, and their coworkers did well enough, perhaps, in their day; but they are back numbers now, and the Bible as illustrated and explained by the GOSPEL ADVOCATE (first page) is the only infallible rule of faith and practice. . . . Is there not a great deal of superficial talk of this kind among the would-be independent thinkers of our day? The writer confesses himself profoundly indebted to Alexander Campbell, and with him it makes a great deal of difference what such men as Luther, Wesley, and Campbell said upon any subject, for they were great men of profound learning and piety.

I have no ambition to play the rôle of an "independent thinker" on religious subjects. In truth, if I rightly understand the matter, no child of God has a right to be an "independent thinker" or to follow an "independent thinker" in matters of religion. The man who claims the right to think independently on the subject of religion is not truly converted to Christ,

and the man who follows "independent thinkers," no
matter how great or how profound in learning and piety
they may be, is "in the gall of bitterness and the bond
of iniquity." The very essence of true conversion is a
complete surrender of the whole man, including the
thinking apparatus, to the will of God as revealed in the
Scriptures. "Except ye be converted, and become as
little children, ye shall not enter into the kingdom of
heaven." (Matt. 18: 3.)

Correct ideas of religion are not to be dug out by the
Herculean efforts of the massive brains of deep and independent thinkers. God has "hid these things from
the wise and prudent, and . . . revealed them unto
babes." (Luke 10: 21.) Even Christ himself did not
claim to be an independent thinker. "My meat is to
do the will of him that sent me, and to finish his work."
(John 4: 34.) The apostles were specifically forbidden
to think independently. "Take no thought how or what
ye shall speak: for it shall be given you in that same
hour what ye shall speak. For it is not ye that speak,
but the Spirit of your Father which speaketh in you."
(Matt. 10: 19, 20.)

The apostles were careful always to make the people
understand that they did not think out their sermons
themselves, but simply delivered the message which God
sent to the world by them. "The foolishness of God is
wiser than men; and the weakness of God is stronger
than men. . . . Not many wise men after the flesh,
not many mighty, not many noble, are called: but God
hath chosen the foolish things of the world to confound
the wise; and God hath chosen the weak things of the
world to confound the things which are mighty; and
base things of the world, and things which are despised,

hath God chosen, yea, and things which are not, to bring
to naught things that are: that no flesh should glory in
his presence. . . . And I, brethren, when I came
to you, came not with excellency of speech or of wisdom,
declaring unto you the testimony of God. For I determined not to know anything among you, save Jesus
Christ, and him crucified. . . . And my speech and
my preaching was not with enticing words of man's
wisdom, but in demonstration of the Spirit and of
power: that your faith should not stand in the wisdom
of men, but in the power of God." (1 Cor. 1: 25 to 2: 5.)

As to those who are not thus gifted with inspiration,
both Christ and the apostles continually urged them to
"pass by all uninspired men and go straight to the
Bible for information on all religious subjects."
"Search the scriptures; for in them ye think ye have
eternal life; and they are they which testify of me."
(John 5: 39.) "These were more noble than those in
Thessalonica, in that they received the word with all
readiness of mind, and searched the scriptures daily,
whether those things were so." (Acts 17: 11.) "But
continue thou in the things which thou has learned and
hast been assured of, knowing of whom thou hast
learned them; and that from a child thou hast known
the holy scriptures, which are able to make thee wise
unto salvation through faith which is in Christ Jesus.
All scripture is given by inspiration of God, and is
profitable for doctrine, for reproof, for correction, for
instruction in righteousness; that the man of God may
be perfect, thoroughly furnished unto all good works."
(2 Tim. 3: 14-17.) "So then faith cometh by hearing,
and hearing by the word of God." (Rom. 10: 17.)

Finally, both Christ and his apostles repeatedly

warned people of the danger of being led away from
the Scriptures by uninspired "independent thinkers,"
and exhorted them to "hold fast the form of sound
words" (2 Tim. 1: 13), and to be not "corrupted from
the simplicity that is in Christ" (2 Cor. 11: 3). "Be-
ware lest any man spoil you through philosophy and
vain deceit, after the traditions of men, after the rudi-
ments of the world, and not after Christ." (Col. 2: 8.)
"But though we, or an angel from heaven, preach any
other gospel unto you than that we have preached unto
you, let him be accursed." (Gal. 1: 8.) "But in vain
they do worship me, teaching for doctrines the commandments of men." (Matt. 15: 9.) It was with
these and other scriptures of like import in mind that I
proposed to "pass by Campbell, Wesley, Calvin, Luther,
and all other uninspired men, and go straight to the
Bible for information on all religious subjects." I see
no reason yet to modify that proposition.

I am not at all disturbed by the *Evangelist's* remark
about "superficial talk." Nor do I raise any question
as to whether "Luther, Wesley, and Campbell . . .
were great men of profound learning and piety." No
matter how great they were, or how profound their
"learning and piety," not one of them ever had a correct idea on religious subjects that he did not get from
the Bible. Some of them, if not all of them, held some
errors in matters of faith and practice contrary to the
Bible. It has always been my understanding that
"Alexander Campbell, Walter Scott, Barton W. Stone,
and their colaborers" urged the people to "pass by all
uninspired men and go straight to the Bible for information on all religious subjects;" but no matter whether
my understanding on this point is correct or not, that is

clearly the proper thing to do. In so far as Campbell, Wesley, Luther, Calvin, and other "great men of profound learning and piety" encouraged and helped people to do this, their lives and labors have been blessings to mankind; but in so far as the life and labors of either or' all of them have tended to divert the minds and hearts of people from the Scriptures and build up sects of partisan followers in religion, they have hindered the gospel, wounded the body of Christ, perverted the truth of God, and darkened the understanding of their proselytes.

The *Evangelist* seems to give undue weight to the alleged greatness of men and supposed profundity of their learning and piety in determining the value of their teaching. The better plan, it seems to me, is to settle all such questions by the word of God. The greatness of the man or the profundity of his learning and piety should not be allowed to cut too large a figure in the case. Some very great men of very profound learning and piety occasionally make egregious mistakes; and when a great man does happen to get between the people and the Bible, he shades the patch and yet bears no fruit himself. In such a case it would unquestionably improve the crop to deaden him. Some very good people think that a little stiffer defense of the word of God and a little less yielding to "great men of profound learning and piety" would greatly improve the tone and policy of the *Christian-Evangelist,* notwithstanding its many other excellencies.

The *Evangelist's* remark to the effect that "the Bible as illustrated and explained by the GOSPEL ADVOCATE (first page) is the only infallible rule of faith and practice" is a little sarcastic, but, withal, pregnant with meaning. It is difficult to get religious partisans and denominationalists, especially those long accustomed to unduly reverence "great men of profound learning and piety," to grasp the idea that the Bible does not need to be "illustrated and explained" by anybody. The point to emphasize here is that God "illustrated and explained" the Bible when he indicted it, and that he gave it, not to "great men of profound learning and piety" to be "illustrated and explained," and then given to common people secondhand, but that he gave it to the people as an "infallible rule of faith and practice" without any necessity for it being further "illustrated and explained" by the first page of the GOSPEL ADVOCATE, Alexander Campbell, John Wesley, Martin Luther, or anybody else. It is a little discouraging to find it necessary to go over these simple elementary principles for the benefit of such papers as the *Christian-Evangelist* and the *Christian Courier* at this late day, but they may yet be taught "the way of the Lord more perfectly" touching these things.

WHAT ARE THE DISCIPLES OF CHRIST?

A few weeks ago the *Western Recorder* expressed the opinion that the disciples of Christ are a denomination and wanted to know what they are if not a denomination. I referred to the New Testament as the only authority on the subject, so far as I know, and suggested that the editor of the *Recorder* might possibly learn what the disciples of Christ are by reading that antiquated document. To that suggestion it makes this reply:

The GOSPEL ADVOCATE comments on our recent paragraph about its denial that the disciples are a denomination, but does not reply to our question. It persists in its
denial, but does not tell us what they are. We really would
like to know. Do tell us, Brother ADVOCATE, just what your
people are. You claim to be Christians; but we all claim
that, and the name "Christian," being already appropriated
to all who accept Christ of all denominations, cannot be
appropriated to one denomination. But you will say: "We
are not a denomination." Then what are you? If we
should call you "Christians," that would be to surrender
our claim to that name, and it would denominate you, and
so would make you a denomination. So if we call you
"disciples," or by any name whatever.

Well, it is a little difficult for a man who has been
associating with Methodists, and Baptists, and Presbyterians, and such like all of his life to understand who
the disciples of Christ, or Christians, are, sure enough,
especially when he will not carefully study the New
Testament, which is the only source of information on
that subject. However, I will make another effort to
explain who the disciples of Christ are. All those and
only those who believe on the Lord Jesus Christ and
obey the commandments of God as taught in the Scriptures are disciples of Christ, or Christians. It is not
necessary for a man to be a Baptist, a Methodist, a Presbyterian, or anything in the whole catalogue of religious
denominations in order to be a Christian, or a disciple
of Christ. All that is necessary is for him to believe
the Bible, obey the Bible, love God, and follow Christ.

WHAT SHALL WE CALL THEM.

The *Western Recorder* is in trouble. It states its difficulty in these words:

The GOSPEL ADVOCATE denies that the disciples are a denomination. We wish it would tell us what they are. We have long been at a loss to know just what to call them so as to be understood and at the same time not to be offensive. Now, we are left in doubt as to what they are. They do not claim to be a church, since each congregation is independent; and if they are not a denomination, what are they?

Well, the New Testament is the only authority I now call to mind on this question. It has much to say about the disciples of Christ. Suppose the *Recorder* look through it carefully and tell us what they seem to be as described in that document. I do not understand that the disciples of Christ, as described in the New Testament, are a denomination, and I am unwilling to be a disciple in any other sense than that in which the term is used in the New Testament. When the *Recorder* wants to speak of the disciples of Christ whom we read about in the New Testament " so as to be understood and at the same time not to be offensive," for instance, what does it do about it? Does it call them " Campbellites?" O, I hope not. Is it ever " left in doubt as to what they are " in the New Testament? I dare say it is not. The question is: Can folks nowadays believe on the Lord Jesus Christ, obey the commandments of God, and be Christians, or disciples of Christ, without joining a party in religion, just as they did in apostolic times? And can the disciples of Christ, or Christians, in any community, form themselves into a church of Christ, keep all the commandments and

11

ordinances of the Lord and attend to their own business, *as a church of Christ,* without becoming a part of a sect, or denomination, in religion, just as folks did in apostolic times? Certainly all these things can be done, for everybody *says* they can, and the Bible clearly teaches that they can. That's the way folks did in apostolic times. Those who did that then were called "disciples of Christ," "Christians," etc. That's the way for the *Recorder* to speak about folks who do that way now "so as to be understood and not to be offensive." Will it do it? Well, I hope so.

THE REPORT OF THE GADSDEN MEETING.

The *Baptist and Reflector* picks a flaw in the report of the Gadsden meeting in these words:

In reporting a meeting recently held by him at Gadsden, Ala., Brother F. D. Srygley says in the GOSPEL ADVOCATE: "There were two immersions [no professions of faith, we presume], and one Baptist abandoned denominationalism [and joined the Campbellites, we presume]."

The *Baptist and Reflector presumes* against facts, as usual. Each of those immersed *professed* to "believe that Jesus Christ is the Son of God." That sort of profession of faith wouldn't count for much in a Baptist meeting, of course, but it gave entire satisfaction to Philip, in Acts 8: 37, and also to Christ, in Matt. 16: 16. And why should the *Baptist and Reflector* presume that a Baptist who abandoned denominationalism joined the Campbellites? The brother admits that a man can be a Christian without being a Baptist, or a

Campbellite, or any other kind of an ist or an ite. If the thing can be done, why does he persist in presuming against facts without any evidence for his presumption that it was not done? Will he please to tell us how a Baptist should proceed when he wants to abandon denominationalism without joining the Campbellites? Baptists frequently ask me how the thing can be done; and if I have not been giving the proper instructions, I should be glad for the *Baptist and Reflector* to set me right.

SPACE ALLOWED ON THE ORIGIN OF THE BAPTIST DENOMINATION.

The *Baptist Helper* accepts the proposition to allow him as much space on the origin of the Baptist denomination in the GOSPEL ADVOCATE as he can find on that subject in the Bible, and proceeds to say:

Now, notice, will you, that John was sent from God; that he was called "the Baptist;" that he preached, and was, therefore, a Baptist preacher; that he baptized those who came as directed by the Baptist preacher. If a Baptist preacher were to baptize any one, F. D. Srygley and all others would be ready to say at once that the one baptized is a Baptist; so also were those baptized by John the Baptist Baptists. Out of the material prepared by John the Baptist, Christ organized his church. See 1 Cor. 12: 28, where it is said: "God hath set some in the church, first apostles," etc. And since those Baptists were thus set in the church, any one can see that it was a Baptist Church.

· It does look like any one could see that, sure enough —that is, if he *wanted* to see it and was determined not to see anything else. But, strange to say, the men who wrote the New Testament did not see it. They never called it the "Baptist Church." They labored all the time under the mistake that it was the church of God, churches of Christ, and such like. At least that is what they *said* it was. Probably their mistake is due to the fact that the *Baptist Helper* was not there to explain it to them. Nor did the writers of the New Testament understand that those baptized by John the Baptist were Baptists. They went to their graves in the mistake that those baptized by John were *disciples* and that as many of them as went into the church of God, or churches of Christ, were *Christians.* At least that is what they *said* they were. "The disciples were called *Christians* first at Antioch." (Acts 11: 26.) They never were called "*Baptists*" anywhere in the New Testament. And, finally, the John the Baptist we read about in the New Testament was not the sort of Baptist that edits the *Baptist Helper.* He preached "the baptism of repentance *for the remission of sins.*" (Mark 1: 4.) The *Baptist Helper* doesn't preach it that way. He calls that "Campbellism."

ANOTHER BAPTIST IN TROUBLE.

Some weeks ago the GOSPEL ADVOCATE offered the *Baptist Helper* "as much space on the origin of Baptists, in the GOSPEL ADVOCATE, as he can find on that subject in the Bible." The *Helper's* effort seems to be unsatisfactory to my beloved brother, Dr. George A. Lofton, of this city, and he comes to the help of the *Helper* in the *Baptist and Reflector* in these words:

I seldom pick up the GOSPEL ADVOCATE that I do not find

some such fling at the Baptist denomination, and I want to
offer one thousand dollars reward to the GOSPEL ADVOCATE
for one passage or expression in the New Testament in which
the title "Christian Church" can be found. "The church of
God" or "the churches of Christ," more commonly the bare
title "church," or "churches," can be found. I find three
times where the title "Christian," used evidently as a term
of reproach by the Gentiles, was applied to the followers
of Jesus; but in no instance does a New Testament writer
employ the word for the purpose of designating a disciple
of Christ, much less a church of Christ. Perhaps I am mistaken; and if so, am hunting for one thousand dollars'
worth of information. I do not object to the title "Christian" as applied to anything that is Christian; it is the
height of assumption to apply it to something that is not
Christian. The Baptist churches are Christian churches,
whether they carry the name or not, if they bear the marks
of the gospel; and you may stick the name "Christian" all
over a church that is not Christian, but that does not make
it Christian. The GOSPEL ADVOCATE, or Elder Srygley, may
not be able to trace the origin of the Baptist churches; he
may not find them by name in the New Testament, but he
can find them there in fact. He would be terribly put to it
to find his so-called "Christian Church," for he well knows
that, beyond Alexander Campbell, his origin would cease
in an unlimited space of nonexistence. A rose by any other
name would smell just as sweet, especially if the name is
a good and characteristic one, as the word "Baptist" is.
You may call a poppy a "rose," however, but it will still
smell like a poppy. The word "Christian" is a beautiful
and sweet word, but it does not make Campbellism smell
any sweeter, nor speak and write any sweeter, nor do any
better. . . . If we are to judge by the teachings and
flings of the GOSPEL ADVOCATE or its editors, Baptists are not
Christians at all. The ordinary reader would be bound to
come to the conclusion, from Campbellite teaching and

preaching, that really there are no other Christians in the world than the followers of Alexander Campbell, called the "Christian Church" and just about sixty-five years old.

It seems from this that Brother Lofton considers it a "fling at the Baptist denomination" to offer "him as much space on the origin of Baptists, in the GOSPEL ADVOCATE, as he will find on that subject in the Bible." Well, the ADVOCATE has made several "flings" of that sort first and last, and its idea is to keep *flinging* in the same direction. If the Baptist brethren don't want the ADVOCATE to "fling" at them, they must get inside of the Bible in matters of religion.

Brother Lofton says "'the church of God,' or 'the churches of Christ,' more commonly the bare title 'church,' or 'churches,' can be found" in the Bible, but he can't find the Baptist denomination. And what is still worse, he can't find "the title 'Christian Church,'" and he offers the GOSPEL ADVOCATE a thousand dollars to find it for him. Brother Lofton ought to save his money and try to reconcile himself to such things as he can find in the Bible. That's the way the GOSPEL ADVOCATE does. When the ADVOCATE failed to find the title "Christian Church" in the Bible, it quit using it. Why doesn't Brother Lofton do that way as to the Baptist denomination? It smacks of rebellion against God to offer a thousand dollars for a title he can't find in the Bible, and at the same time refuse to use the titles he can find in the Bible without money and without price. The GOSPEL ADVOCATE wouldn't give fifteen cents for anything it can't find in the Bible in the way of religious doctrine or titles. But why should Brother Lofton give a thousand dollars to find the title "Christian Church" in the Bible? He ad-

mits that he has found several titles in the Bible which
he will not use, and he persists in using the title "Baptist Church," which he admits is not in the Bible at all.
What difference does it make with him whether a thing
is in the Bible or not? He pays no attention to what
the Bible says, anyhow. He admits that he is outside of
the Bible (" *by name* ") when he gets into the Baptist
denomination; and if he really wants to get to the Bible,
he needn't squander a thousand dollars to get there.
He can come to it any time he pleases, and it will not
cost him a cent.

Brother Lofton relies upon his *ipse dixit* against some
very stubborn facts, when he says: " I find three times
where the title ' Christian,' used evidently as a term of
reproach by the Gentiles, was applied to the followers of
Jesus; but in no instance does a New Testament writer
employ the word for the purpose of designating a disciple of Christ." This is a very lame excuse for re-
fusing to use titles he finds in the Bible, and a flimsy
pretext for using titles he cannot find in the Bible.
Does Brother Lofton, in all seriousness, refuse to use the
term " Christian " because he thinks the Gentiles used
it as a term of reproach. If so, why does he object to
the people he calls " Campbellites " using it, and why
is he so anxious for everybody to understand that Baptists and many others who do not call themselves " Christians " are really Christians " *in fact?* " Or does
Brother Lofton seriously decline to use the title " Christian " because he thinks no New Testament writer ever
employed the word to designate a disciple of Christ?
If so, it is difficult to understand why he uses the title
" Baptist denomination " constantly, when he well
knows that no New Testament writer ever employed

that term to designate anything. The fact is, Brother Lofton is something more than a Christian, and he has to use a title he can't find in the Bible to indicate it. He belongs to something more than "'the church of God,' or 'churches of Christ,' more commonly the bare title 'church,' or 'churches,'" and he has to use titles he can't find in the Bible to indicate the thing he belongs to, which is not in the Bible. He is a Baptist more than a Christian, and he belongs to the Baptist Church more than the church of God. There are no titles in the Bible to designate the Baptist denomination, for the simple reason that the Baptist denomination is not in the Bible. The titles that are in the Bible will not designate things that are not in the Bible. Brother Lofton is, therefore, compelled to use titles he can't find in the Bible so long as he holds to things which are not in the Bible, and he is displeased because some folks refuse to be anything but Christians, or to belong to anything but the church of God. "And the disciples were called Christians first in Antioch." (Acts 11: 26.) A New Testament writer uses the word "Christians" here to designate disciples of Christ, and it is doubtful whether the Gentiles ever used it as a term of reproach. "If a man suffer as a Christian, let him not be ashamed; but let him glorify God in this name." (1 Pet. 4: 16, Revised Version.) Peter was a New Testament writer, and not a Gentile, either, and he used the word "Christian" in this case, not as a term of reproach, but to designate disciples of Christ, whom he exhorted to glorify God *"in this name."* No New Testament writer ever exhorted anybody to glorify God in the name "Baptist." In fact, God can't be glorified in the Baptist name.

Brother Lofton says the GOSPEL ADVOCATE may not find the Baptist churches " by name in the New Testament, but he can find them there in fact," and " a rose by any other name will smell just as sweet." Certainly " a rose by any other name will smell just as sweet; " but how would the man smell, for instance, who would say a rose is a hollyhock? It wouldn't damage the smell of the rose, of course, but wouldn't it give a disagreeable odor to the veracity of the man who thus prevaricated about it? Brother Lofton admits that God says the churches we read about in the New Testament are " ' the church of God,' or ' the churches of Christ,' more commonly the bare title ' church,' or churches.' " But Brother Lofton says they are Baptist churches. It seems to me that this springs a question of veracity between Lofton and the Lord. And how much is Brother Lofton's testimony worth as to what those churches were " *in fact*," after the Lord thus flatly contradicts him as to what they were " *by name?* " Can a man who misses the truth that far " *by name* " be relied upon to fairly represent things " *in fact?* " No one objects to the title " Baptist Church " when applied to anything that is a Baptist church. It is well to call things by their right names. But when God says things are " ' the church of God,' or ' the churches of Christ,' more commonly the bare title ' church,' or ' churches,' " what right has Brother Lofton or anybody else to say they are Baptist churches? It is not a question now as to whether any particular church in this age and country is the church of God. The question is, whether the churches we read about in the New Testament are what God says they are—viz.: " ' The church of God,' or ' the churches of Christ,'

more commonly the bare title ' church,' or ' churches.' "
That is what God says they are, but Brother Lofton says they are Baptist churches. There is some
excuse for mistake when it comes to applying names
to churches in this age and country. A man might erroneously conclude that certain churches nowadays are
churches of Christ, when, in fact, they are nothing of
the kind. But what excuse has Brother Lofton for saying the churches of the New Testament are Baptist
churches, when God says they are churches of Christ?
The man who thus flatly contradicts the Lord as to the
name of things would probably walk defiantly over God
whenever he pleases in other matters. In changing the
name of New Testament churches from " churches of
Christ " to " Baptist churches," Brother Lofton takes
a liberty with the Lord's churches which he would not
suffer any man to take with Baptist churches. What
would he say, for instance, if I should impertinently
declare that the churches which he calls " Baptist
churches " are, in point of fact, Catholic churches?
He would resent—and very properly, too—such imper-
tinence. Then why should he presume to take liberties
with God's churches which he would not allow any man
to take with Baptist churches? He has a right to
change the name of " Baptist churches " to " churches
of Christ," if they will conform to the requirements
of the New Testament in all matters of doctrine and
practice, but he has no right to change the name of
" churches of Christ," in the New Testament, to " Baptist churches." The New Testament must not be
changed. Brother Lofton can come to it or stay away
from it, just as he pleases, but he cannot bring it to him.
Brother Lofton has also overlooked some important

differences "*in fact*" between the churches we read
about in the New Testament and the Baptist churches
in this country.

The churches of the New Testament came together on
the first day of the week to break bread among other
things. (Acts 20: 7; 1 Cor. 16: 1, 2; 1 Cor. 11: 20-29;
Heb. 10: 25.) Baptist churches in this country don't
do that way.

The churches of the New Testament never called
mourners, and hence never left any "mourners on the
ground." Baptist churches in this country often do
both.

The churches of the New Testament held this doctrine: "Repent, and be baptized every one of you in
the name of Jesus Christ for the remission of sins."
(Acts 2: 38.) "Arise, and be baptized, and wash away
thy sins, calling on the name of the Lord." (Acts 22:
16.) "Go ye into all the world, and preach the gospel
to every creature. He that believeth and is baptized
shall be saved; but he that believeth not shall be
damned." (Mark 16: 15, 16.) The Baptist churches
in this country hold no such doctrine as that; they call
that "Campbellism."

Each local church of the New Testament was independent of all other local churches. There was no such
thing as a denominational federation of churches in a
partisan brotherhood, excluding from its sectarian fellowship a large proportion of recognized Christians.
The churches of the New Testament were not combined
into associations, district and general conventions, and
such like. The Baptist churches in this country are
organized into both associations and general conventions.

Each New Testament church had a plurality of eld-

ers.   (Tit. 1: 5; Acts 20: 17.)   Baptist churches in
this country never have more than one elder to a church,
and usually they have but one elder for several churches.

The churches of the New Testament included all
Christians.   There was no such thing in New Testament times as a Christian who did not belong to the
church.   The same things which made folks Christians
added them to the church in those days.   Baptist
churches in this country have one way to make Christians and an entirely different process to add them to the
church.   Moreover, the Baptist churches includes but a
very small proportion of the Christians in this country,
according to their own admissions.

There are other important differences between the
churches of the New Testament and Baptist churches
in this country, but these are sufficient to show that
Brother Lofton misses the truth as far " *in fact* " as he
misses it " *by name.*"

The GOSPEL ADVOCATE cares nothing about anything
which Alexander Campbell or any other uninspired man
ever started in religion.   It is all one with the ADVO-
CATE whether such things are sixty-five years old or
sixty-five hundred.   Nor does the ADVOCATE ask Brother
Lofton or anybody else to join " the so-called ' Christian
Church,' " which ceases " in an unlimited space of nonexistence beyond Alexander Campbell."   The ADVOCATE
cares nothing about anything in religion which is not
clearly taught in the Bible.   Brother Lofton ought not
to pay any more attention to that sort of a " so-called
' Christian Church.' " than to the so-called " Baptist
Church " or any other kind of a so-called " church " that
he can't find in the Bible.   The thing for him to do
is to get out of the Baptist denomination, which he ad-

mits he can't find in the Bible, and stick close to the Bible in all matters of religion, and belong to nothing but "'the church of God,' or 'the churches of Christ,' more commonly the bare title 'church,' or 'churches,'" which he says "can be found" in the Bible.

The ADVOCATE has never said that "Baptists are not Christians at all," or that "there are no other Christians in the world than the followers of Alexander Campbell." The ADVOCATE's point is that people can be Christians and be saved without being either Baptists or followers of Alexander Campbell. Brother Lofton admits all this. Then why should any one be a Baptist or a follower of Alexander Campbell? The ADVOCATE is laboring and praying to get Baptists, Methodists, Campbellites, Presbyterians, Episcopalians, and all other denominationalists to give up their unscriptural denominationalism and be simply Christians, or disciples of Christ, such as we read about in the New Testament, and belong to nothing but "'the church of God,' or 'the churches of Christ,' more commonly the bare title 'church,' or 'churches,'" just as folks did in New Testament times, before the Baptist denomination or any other denomination was ever heard of. To this end, the ADVOCATE earnestly exhorts Brother Lofton to lay aside his superfluity of Baptist naughtiness and be simply a Christian, or disciple of Christ, while he lives and go to heaven when he dies.

> While the lamp holds out to burn,
> The vilest sinner may return.

DR. LOFTON'S OFFER OF A THOUSAND DOLLARS.

The *Baptist Helper* publishes Dr. Lofton's offer of a thousand dollars to the GOSPEL ADVOCATE " for one passage or expression in the New Testament in which the title ' Christian Church ' can be found," and suggests that if the ADVOCATE should fail to find such " passage or expression," it would " be well for them and their followers, country newspapers and correspondents, weak-kneed Baptists, and all others to quit using it." To be sure. And if the *Baptist Helper* and Dr. Lofton should fail to find " one passage or expression in the New Testament in which the title " Baptist Church " can be found, would it not be well for " weak-kneed Baptists and all others to quit using " that title, too? Brother Lofton and the *Baptist Helper* seem to think it is a grave offense in the GOSPEL ADVOCATE to use a title not found in the New Testament, but eminently proper for Baptists to use all sorts of things they can't find in the Bible.

" RIGHT, SO FAR AS THE SCRIPTURES GO TO SHOW."

My beloved brother, George A. Lofton, the Baptist, called out an article in these columns a few weeks ago by offering, in the *Baptist and Reflector,* a thousand dollars " for the title ' Christian Church ' to be found in the Bible." Not many days afterwards he made a four-column effort to reply to the ADVOCATE in the *Baptist and Reflector,* and, after reading his article, I felt inclined to let the case go to the public without further argument, but changed my mind and concluded to make a few more remarks, " for the satisfaction of the Baptists and a few others," in deference to the following suggestion from Gillum E. McCorkle, of Newbern, Tenn.:

I see you have silenced George A. Lofton's battery, and now he tries to play around with his small arms. He is small game, anyway, and I don't think you can afford to waste any ammunition on him; but, for the satisfaction of the Baptists and a few others, I will advise you to '*sock it to 'em.*' The Methodists and Cumberlands will read Lofton's pieces out loud, but will not read yours at all.

Of course, I must depend upon the brethren and friendly sinners who love fair play to read my articles to the Baptists, Methodists, Cumberlands, and others who are disposed to boycott the truth and quarantine against the word of the Lord.

Brother Lofton begins his article with a restatement of his offer of a thousand dollars " for the title ' Christian Church ' to be found in the Bible," and says:

The GOSPEL ADVOCATE's reply is this: '*When the ADVOCATE failed to find the title 'Christian Church' in the Bible, it quit using it.*'' This ends the Campbellite claim to the title " Christian Church," so far as the authority of the GOSPEL ADVOCATE is concerned; and, unquestionably, the ADVOCATE is right, so far as the Scriptures go to show.

The ADVOCATE never tries to be right any further than " the Scriptures go to show." The trouble with Brother Lofton and his Baptist brethren is they admit they are not right and refuse to get right—" by name " —" as far as the Scriptures go to show," but insist that they are right where the Scriptures do not go to show. What the ADVOCATE has said on this subject does not end "the Campbellite claim to the title 'Christian Church'" more conclusively than it ends the Baptist claim to the title "Baptist Church." If the position of the ADVOCATE is so satisfactory to Brother Lofton against the Campbellite claim to the title "Christian Church," why is it not just as conclusive against the Baptist claim to the title "Baptist Church?" Brother Lofton seems to think the Campbellites have no right to get outside of the Bible; but the Baptists are under no obligation to pay any attention to anything "the Scriptures go to show." The ADVOCATE simply sticks to the Bible, and has no more to do with Campbellites when they get out of the Scriptures than it has to do with Baptists before they get in the Book. The Scriptures go about as far to show against the Baptists as the Campbellites on this question. The title "Christian Church" is no further outside of the Bible than the title "Baptist Church." The Campbellites can probably see the force of the ADVOCATE's argument against the Baptists about as clearly as Brother Lofton can see it against the Campbellites, and everybody else can see that it knocks the Campbellites and Baptists both into a cocked hat.

Brother Lofton's next point is stated in these words:

The question now arises: To what church do the editors of the ADVOCATE belong? All the Campbellite churches in this city or this country pose under the title "Christian;" and the editors of the ADVOCATE belong to a church so named by itself, unless it has recently changed its title. Otherwise the editors of the ADVOCATE must belong to no church or a church of their own making and naming. Surely after this voluminous editorial they do not belong to the Christian Church.

The editors of the GOSPEL ADVOCATE belong to the church we read about in the New Testament. Brother Lofton told us in his former article that " ' the church of God,' or ' the churches of Christ,' more commonly the bare title ' church,' or ' churches,' " can be found in the Bible; but neither the Christian Church nor the Baptist Church is so much as named in the Scriptures. The editors of the ADVOCATE belong to that church which Brother Lofton says he can find in the Bible; and the trouble is to find out why Brother Lofton does not quit his Baptist naughtiness, which he admits he can't find in the Bible, and belong to the church he can find in the New Testament.

The brother's next point is to this effect:

What a hard time the Campbellites have had over their name—" Disciples," " Reformers," " Christians," etc.! And now comes the GOSPEL ADVOCATE trying to ignore Alexander Campbell and formally renouncing even the title " Christian!" What next? The only safe and certain name char-acteristic and definitive of the church to which the editors of the ADVOCATE belong is the patronymic of their father and founder, " Campbellite." The denomination is too young to be called the " church of Christ," or " church of God;" and its origin and nature are such, doctrinally and spiritually speaking, as to forbid that title. The title " Christian " is misnomer enough, and let it not be that a greater mistake shall follow. " Campbellite" is the only significant name which can crown the system of religion advocated by the ADVOCATE, unfortunately and erroneously called " GOSPEL ADVOCATE."

The Campbellites do seem to be having a hard time of it " over their name," sure enough; and, what is still worse for Brother Lofton, the Baptists are in the same hard row of stumps on this point. The fact is, when-

12

ever people undertake to go further than "the Scriptures go to show," in matters of religion, "over their name" or anything else, they will have "a hard time," no matter whether they are Campbellites or Baptists. "The only safe and certain" thing is for Campbellites and Baptists and everybody else to give up everything in religion which they can't find in the Bible and try to get along with such "patronymics" as the New Testament furnishes. The GOSPEL ADVOCATE is not trying any harder to ignore Alexander Campbell than George Lofton. It repudiates them both as authorities in matters of religion for the same reason—viz.: they are not inspired. When Brother Lofton says the ADVOCATE has renounced "even the title 'Christian,'" nothing but a charitable perversion of his language can possibly bring him within the limits of the truth. The ADVOCATE renounced the title "Christian Church" because it is not in the New Testament, and distinctly protested against Brother Lofton's effort to renounce the title "Christian" because it is used by New Testament writers with approval. At this point the brother pauses for breath and exclaims: "What next?" Well, if there is nothing else before the house, suppose we ask Brother Lofton and his Baptist brethren whether they are willing to lay aside their unscriptural "patronymics" and other incendiary "tenets" and content themselves in religion with what "the Scriptures go to show?" Brother Lofton need not trouble himself to think out a suitable name for the denomination the editors of the ADVOCATE belong to. They belong to no denomination. The only thing they belong to or feel any interest in, as to matters of religion, is "'the church of God,' or 'the churches of Christ,' more commonly the bare title

' church,' or ' churches,' " which Brother Lofton says
can be found in the New Testament, and they are fully
determined that neither Brother Lofton nor anybody else
shall lead them away from the Bible, even so far as to
change the name of things.

The brother next explains:

We are called " Baptists " simply because we baptize and
for the same reason that John was called " the Baptist "—
a title given by the Scriptures. . . . I am both a Baptist
and a Christian, and so of the church to which I belong, if
we have the marks of the gospel. If so marked, Baptist
churches are the churches of Christ; and if so, then the
New Testament churches were, in fact, Baptist churches,
though not technically so called at the time. . . . It
must be remembered, too, that the title " Baptist " was
never assumed by us. It was given to us, however properly, by our enemies."

If Brother Lofton and his brethren are so willing to
be called " Baptists " " for the same reason that John
was called ' the Baptist,' a title given by the Scriptures,"
why is it that they are not also willing to be called
" Christians " for the same reason that " the disciples
were called Christians first in Antioch "—" a title given
by the Scriptures? " (Acts 11: 26.) The disciples
never were called " Baptists " at all anywhere in the
New Testament. Brother Lofton and his brethren are
not called " Baptists " because they baptize. The editors of the GOSPEL ADVOCATE baptize " and preach the
baptism of repentance *for the remission of sins* " (Mark
1: 4), just as John did, and nobody calls them " Baptists." If John lived in these days and preached such
doctrine as that, Brother Lofton would call him a
" Campbellite." Moreover, the title " Baptist " never

was "given by the Scriptures" to anybody but John. Not one of those John baptized is ever called a "Baptist" in the New Testament. "Jesus made and baptized more disciples than John (though Jesus himself baptized not, but his disciples)." (John 4: 1, 2.) And yet Jesus and his disciples are never called "Baptists" in the Bible. If "the patronymic of their father and founder, ' Campbellite,' " is such a " safe and certain name, characteristic and definitive of the church to which the" Campbellites belong, why is not the patronymic of their Father and Founder, " Christian," just as " safe and certain name, characteristic and definitive of the church to which the" disciples of Christ belong? Campbellites and Baptists nowadays, and Jesus and his disciples in New Testament times, all baptize. Then why call some of them " Baptists," others " Campbellites," and others " Christians?" Brother Lofton says " our enemies " gave us the name " Baptist " *properly.* How does he know they did it properly? The Bible doesn't say it is proper at all to call the people of God " Baptists." Brother Lofton seems to think our friends who wrote the New Testament acted very improperly when they called the disciples " Christians," but our " enemies " did exactly the proper thing the first effort they made to give us a name. He evidently has more confidence in the judgment of the devil than the wisdom of God when it comes to naming the disciples of Christ. The ADVOCATE does not propose to allow " our enemies " to pervert the right way of the Lord by setting aside the names which the writers of the New Testament gave the disciples and imposing upon us names of their own choosing; and if Brother Lofton and his Baptist brethren have decided to meekly surrender to " our enemies," throw away the Bible, and let the devil run the whole country, they may as well prepare for a tussle with the GOSPEL ADVOCATE. The brother still insists that "Baptist churches are the churches of Christ; and if so, then the New Testament churches were, in fact, Baptist churches." He is anxious enough to make it appear that he is in harmony with the New Testament. The trouble is, he wants to change the Bible instead of the Baptists in order to prevent a clash. A schoolgirl can see that *something* must be changed, and Brother Lofton is moving heaven and earth to hold the Baptists steady and change the Bible. If " Baptist churches are the churches of Christ," why doesn't Brother Lofton call them that? Who changed the name from " churches of Christ " to " Baptist churches? " Brother Lofton says " our enemies " did it. And where were Lofton and the whole Baptist concern, and what were they doing, while " our enemies " were thus tampering with the word of God? And why is he now joining in with " our enemies " against the GOSPEL ADVOCATE and the Lord, instead of standing up like a man for the pure speech of the New Testament against the world, the flesh, the devil, and the Baptists? Of all the " enemies " who have corrupted the pure speech of the Scriptures by offensively thrusting upon the people of God ugly and insulting names unauthorized by the New Testament, the GOSPEL ADVOCATE has never yet struck a tougher specimen than George A. Lofton.

BROTHER LOFTON ON THINGS IN FACT.

After showing that Baptist churches differ from New Testament churches "by name"—a thing which Brother Lofton, by the way, freely admits—the GOSPEL ADVOCATE undertook to show that Baptist churches also differ from the New Testament churches in many respects "*in fact.*" Having disposed of his effort to reply, as to the names of things, in these columns last week, it is in order now to consider the brother's attempt to bend the New Testament churches to fit the Baptist pattern *in fact.*

The ADVOCATE reminded Brother Lofton that New Testament churches differed from Baptist churches in that "the churches of the New Testament came together on the first day of the week to break bread, among other things." To this the brother replies: "Baptists always celebrate the Lord's Supper on the first day of the week, though not on *every* first day; and it cannot be proven from the Scriptures that the law required *every* first day." It is hardly necessary to prove "from the Scriptures that the law required *every* first day." The fact is, there is but one first day of the week. Brother Lofton talks as though the week had ten or twelve first days. There is precisely the same requirement to "celebrate the Lord's Supper," as Brother Lofton puts it, *every* first day that there is to observe *every* first day at all, in any way. The law said: "Remember the Sabbath day, to keep it holy." If Brother Lofton had lived in those days, he probably would have said: "It cannot be proven from the Scriptures that the law required *every* Sabbath day." The fact is, there is but one Sabbath day. There is, also, but one first day. Celebrating the Lord's Supper, as Brother Lofton calls it, is simply one of the things we are required to do by way of remembering or observing the first day.

The ADVOCATE next made the point that Baptist churches differ from New Testament churches in that " the churches of the New Testament never called mourners, and hence never left any mourners on the ground. Baptist Churches in this country often do both." To this Brother Lofton replies:

I see that Dr. Lin Cave recently, in a revival at the Christian Church on Vine Street, this city, had some mourners, or inquirers, forward for prayer; and I do not conceive that there is any Campbellite mind so weak as to infer that this action on the part of Dr. Cave vitiated or destroyed the integrity of his church as a gospel institution.

Lin Cave is not a Doctor, and neither did he call any " mourners, or inquirers, forward for prayer " during " a revival at the Christian Church on Vine Street, this city," or at any other time or place. While Brother Vernon was preaching for that church in a protracted meeting, some mourners, who had been befuddled by the unscriptural preaching and practice of Baptists and others, when they ought to have been reading the Bible and obeying the gospel, came forward for prayer; but Brother Vernon and Brother Cave expounded unto them " the way of the Lord more perfectly," just as the ADVO-CATE is now trying to do for Brother Lofton. It is no unusual thing for such men as Brother Vernon and Brother Cave to have to pull good folks out of the unscriptural ideas they have learned from Baptists and others. Dr. Ananias once had a mourner, or inquirer, forward for prayers, too, and he told him to " arise, and be baptized, and wash away thy sins, calling on the name of the Lord." (Acts 22: 16.) Dr. Cave and

Brother Vernon settled the mourner question in the same way; but this is not according to "Baptist usage." But suppose Dr. Cave should go to calling mourners and leaving mourners on the ground in genuine Baptistic and unscriptural style; what then? If Dr. Cave and "his church" should depart from the New Testament in doctrine or practice, they wouldn't be any better than Dr. Lofton and his church. There might not be "any Campbellite mind so weak as to infer that" calling mourners and leaving mourners on the ground would vitiate or destroy the integrity of either Dr. Cave's church or Dr. Lofton's church "as a gospel institution." When a mind gets weak enough as to the teaching of the Bible to be a Campbellite or a Baptist, there is no telling what it will "infer," but the ADVOCATE makes bold to say such an action on the part of either Dr. Cave's church or Dr. Lofton's church would mark a wide departure from the New Testament churches. When the ADVOCATE undertakes to settle a question of doctrine or practice in matters of religion, it has no time to waste on Dr. anybody or his church this side of the New Testament. The question is: What did Dr. Paul and Dr. Peter and their churches do and say about it?

The ADVOCATE stated that Baptist churches differ from New Testament churches on another point, in that "the churches of the New Testament included all Christians. There was no such thing in New Testament times as a Christian who did not belong to the church. The same things which made folks Christians added them to the church in those days. Baptist churches in this country have one way to make Christians and an entirely different process to add them to the church." To this Brother Lofton replies:

Thank God, Baptist churches do not make Christians. God makes Christians. They are added to the church by baptism at the hands of the ministry. . . . It is not true that all Christians in apostolic times were included in the churches. I would like to know what church the eunuch belonged to after Philip baptized him. Doubtless thousands like the eunuch and others I could mention were unaffiliated with any church.

It is hardly necessary to thank God that Baptist churches do not make Christians. Come to think about it, Baptist churches are not trying to make Christians. The thing to thank the Lord for is that God doesn't make Baptists. God makes Christians, and the Baptist preachers and churches make Baptists. However, this Baptist manufactory is a modern industry which is not mentioned anywhere in the New Testament. God made Christians in New Testament times, "and the Lord added to the church daily such as should be saved." (Acts 2 : 47.) The Lord did it all, you see, and by the same process, just as the ADVOCATE said. Brother Lofton wants to know what church the eunuch belonged to when Philip baptized him. He belonged to the same church the editors of the GOSPEL ADVOCATE belong to, of course. That's all the church there was in those days, and all Christians belonged to it. Brother Lofton said, in his former article, that " ' the church of God,' or ' the churches of Christ,' more commonly the bare title ' church,' or ' churches,' can be found " in the New Testament in those days. That's the church the eunuch belonged to when Philip baptized him. Brother Lofton certainly does not think the eunuch was baptized without getting into any church at all. What else could he have been baptized for? Baptists all contend that

baptism is "the door into the church." "God makes
Christians; they are added to the church by baptism at
the hands of the ministry." (Lofton.) "Baptized
into Jesus Christ." (Rom. 6: 3.) "The head over all
things to the church, which is his body." (Eph. 1: 22,
23.) "For as the body is one, and hath many members, and all the members of that one body, being many,
are one body, so also is Christ. For by one Spirit are
we all baptized into one body." (1 Cor. 12: 12, 13.)
The eunuch was baptized into that one body. So, also,
were the editors of the GOSPEL ADVOCATE and everybody
else who has ever been baptized at all. That is the body
which Brother Lofton found in the New Testament
called "'the church of God,' or 'the churches of Christ,'
more commonly the bare title 'church,' or 'churches.'"
The Baptist denomination is nothing more than a one-
horse faction or sect, like the Campbellite denomination
and all other denominations, which well-meaning, but
misguided, folks have started since the New Testament
was written.

The ADVOCATE noted another difference between Baptist churches and New Testament churches in these
words:

There was no such thing as a denominational federation
of churches in a partisan brotherhood, excluding from its
sectarian fellowship a large portion of recognized Christians. Baptist churches in this country are organized into
both associations and general conventions.

To this Brother Lofton replies:

Alas, I see that the Campbellites hold conventions, just
like the Baptists. . . . We have associations and conventions for advising, educational, benevolent, or missionary purposes, composed of messengers from the churches

and other bodies, according to expediency; and we think we
find a gospel precedent (Acts 15) in the council held at Jerusalem—a precedent which the early Christians followed,
and which even the Campbellites themselves are beginning
to follow, GOSPEL ADVOCATE or no GOSPEL ADVOCATE.

The brother is in error again. The "Campbellites,"
as he calls them, do not claim to follow that precedent,
if I rightly understand them, •in their conventions.
"The method of the Methodists" seems to be the precedent upon which they principally rely. With few exceptions, they are too well informed in the Scriptures
to consider the council at Jerusalem (Acts 15) a precedent for "conventions for advising, educational, benevolent, or missionary purposes, composed of messengers
from the churches and other bodies, according to expediency." They know the convention at Jerusalem referred to in Acts 15 was not a mere advisory gathering
"according to expediency" at all, but a meeting with
the inspired apostles to settle an important question of
doctrine which could not be settled any other way. The
New Testament was not yet written, and hence it was
necessary to appeal to the college of inspired apostles at
Jerusalem to settle a dispute that arose in the church
at Antioch over the question of circumcision. It is
worthy of note that Brother Lofton tries to prove his
doctrine on this point, as well as on the mourners'-bench
question, by the "Campbellites," as he calls them. In
view of the opinion he has of Campbellites, he must
be hard pressed for evidence when he gives up the Bible
and relies upon them for proof. The ADVOCATE has
observed before that Baptists and Campbellites are much
more like each other on this general-convention question than either of them is like the New Testament

churches. When either of these denominations argues
this general-convention question, it always proves its
position by the other, but neither one of them ever
quotes any scripture for proof. It is doubtless a great
consolation to each of them to know it is as good as the
other. "Misery loves company." But all this effort
to prove their practices by each other is not worth a
cent in a controversy with the GOSPEL ADVOCATE or anybody else that sticks to the Bible. What good does it do
to say the Campbellites hold conventions, "GOSPEL AD-
VOCATE or no GOSPEL ADVOCATE?" The exact truth
is that Campbellites and Baptists both have taken the
bits in their teeth and determined to form denominational associations and hold general conventions, Bible
or no Bible, as well as GOSPEL ADVOCATE or no GOSPEL
ADVOCATE; but the answer to all this is that the GOSPEL
ADVOCATE has made up its mind to stick to the Bible,
Baptists or no Baptists, Campbellites or no Campbellites. Now, let us see who will get the best of the tussle
in the end.

THE BASIS OF UNION.

A correspondent in the *Church Union* quotes Bishop
Wilmer as saying he delighted in the union of all of
God's people, and was ready at any time to do all in
his power to bring about such union. When asked on
what basis he preferred such union, he very promptly
said : "On that of the first three centuries." Upon this
the correspondent referred to suggests that the editor
of the *Church Union* appoint a commission to "report a
basis of union founded on principles on which all were

agreed before our present unfortunate divisions began."
To this suggestion the editor replies:

We decline to move in the appointment of any such commission, not only because we claim no authority for such
work, but also because we doubt the wisdom of it. The
"first three centuries" embrace two centuries after the
apostles had been called from the earthly church to the
Zion that is above. After their departure, as one of them
predicted, grievous wolves entered in, not sparing the flock;
and though the second and even the third century may be
studied by us for instruction and for quickening, they afford us no authority whatever. Those two centuries, as
well as the nineteenth and every other period, must be
judged by the divine standard given by the Holy Spirit
through Christ's apostles, the last of whom died near the
close of the first century. We commend to our esteemed
correspondent and to all lovers of union in the church that
each appoint himself on a committee to study the "basis
of union" on which the church was agreed and which may
be found between the first verse of the Gospel according to
Matthew and the benediction that closes the book of the
Revelation.

This is decidedly good preaching, and, coming from
the source it does, it should greatly encourage those who
have been at work along that same line since Mr. Campbell preached his celebrated sermon on the law. Brethren, the world *do move.*

UNION BETWEEN BAPTISTS AND DISCIPLES.

The *Western Recorder,* a Baptist sort of a Christian
journal, solves the mooted question of union between
Baptists and Disciples thus:

If any Disciple wishes to "unite" with the Baptists in sincerity and in truth, instead of crying for "union" in all. the papers which will give him space, let him go to the nearest Baptist church and relate his experience. That is the only way to unite with the Baptists, as any man of intelligence ought to know.

To which the GOSPEL ADVOCATE feels disposed to reply: If any Baptist wishes to "unite" with the New Testament in sincerity and in truth, let him preach to the people: "He that believeth and is baptized shall be saved." (Mark 16: 16.) "Repent, and be baptized every one of you in the name of Jesus Christ for the remission of sins." (Acts 2: 38.) "Arise, and be baptized, and wash away thy sins, calling on the name of the Lord." (Acts 22: 16.) "For as many of you as have been baptized into Christ have put on Christ." (Gal. 3: 27.) "The like figure whereunto baptism doth also now save us." (1 Pet. 3: 21.) "Except a man be born of water and of the Spirit, he cannot enter into the kingdom of God." (John 3: 5.) "And he took them the same hour of the night, and washed their stripes, and was baptized, he and all his, straightway." (Acts 16: 33.) "And as they went on their way, they came unto a certain water; and the eunuch said, See, here is water; what doth hinder me to be baptized? And Philip said, If thou believest with all thine heart, thou mayest. And he answered and said, I believe that Jesus Christ is the Son of God. And he commanded the chariot to stand still: and they went down both into the water, both Philip and the eunuch; and he baptized him." (Acts 8: 36-38.) If the Baptists will unite with the folks we read about in the New Testament in such preaching and practice as this, they will be all right, no matter what the Disciples in these modern times may or may not do or say.

GROUND OF CHRISTIAN UNION.

In the same issue of the *Western Recorder* which contains the proposition to unite " on the Bible, and the Bible alone," I notice an editorial on "Articles of Faith " containing these words:

> After some search we have found a most admirable compendium of Baptist belief. It covers the whole ground of the great doctrines, and it covers it very clearly and very briefly. There isn't a single uncertain note in this blast of the gospel trumpet. These articles are those adopted by the Eutaw Place Church, in Baltimore, and were prepared by Prof. F. H. Kerfoot, of our seminary. . . . The Book Concern, at our request, has agreed to publish them in a tract form and sell them at one dollar per hundred. Already more than one thousand have been ordered by brethren who happened to be in and heard they were to be published. Every church ought to present one to every member and Sunday-school scholar.

I protest. This is not right. The *Recorder* and I have agreed to unite " on the Bible and the Bible alone," and that paper has no right to violate the terms of the union by seeking to work off on its readers a lot of this cheap Baptist wadding. If we *must* have some "Articles of Faith " besides the Bible, I claim the right to take a hand with Professor Kerfoot in fixing them up. He is a very good man and a very learned man, too, I doubt not, but what right has he to fix up other peoples' "Articles of Faith?" How does he know what other folks believe? As I understand this matter, God has written "Articles of Faith" for all Christians. That is exactly what the Bible is—"Articles of Faith," written by inspiration of God for all Christians. Does the *Recorder* think Professor Kerfoot can beat God on a little job like this?

RESOLUTION ON CHRISTIAN UNION.

Our Baptist brethren, in convention assembled, recently passed some resolutions on Christian union. The main idea in the resolutions seems to be that the Baptists are ready and willing to unite with all Christians who will unite with them. The *Guide* and the *Standard* have spoken of the resolutions and notified the Baptist brethren that the Disciples (with a big " D ") are also ready to unite with all Christians who will unite with them. This is encouraging progress toward Christian union, and the only thing that prevents the consummation of the business is that the Baptists don't seem willing to unite with the Disciples, and the Disciples, in like manner, seem unwilling to unite with the Baptists. Each body is perfectly willing for the other to unite with it, but neither is willing to unite with the other. Now, if both institutions will disband as institutions and leave the people free to be Christians, as individuals, and to worship God and attend to their own business as local congregations, without general denominational organization or supervision, the whole thing will unite itself.

WE OUGHT TO AGREE AMONG OURSELVES.

The *Baptist and Reflector* refers to the differences and discussions among " us as a people," and suggests that we ought to agree among ourselves and quit arguing with each other before we push " our plea " for the union of all Christians on the Bible much further. The brother errs, not knowing the Scriptures. Because we differ in opinions and argue questions among ourselves, it does not follow that we are not united as Christians on the Bible. We have never proposed or desired to unite Christians in any institution that is too narrow to allow them to differ in opinion or argue with each other. We are in favor of giving everybody room to think and liberty to speak for himself. For myself, I am opposed to any institution that allows no one but the bosses and grand moguls to entertain an idea or express an opinion. For the life of me, I can't see that I am under any more obligation to agree with Alexander Campbell than he to agree with me. I would never unite with him or anybody else on the Bible on any other condition than that I am as free as he to study the Bible. This is the only kind of union we have ever proposed, and it is the only kind that is practicable or right among men. Whenever it comes to human organizations in which no one but the framers of doctrinal standards are allowed to do any thinking, I beg to be excused. My thinking apparatus is not very large, I admit, but I claim all the room the Bible allows me in which to operate it. The *Reflector* evidently thinks that because every man, with us, is free to think for himself and to differ from and argue with everybody else, *therefore* we are not united. That is an error. We are united, and the beauty and strength of the union is to

13

be found largely in the fact that it is a union in Christ wherein every one is allowed to study the Bible and think for himself, without being amenable to ecclesiastic authorities or doctrinal standards of human make. The *Reflector* seems to have the old, bigoted idea that if a man should happen to differ from me and undertake to argue a question with me, he must get out of my church and start a little concern of his own. That has been the trouble with religious bigots all along the ages. It takes just such bigotry as that to build up denominations·and keep Christians apart. "We as a people" are a rather contentious set, I admit, but we have not yet given in to that idea. It is just at this point I file my objection to the Baptist Church. One must accept its doctrinal standards, written by uninspired men, or get out of it. Here is the *Baptist and Reflector*, for instance. It could think out some very good ideas of its own and express them in very creditable English if it only had room. But, my! Wouldn't the Baptist bosses sit down on it with a crash if it should happen some day to think a little thought all my itself, without consulting the doctrinal standards? The basis of our union ought always to be as broad as the conditions of salvation. No man has any right to make his plea for union narrower than this. It is wrong to make anything a condition of fellowship which is not essential to salvation. We draw the line here. That which will damn a soul and separate us in the next world should divide us in this; nothing else should.

There are a few men among us who are trying very hard to "organize" the thing called "us as a people," so as to shut off all investigation and stop all discussion; but they are entirely too narrow in their ideas to fairly represent this reformation. They say that if something of this kind is not done very soon, "our plea" will burst into smithereens, "our organized mission work" will break all to flinders, and "we as a people" will go to smash on general principles; but I think not. The shortest route I know to such a crash is to organize us and undertake to compel us all to quit thinking and arguing and accept the conclusions and carry out the plans of "leading men and papers," without the liberty to conceive an idea or express an opinion of our own.

THE BASIS OF UNION AS BROAD AS THE CONDITIONS OF SALVATION.

Some weeks ago, speaking of Christian union, I said:

The basis of our union ought always to be as broad as the conditions of salvation. No man has any right to make his plea for union narrower than this. It is wrong to make anything a condition of fellowship which is not essential to salvation. We draw the line here. That which will damn a soul and separate us in the next world should divide us in this; nothing else should.

The *Baptist and Reflector* replies to this by saying that "the Bible lays down only two conditions of salvation—repentance and faith," and argues that most Baptists, Methodists, Presbyterians, Episcopalians, etc., have complied with these conditions, and should, therefore, be admitted into the union. "What kind of union would that be?" Well, if the *Baptist and Reflector* is right about it, and all these folks have complied with the only two conditions of salvation which the Bible lays down, which I do not admit, a union of them all in this world would be, so far as I can see, exactly the "sort of union" we will have to put up with in heaven, and we might as well be getting used to it! However, the *Baptist and Reflector* goes on to say:

But the ADVOCATE would claim that *baptism is also essential to salvation.* If so, it distinctly admits that the lack of baptism will damn a soul and separate us in the next world—the clearest admission of belief in water salvation we have seen for some time.

Yes, I have seen no clearer "admission of belief in water salvation" since the *Baptist and Reflector* said the man who persistently neglects or refuses to be baptized after he is fully informed as to the teaching of the Scriptures touching that ordinance cannot be a Christian while he lives or go to heaven when he dies, " *because such refusal shows that his heart is not right, his faith is not genuine."* But it has not been so very long since the *Baptist and Reflector* made that statement, after all; it hasn't been a year yet! It will be a long time till he sees any clearer "admission of belief in water salvation" than that on this page. Finally, he says:

You mix up a lot of Baptists and Methodists and Presbyterians and Episcopalians and Catholics into one organization, each with his peculiar ideas of church government, of falling from grace, of predestination, and such like, and what kind of a union have you got?

Well, a pretty bad mess of it, I admit; but if they are all going to heaven, they will have to be mixed up there; and if we must spend eternity in such a muddle, I think we ought to try to put up with it the few years we are on earth! But I have never said anything about mixing up Baptists, and Methodists, and Presbyterians, and Episcopalians, and Catholics "into one organization." My idea is that there ought not to be any Baptists, or Methodists, or Presbyterians, or Episcopalians, or Catholics in this business. They ought to be Christians—every mother's son of them! And as for mixing them in one organization, my idea is for all of them —*as Christians*—to put in their time doing the will of my Father who is in heaven, *as taught in the Scriptures*, and let all this big church-organization business go to the dogs. The doing of those things which God, in the Scriptures, has required will constitute all the organizations in the way of churches that we need, and mix us all in them just as we ought to be mixed, too. That's my idea.

GOOD WORDS AND FAIR SPEECHES ON CHRISTIAN UNION.

My beloved Brother Nichols—John H. Nichols—sets himself down in the *Arkansas Methodist* in these words:

Every fellow wants "peace and union," but he wants them on his own terms. "Good words and fair speeches" are abundant, because they are cheap. A man cries to the multitude: "Come and join me on the Bible and be a Christian—not a Baptist, Methodist, or Presbyterian, but simply a *Christian*." These are "good words and fair speeches," but "by their fruits ye shall know them." Few men of modern times have been louder in their cries for "union on the Bible" than has been the first-page editor of the GOSPEL ADVOCATE, a Campbellite paper published in Nashville, Tenn. He plants himself on the Bible in this language: "I have accepted the Bible just as the Holy Spirit

wrote it, without any reference as to how Alexander Campbell or anybody else understood it." (GOSPEL ADVOCATE,
April 15, 1891.) These are " good words and fair speeches,"
and no doubt the editor thinks they are true, and they may
be true; but it is a little remarkable what a similarity
there is between the way the editor understands the Bible
and the way Alexander Campbell understood it.

In another place he finds where I said, "The man or
church which goes into anything I believe to be contrary to the teaching of the Father by the Spirit,
through the Scriptures, must part company with me,"
and straightway he cries, "Perhaps nothing would be
more offensive to the editor than to propose the Methodist 'Discipline' as the basis of union on the Bible;
but the thing is solid and all right if you will just
make the editor's belief the basis of union," and much
more of the same sort of talk. Now, if Brother Nichols
will just lay aside the Methodist "Discipline" a few
moments and allow his overworked brain to cool off, I
think we can come to a better understanding of this
whole matter. Surely he would not ask me, or anybody
else, to do what I believe to be " contrary to the teaching
of the Father by the Spirit, through the Scriptures,"
in order to unite with him or anybody else in a thing
which he does not believe himself it is necessary for anybody to do in order to be a Christian or to go to heaven.
Now it so happens that I believe the Methodist " Discipline," as well as the whole Methodist concern, for that
matter, is "contrary to the teaching of the Father by
the Spirit, through the Scriptures," and it happens also
that Brother Nichols and everybody else believe that a
man can be a Christian while he lives and go to heaven
when he dies without believing the Methodist " Disci-

pline " or joining the Methodist Church. I cannot see, therefore, why he or anybody else should offer the Methodist " Discipline " as a basis of union or ask any one to join the Methodist Church. Brother Nichols and everybody else admit that a man can obey every command God has ever given without believing the Methodist " Discipline " or joining the Methodist Church. I suppose the Methodist " Discipline " and the Methodist Church are very good things of the sort for those who like that sort of things and have time and inclination to follow after things which are not at all necessary to make Christians or save souls, but I am busy these days attending to the things which God has required and without which a man can neither be a Christian nor go to heaven. I am not at all concerned about matters which I do not have to believe or do in order to be a Christian or go to heaven. I confess, therefore, that I am gradually drifting into a widespread and rapidly diminishing interest in the whole Methodist concern. And I don't see why even Brother Nichols should strain himself trying to believe the Methodist " Discipline " and belong to the Methodist Church, when he can be a Christian and go to heaven without it. Now, if he stood any chance at all to get a job as Bishop or something of the sort, there might be some sense in his course, but he will never get above the rank of a one-horse circuit rider or a six-for-a-nickel station preacher. It ought to satisfy the ambition of a man of his caliber to be a Christian while he lives and go to heaven when he dies. That is the way it looks to me.

THE BAPTISTS CATCH A BEAU.

Some time ago I said:

I love the Baptists for their devotion to the word of God, their steadfastness in holding uncorrupted the sacred ordinance of baptism, their splendid record on the question of congregational church polity, their magnificent fight against ecclesiastic encroachments upon the liberty of the individual conscience—all these things, and many others, I admire in them; and I am not without hope that we may yet understand each other better and love each other more.

Whereupon the *Baptist Helper* remarks:

Now, if Mr. Srygley has stated his honest convictions, and has only one purpose, and that to glorify God, why doesn't he leave the denomination devoted to its own interpretations of the word of God, and grossly corrupting the sacred ordinance of baptism, and governed by elders, and denying liberty of conscience, etc., and unite with those that he so highly commends and so dearly loves?

It would seem from this that the Baptists, in so far as they are represented by the *Baptist Helper,* are not used to being "so dearly" loved. Indeed, they act as though they never had a beau before. Such an experience has quite unnerved this antique maiden, and she is all in a flutter to know why he doesn't marry her on the spot. She must be getting on the shady side of matrimonial probabilities. If I ever get out of this scrape without a damage suit for breach of promise, I will be cautious how I compliment the old spinster in future. But, seriously, if the *Baptist Helper* will be calm and listen to a few words of rational explanation, it will be surprised and mortified to discover what a spectacle it is making of itself. "Mr. Srygley has stated his honest convictions, and has only one purpose, and that to glorify God;" but he fails to see how it would glorify God to join a party or denomination in religion which is not so much as named in the Bible, and which excludes from its fellowship the vast majority of God's spiritual children, according to its own admission. It is needless to ask why Mr. Srygley doesn't "leave the denomination devoted to its own interpretation of the word of God," etc., etc. Mr. Srygley is not in any denomination. "His honest convictions" are that all denominations in religion are wrong. They are schisms in the body of Christ, and the New Testament condemns them as clearly as it condemns adultery. There is no such thing known in the New Testament as a denomination which excludes from its partisan fellowship any of the disciples of Christ. While I love the Baptists for many things they believe and practice, all those things can be maintained in doctrine and deportment just as well without joining the Baptist denomination as they are believed and practiced by the Baptists themselves. They were successfully observed by Christians in New Testament times before the Baptist denomination was ever heard of, and they would not be affected in any way if the whole Baptist denomination should be annihilated to-morrow. I have often said, and now say again, that I love the Methodists and Presbyterians for many things which they believe and practice; but all those things existed hundreds of years before the Methodists and Presbyterians were ever heard of, and they would continue to flourish as long as people reverence the Bible if the Methodist and Presbyterian Churches were obliterated to-day. I love the Baptists, Methodists, Presbyterians, and every other kind of denominationalists for everything they advocate which the Bible teaches; but for the many things they believe and practice which the Bible does not teach, I have no sympathy at all; and for their sectarian narrowness, partisan bigotry, and denominational intolerance especially, I have a strong and constantly increasing aversion.

CHURCH SUCCESSION.

The Baptist brethren who are trying to make out a case of church succession find it necessary to prove that Roger Williams did not start the first Baptist church in America. This raises a howl from Roger's old friends and admirers among the Baptists, and they use some vigorous words against those who would pluck the tail feathers out of Brother Williams' honor, even after the United States has built a monument to him and all the world has praised or cursed him for more than a century, according as they liked or disliked Baptist religion, for saddling his theology upon this otherwise goodly land in the tender years of the country's helpless infancy. But Roger must go. He is in the way of the succession builders; and when they undertake to make a chain of succession out of their bag of disconnected and contradictory links, Roger Williams, Simon Peter, Paul, and the Lord Jesus Christ may as well stand aside.

BAPTIST CHURCH SUCCESSION.

My beloved Brother Grime, of the Baptist variety, earnestly protests against some things I said about the

Baptist doctrine of succession, and wastes much space in a Baptist paper trying to prove what he ought to know is not true—viz., that there has been a regular and uninterrupted chain of Baptist churches from the days of the apostles to the present time. His theory is that each Baptist church is connected with some other Baptist church by authority of which it was founded, and that this chain of churches has an absolute monopoly of the ordinances in religion. No man or church outside of this chain of churches is authorized to administer baptism or partake of the Lord's Supper. To prove that there is such a succession of churches reaching clear back to the apostles, Brother Grime challenges me to name the time and place where the first Baptist church was organized, and open the columns of the ADVOCATE to him to prove that I am wrong about it. I am not at all sure I can state when and where the first Baptist church started. My religious reading has been mainly in the Bible, all of which was written several years before such a thing as a Baptist church was ever heard of in the world. I don't know exactly how long Brother Grime's chain of succession may be, but I undertake to say the far end of it doesn't reach to the Bible. If he thinks he can find any mention of the Baptist Church in the Bible, I will cheerfully " open the columns of the ADVOCATE " wide enough for him to name the book, chapter, and verse where such reading may be found. Speaking of this succession business, I venture to say Brother Grime cannot trace the succession of the church of which he is a member himself as far as one hundred years back toward the apostles. Let us see. He is a member, say, of Shop Springs Baptist Church. Now tell us by authority of what Baptist church the

Shop Springs Baptist Church was established; then tell us by authority of what Baptist church that church was established, and so on back. Just see how far back you can go by way of experiment, and be sure you give exact dates and all particulars in each case. Brother Grime may humbug a few of his Baptist brethren on this succession business in religion, but he could not sell a Jersey heifer to any Baptist farmer in Middle Tennessee, *as a registered animal,* that did not have a better pedigree than he can make out for any Baptist preacher or church in the State. His chain of succession is a beautiful thing theoretically, but for all practical purposes it is too short at both ends and in too many pieces in the middle!

THE BAPTIST GLEANER ON CHURCH SUCCESSION.

The *Baptist Gleaner* talks at me on this wise:

If you had written, "The churches which we read about in the New Testament went down in *all* places," you would have said what your theory requires. But if there were some places where these New Testament churches did not go down, then in these places those churches still stand, and an unbroken succession can be traced through them. Will you kindly name the places where the New Testament churches did not go down?

I have no theory in religion but the Bible. Will the brother please cite chapter and verse when he undertakes to state what my "theory requires?" I like to read it for myself. I have known for a long time that he is hard pressed for evidence of "an unbroken succession," but I hardly expected him to try to prove it by

me. I am compelled to say I can give him no help in
that line. I cannot name any places just now where the
New Testament churches did not go down; but if called
upon suddenly and even unexpectedly to name a place
where Baptist churches did not go up, I would promptly
say the New Testament, at a venture. There are no
such churches mentioned in that book.

THE BIBLE RULED OUT OF THE CHURCHES.

"The Supreme Court of the State of Wisconsin,"
says the *Cumberland Presbyterian,* "has ruled the Bible
out of the public schools of the State because it is a sectarian book." Yes, and our denominational brethren
have "ruled" it out of their churches and substituted
their creeds and confessions of faith for it because it is
not a sectarian book. Truly, between the Supreme
Court on one hand and sectarianism on the other, the
Bible is in a hard row of stumps; but, for one, I am going to stick to it, even if it is "ruled out" of every
school and church in the world!

I am just in receipt of the following from John H.
Nichols, of Unionville, Tenn.:

In the GOSPEL ADVOCATE of June 4 your first-page editor
quotes from the *Cumberland Presbyterian* as follows: "The
Supreme Court of the State of Wisconsin has ruled the Bible out of the public schools of the State because it is a
sectarian book." The editor adds: "Yes, and our denominational brethren have 'ruled' it out of their churches and
substituted their creeds and confessions of faith for it because it is *not* a sectarian book; . . . but, for one, I
am going to stick to it, even if it is 'ruled out" of every

school and church in the world." Well, he who sticks to the Bible will not bear false witness against his neighbors, and I like to keep reasonably well up in regard to all the *denominations;* but the editor has stepped in ahead of me here, and I write for information. Will the editor be so kind as to tell me through the ADVOCATE what "denominational brethren have ' ruled'" the Bible "out of their churches and substituted their creeds and confessions of faith for it?" If you will not publish this, please return it to me.

Brother Nichols still thinks I have failed to show that the denominations have ruled the Bible out of their churches and substituted their creeds and confessions of faith for it. He is particularly anxious to show that the Methodists have not done this, and quotes from the " Discipline" the statement that " the Holy Scriptures contain all things necessary to salvation, so that whatsoever is not read therein, nor may be proved thereby, is not to be required of any man, that it should be believed as an article of faith, or be thought requisite or necessary to salvation." This is no news to me. I was aware the Methodist " Discipline" contained that statement. The same statement in substance may be found in every creed or confession of faith in the world. Brother Nichols need not rush to the defense of the Methodist " Discipline." The *Arkansas Baptist* will look after that document. What I want Brother Nichols to do is to show that the doctrine and practice of the Baptist Church is in harmony with the Scriptures. He has said no denomination has ruled out the Bible, substituting its creed or confession of faith for it. I mention the Baptist denomination as one that has done that. The *Arkansas Baptist* has also said no denomination has ruled out the Bible and substituted a creed or confession of faith for it. To the Baptist brother I mention the Methodist denomination. To be candid, now, brethren, *you* know that *somebody* has ruled out the Bible. No sensible man can believe that *all* the denominations in the world are teaching just what is in the Bible and nothing else. To justify the Methodist "Discipline," Brother Nichols says:

When I read what you have to say on religious subjects on the first page of the GOSPEL ADVOCATE, I suppose you believe what you write; so I take it for your *creed* on those points. What more right have you to publish your creed on the first page of the GOSPEL ADVOCATE than I have to publish mine in a little book, anyhow? How would you go about proving there is any more Bible authority for a GOSPEL ADVOCATE than there is for a Methodist "Discipline," eh?

I do not object to Brother Nichols publishing what he believes in a little book. I concede to every man the right to state what he believes in private conversation, from the pulpit, through a paper, or in a book. But the Methodist "Discipline" is something entirely different from this. It was not written by Brother Nichols. The rulers of the Methodist Church wrote it, and they compel him to swallow it or get out of the Methodist Church. This is the point I make against it. No man or set of men has any right to state my faith for me. And for a small proportion of the professed people of God to get together and formulate a doctrine and then organize themselves into a church unknown to the Bible to propagate their form of doctrine and build up their little close corporation or ecclesiastical trust, and at the same time deny fellowship with every man who cannot swallow their creed, is an unwarranted interference with the liberties of the people of God which I cannot indorse. Brother Nichols talks about writing his faith in a little book. I should like to see him try it. Why, God bless you, he has nothing to do with writing his faith. The bosses of the Methodist Church write it for him, and change it to suit themselves whenever they wish without consulting him about it; and he has to swallow it just as they fix it up, no matter how absurd it may seem to him, or else get out of the Methodist Church and hunt another job.

The doctrinal column of the *Arkansas Baptist* abuses me for a statement which recently appeared on this page to the effect that our denominational brethren have ruled the Bible out of their churches and substituted their creeds and confessions of faith for it because it is not a sectarian book. After much abuse, the brother says: "Will you name any church that has ruled out the Bible on any pretext whatever? Name one, please." O, yes, I could mention several; but just now the name of the Methodist Church occurs to me. As I understand this matter, our Methodist brethren have substituted their book of "Discipline" for the Bible as an expression of their faith on all questions of doctrine, as well as a book of discipline on all matters of deportment. How does the doctrinal editor of the *Arkansas Baptist* understand this? When my good Brother Nichols, of the Methodist Church, "kicked" against that innocent-looking little paragraph, I put him to defending the Baptist brethren. Now I have got the *Arkansas Baptist* set for the defense of the Methodist "Discipline," infant sprinkling and all. No doubt these brethren would like to "swap work," but I can't allow that. They have both "pitched into" me for making the statement, and each of them has broadly intimated that I was mistaken about it. In fact, they have both laid themselves out to assert that no denomination has "ruled out" the Bible. It comes rather hard on a Baptist to defend Methodism, and a Methodist to defend Baptistism, as in strict agreement with the teaching of the Bible, but there is no help for it now. They will have to "grin and endure it."

Referring to my statement that the denominations have ruled the Bible out of their churches, the *Arkansas Baptist* thinks "they have done no such thing, and the first-page editor knows it." As to the Methodists, our Baptist contemporary frankly admits that they "hold some erroneous notions, and some doctrines that cannot be proved by the Bible," but argues that "it does not follow that they have ruled the Bible out of their church." Friend Nichols makes exactly the same point as to the Baptists, and both of them think my "statement was severely reckless," and advise me to be "a little more careful in future." So, according to my critics, I am due the denominations a retraction and an apology, which I cheerfully make. As the case now stands, I am authorized, by all the representatives of denominations who have spoken on this question, to state that the denominations all retain the Bible in their churches, but that not one of them agrees with it in doctrine and practice. This is what I intended to say at the beginning; but as my language was understood to convey a different idea, I cheerfully withdraw it and state myself now exactly in the language of the representatives of the denominations themselves. This puts the matter beyond cavil or criticism. And now that the representatives of denominations who have spoken on this

14

question establish, by their own unsolicited testimony, the fact that no denomination agrees with the Bible in doctrine and practice, it seems pertinent to inquire whether those denominations propose in future to conform their doctrine and practice to the teaching of the Bible. As my friends Hall and Nichols assure us that neither the Baptist nor the Methodist denomination agrees with the Bible in doctrine and practice, it seems eminently proper for them to undertake to set these two denominations right. They have been working zealously, but not wisely, along this line for several years. Hall is a Baptist and works hard to set the Methodists right, while Nichols is a Methodist and labors without ceasing to correct the errors of the Baptists. I suggest a change. How would it do for each one to correct his own denomination?

Some weeks ago I stated, in substance, that the denominations have ruled the Bible out of their churches and substituted their creeds and confessions of faith for it. Brother Nichols promptly denied the statement, asserted that no denomination had ruled out the Bible, and asked me to name one denomination that had done such a thing. I named the Baptist. Brother Nichols is a Methodist. Just as I expected, this "spiked his gun." He has been trying ever since to get to prove that the Methodist denomination has not ruled out the Bible, but I insist on holding his attention to the Baptists. That is his job. The *Arkansas Baptist* will look after the Methodist brethren. And because I decline to hear him in defense of the Methodist denomination he loses his temper and writes me that I am acting the part of "witness, judge, attorney, and jury" in this case, O, no! I don't need any witness, judge, jury, or

lawyer yet. What I do need just now is an opponent.
Brother Nichols has said no denomination has ruled out
the Bible and substituted its creed or confession of faith
for it. I have named the Baptist denomination as one
that has done this, and until he is willing to try to show
that in doctrine and practice the Baptists are in harmony with the teaching of the Scriptures, he is not on
docket in this case at all. But as he seems so very anxious to show that the Methodist Church has not ruled
out the Bible and substituted its creed for it, I will
point out the things in which the Methodist " Discipline " differs in doctrine from the Bible and give him
an equal division of space with me in the ADVOCATE to
defend his " Discipline," provided he will secure the
publication of our articles in some Methodist paper of
as large circulation as the ADVOCATE has.

Friend Nichols seems to be pretty well used up. He
started out to prove that no denomination has ruled the
Bible out and substituted a creed or confession of faith
for it. At his first answer the thing wilted on him hopelessly. His bristles were up to defend the Methodist
denomination, but he laid his foundation too broad. He
said no denomination had done such a thing. This
left me entirely free to select the ground for the fray,
and so I set him for the defense of the Baptist denomination. This has proved the biggest job of his life.
After worrying with it till he is completely fagged out,
he sends me a stamped, self-addressed envelope, and asks
me to return his manuscript. Sorry I can't comply,
but his manuscript has not been preserved. I published
it all in the ADVOCATE save one article, and I extracted
liberally from that. It is gone beyond recall now, my
dear. I felt satisfied you would wish you had that

manuscript back before you got through with the job, when you wrote first, but really I didn't expect you to confess it. Well, this may be a lesson to you in future. Hereafter when you write an article of that kind, it would be well to consider before you send it off whether you are liable to wish you had it back after it is gone. The ADVOCATE is open to you at any time (1) to show that the Baptists, in doctrine and practice, agree with the Scriptures, or (2) to show that the Methodist "Discipline" is in harmony with the Scriptures in teaching, provided, under this second head, that you secure the publication of our articles in some Methodist paper of as large circulation as the ADVOCATE.

TENNESSEE RIPE FOR CONVENTION WORK.

My beloved Brother John A. Stevens, State evangelist of Mississippi, whatever that may mean, snatches time from his arduous official duties to write about me in *The Messenger* on this wise:

It will take our friend three hundred first pages to convince us that he hasn't told a "*Jacob*" about Tennessee being "practically unanimous in opposing the society." No man knows better than F. D. Srygley that Tennessee is yellow with ripeness for this coöperative convention work.

This makes two times I have been accused of lying in one week—once by Brother Stevens and once by the *Christian-Evangelist*. This is decidedly refreshing, especially when the facts are clearly in my favor; but if they can afford it, I will try to endure it. There is nothing like getting used to a thing. Those who took the uppermost seats and thanked God that they were not mean and bad like other folks were not noted for kindness and courtesy in their bearing toward common people even in New Testament times, and it is possibly well enough to allow sufficient latitude in gentlemanly etiquette for State evangelists and metropolitan journals to show clearly the distinction between themselves and common Christians in these modern days. But, in all seriousness, I beg to assure Brother Stevens that I haven't told a "*Jacob*" about the societies since I quit trying to work them up and operate them. Why should I? It is wholly immaterial with me whether they run or not. I am no State evangelist. I do not raise the question as to the right of individuals or churches to work through such societies. Brother Lipscomb will argue that branch of the subject. I am set for the defense of their right to stay out. Brother Stevens will doubtless admit that any man can be a Christian, obey every command God has ever given, and be saved without having anything to do with "this coöperative convention work." My idea is, therefore, "with charity for all and malice toward none," to stand aloof from everything not clearly required by the Lord which causes "envy, strife, and division" among Christians and in churches, attend to my own business, "fear God and keep his commandments" while I live and go to heaven when I die, and let State evangelists, who are hired to run "this coöperative convention work," tell the "*Jacobs*" about it, if anything of that sort must be told. And as to Tennessee being "yellow with ripeness" for that sort of thing, it strikes me that the laborers, after two years hard gleaning, have brought in a very small sheaf for such an inviting field. There must be something wrong with the harvesting machine. The laborers toil early and late, but somehow the grain seems to shatter; and when the reapers come together in annual convention to winnow the year's gleaning, there are too many shucks for the number and size of the nubbins.

THE SIZE OF THE CHANGE.

The *Christian Courier* expresses the opinion, as to the writer of this page, that "since his last great change, he has seemed to seek opportunities to destroy the things which he once preached." The reference is to my position, past and present, touching what is called "organized mission work," of course. I am disposed to think that the *Courier* is in error as to the size of the alleged "change." It is probably not as great as the *Courier* seems to think. In truth, I am a little doubtful whether it is as great as it ought to be. By way of correction as to the size of the "change," I would suggest, that (1) I was not as bad as some folks seem to think before the "change," and (2) I am probably not as good as others suppose since the "change." In the days when the senior editor of the *Courier* and I were true yokefellows in "State work" and a few other things, I spent much time, when not engaged in preaching the gospel, trying to keep a few ultra spirits from introducing methods of work not required by the Scriptures which would stir up "envy, strife, and division" among the brethren in Texas. At the State meeting which assembled in Fort Worth early in the eighties, when I was living in Texas, I had the honor to be one of a committee of five—T. W. Caskey, Charles Carlton,

John T. Poe, and C. M. Wilmeth were the other four—
on "plan of work." In the committee I made the point
that as Caskey, Carlton, and myself, as well as the most
ultra society man in the State, could work under any
plan, it was but brotherly to allow Brother Poe and
Brother Wilmeth, as representing a large constituency,
to suggest the method that they could conscientiously
adopt, and not ask them to do what they honestly believed to be contrary to the teaching of the Bible.
Caskey and Carlton made the same point, and the committee easily brought in a report on which all agreed.
We had a brotherly handshaking all around; the beloved
veteran chairman, Thomas Moore, tried to talk, but
broke down in a gush of godly tears, and the session
ended with a season of refreshing from the presence of
the Lord. About two years later, and after I had left
the State, a few ultra spirits broke away from conservative moorings and inaugurated a factional movement
which has kept up a row in Texas ever since. If I
rightly understand myself, I was not mean enough even
before what the *Courier* calls my " great change " to follow those few well-meaning, but rash and ill-balanced,
brethren into such a factional movement against the
protest of such men as the late lamented Dr. C. Ken-
drick, who was present and, with tears in his eyes, besought the brethren not to press their preference as to
a method of work against the sincere convictions of their
brethren to such ruinous results. If the *Courier* will
carefully read all I have said since what it calls my
" great change," it will probably be surprised to find me
still working along the safe and conservative line so ably
advocated at Fort Worth by President Clark, Thomas
Moore, T. W. Caskey, Charles Carlton, and a host of

others. I have always understood that Christians and churches have a perfect right to stay out of these societies if they want to, and I am still set for the defense of their right to stay out. As everybody admits that a man can be a Christian, obey every command God has ever given, and be saved without joining a society, I don't see why the *Courier* should consider it such a " great change " for a man to drop out of such societies every now and then and worship without them like folks did in New Testament times.

KEEPING THE REFORMATION ON THE TRACK.

The following paragraph from one of Brother Wilmeth's heaviest editorials in the *Christian Preacher* comes just in time to vindicate me against the charge of some of my old-time friends that I have gone against them touching certain methods of church work and have followed after such men as Wilmeth and Lipscomb:

> But we would not risk Brethren F. D. Srygley and A. P. Aten to run a wheelbarrow for us with any hope they would keep it on the track. Brother Srygley is learning, it is true, and is saying some good things; but some men are always learning and never coming to a knowledge of the truth. We need men now with backbone and well-defined Bible faith.

I am no great stakes in the wheelbarrow business, I admit, and as for keeping this reformation "on the track," I gave up that job years ago. It takes all my time now to preach the gospel to the world, fight the devil in the church, and keep in a good humor with the brethren who criticise me on the right hand and on the left.. I am willing to do all I can in my feeble manner to push the thing along, but I must depend on such men as Brother Wilmeth to keep it "on the track;" and if they should let it slip a cog or jump the track, this glorious reformation will inevitably be smashed into smithereens.

ANOTHER MAGAZINE TOUCHED OFF.

Brother John A. Stevens, ex-State evangelist of Mississippi, and pastor-elect of Chattanooga, Tenn., philosophizes thus in *The Messenger:*

It seems that the *Standard* people have gotten the ADVOCATE people into a sort of an awkward shape. It looks quite bad on paper at first sight. In fact, I look upon the whole affair simply as a misfortune. I don't blame my friends, Srygley and McQuiddy, for making an effort to change the policy of the ADVOCATE. They doubtless believed at that time that the ADVOCATE's policy was harmful, and that the methods which the Standard Publishing Company was forward to give to the world were the most effective methods of converting the ADVOCATE into a missionary paper. So the effort, though made in a questionable way and resulting in a failure, was a laudable one. We should throw a mantle of charity over any mistake that our brethren might honestly make. When the question is asked why Srygley and McQuiddy remained on the paper for five years with its present policy, after going on the paper for the express purpose of smothering said policy to death, I answer that it is possible that their views underwent a radical change after beginning work on the paper. This is a charitable view to take of the matter under the circumstances, but just such a view as charity would take. In the event that their minds have undergone a change relative to the missionary question, they have not been found to be unfaithful to their convictions in what they have written on the subject. The *Standard* did perfectly right in publishing the correspondence under the circumstances. Evidently our Advocate friends did not think that the *Standard* was still in possession of this magazine of correspondence, else they would have let up about the *Standard* being a monopoly before they induced it to touch off this magazine of correspondence. But bought wit is the best of all, and it is to be hoped that it will all turn out for the best interests of the church and the glory of God.

As the public in general, and Brother Stevens in particular, seem to be greatly concerned about that radical change in my " views," perhaps a few words of explanation would not be ill-timed. To make the matter clear, it will be necessary to publish a few private letters from Brother Stevens; but I take it for granted he will think I " did perfectly right in publishing the correspondence under the circumstances," and no one else has any cause to complain.

I " went on the paper" November 1, 1889. A few weeks before that date Brother Stevens went to San Antonio, Texas, to preach the gospel in destitute places under some boards. May 8, 1890, only a few months after the effort to smother " said policy to death" had been begun, and before any considerable progress had been made in the good work, Brother Stevens wrote me as follows:

I am a little tired of being under three boards—" general," " State," and " local church board." I am not stuck on a great many things that you would suppose I was. For instance, a man has to create certain sentiments, circulate certain papers, use certain Sunday-school literature, write in certain periodicals, etc., etc. . . . Red tape I despise. Foolishness I hate. Bigotry is from hell. Ringism is contrary to what I believe to be religious equity. Ostracism is wickedness. Partyism is ungodliness. I don't know how it is over among the " fogies," but the air is full of it over this way. I am tired. Let me get a good breath. Three boards are unbearable.

Of course I had to stop smothering the policy of the GOSPEL ADVOCATE to death on receipt of this letter and try to keep the boards from smothering Brother Stevens to death. Accordingly I pulled him out from under that San Antonio board pile and arranged for him to hold a few meetings over in Tennessee " among the fogies " and " get a good breath." A few months after the date of the above letter, he left Texas and labored successfully in protracted meetings at Jackson, Henderson, and Murfreesboro, Tenn. While he was at Henderson, I notified him that some of " the fogies " suspected he was trying to introduce organs, societies, and such like, and, consequently, felt inclined to put him back under the board pile. With the horrors of his late San Antonio experience fresh in his mind, he promptly wrote as follows, under date of October 26, 1890:

I guess there is not much danger of my preaching anything but the straight old gospel. All that even McGary said about me was that my conclusions were wrong on one passage only. If I keep right and only butcher one passage in the future, it will be better work than I have ever done in the past. But I guess you mean for me to preach the straight old gospel and not crook off and preach organs, societies, etc. Well, beloved, rest in peace on that line. I never speak of these things. They are no part of my protracted-meeting stock in trade.

A short time before he left Tennessee he had a call
from the Mississippi State Board to become State evangelist, on condition that he would raise his own salary.
He showed me the call and asked my advice. We both
thought it would be better to be *on* a board in the capacity of State evangelist than to be under a pile of
boards in the capacity of a common sort of a preacher;
but still his late San Antonio experience prejudiced him
against the whole board business, and hence he asked
the Mississippi Board to give him time to consider the
matter. Meantime he asked me to do all I could to
find a better job for him. Under date of December 4,
1890, he wrote me from Texarkana, as follows:

·I am holding Mississippi at bay. Will put them off as
long as I can, but think they will require a decision in a few
days.

If he could have held Mississippi "at bay" a few
days longer, we might have found a better job for him,
but the board forced·a decision before anything better
could be found, and he reluctantly consented to "create
certain sentiments, circulate certain papers, use certain
Sunday-school literature, write in certain periodicals,
etc., etc.," for the boards once more, and raise his own
salary into the bargain.

Soon after he became State evangelist for Mississippi,
and before I had made any considerable headway smothering the policy of the GOSPEL ADVOCATE to death, I
was interrupted and called to his assistance again by the
following letter, which he wrote from Senatobia, Miss.,
February 3, 1891:

MY DEAR BROTHER SRYGLEY: I am here, and big blue if
I would acknowledge it. We have about eight members,

and I can find three pairs that will not speak on the streets or in the church. How is that for cussedness? Of course the membership can't attend regularly for fear they will meet each other and have to speak. This is the kind of work I am engaged in. Isn't it awful? . . . They have everything comfortable, fine, and stylish for me. They are keeping me in a fine stall and poking the corn, and fodder, and oats, and bran to me, and keeping my fetlocks trimmed and the witches out of my mane, etc. Physically, I am fat as a hog; but spiritually, I am down on the lift. I would enjoy a teaspoonful of thin spiritual gruel now better than all the fleshpots of Egypt. I am physically foundered, but spiritually gutted. Srygley, this whole State is in a terrible fix, so far as we are concerned. . . . In organization circles Mississippi has a big name, but the brethren don't understand that it is all on paper. There is absolutely no missionary organization in Mississippi, nor ever was. My idea of organization is for the people to band themselves together to send the gospel to destitute places. Paper organization, agreed upon by a few, is simply an effort, that's all, and that's just all we have. . . . Did you ever notice that nearly all little, weak churches in the world are in favor of missionary societies? They want help. . . . Being broken down in the loins spiritually, I will get you to write me a tar plaster to put on them, that I may get up and walk by faith.

On receipt of this letter I dropped everything else for the time, of course, and, after prayerful meditation, wrote such a "tar plaster" as the symptoms seemed to demand. Soon afterwards he wrote, under date of February 26, 1891, the following letter, which clearly indicates that the remedy was a success and the patient was on the high road to recovery:

Dear Brother Srygley: Your kind and very comforting and encouraging letter of the 24th is at hand and contents fully noted. I needed just such a letter from just such a man. I don't know how it came about, the Lord knoweth, but you have become the rock under which my earthly anchor fastens. . . . I had not thought till I read your letter just what I was troubled about. I know now that it was my reputation. Well, I will take your advice and let the reputation go, and serve the blessed Lord to the best of my ability and leave results with him. . . . I read twenty-two chapters from Paul yesterday, and prayed an unusually long and earnest prayer to God while alone in my room, and preached a number-one sermon last night. I tell you, Srygley, there is more in humble prayer and earnest, hopeful trust in God than anything else in this world. I don't think I will ever get blue any more. . . . If headquarters turns the dogs loose because I like Dave Lipscomb, good. I am ready to be offered up. I love R. Moffett supremely, but I love David Lipscomb, too; especially do I have the utmost respect for him as an honest, noble-hearted Christian gentleman.

It is scarcely necessary to say the "tar plaster" I wrote was simply a suggestion that the patient "let the reputation go and serve the blessed Lord, . . . and leave results with him." And, as a sanitary precaution, he was further advised to read and meditate upon the word of the Lord and rely more upon "humble prayer and earnest, hopeful trust in God" than upon "paper organization agreed upon by a few" for success. In an extensive practice upon "organized effort" in chronic and constitutional troubles peculiar to children of weakly parents, this simple remedy has never failed to act like a charm in every case where the patient could be induced to swallow the dose.

Brother Stevens is not the only advocate of "State work" for whom I have had to furnish "tar plasters" and "spiritual gruel" during the few years of my humble life as a preacher. At one time or another I have had "organized effort" in almost every State in the South "broken down in the loins," "spiritually gutted," and "down on the lift" on my hands for treatment. After observing carefully the effects of "State work" upon the spiritual health of hundreds of such patients as Brother Stevens, and noting the absence of anything like "organized effort" in the New Testament, my "views" very naturally "underwent a radical change," and I retired from the practice.

WE WILL NOT ASK HIM TO COME DOWN.

The following card comes from F. D. Pettit, Chillicothe, Mo.:

DEAR BRETHREN: The good brother who suggested me as a possible permanent reader of the GOSPEL ADVOCATE was mistaken in his man. Your constant opposition to the great host of loyal disciples because their plans for missions do not harmonize with yours is only a cause of ill will and division. The charges you make of extravagance of such self-sacrificing and godly men as Brother McLean are uncalled for. By their fruits you shall know them. Do your work as you please, but do it. You are as sectarian in your demands as the sects you denounce. Show us some worthy fruits before you ask us to come down with you.

Along the line of the fable about the boy up the apple tree, in the old blue-backed spelling book, we will not ask the brother ". to come down." The better plan is to "fetch him" with a few stones in the way of New Testament teaching. We make no opposition to "the great host of loyal disciples" or anybody else "because their plans for missions do not harmonize with" ours. The opposition we make is to plans which do not harmonize with the New Testament. We have no plans of our own. We have no ill will toward anybody, and we do not intend to allow any division to come between us and anybody who sticks to God and the Bible. It is our duty and purpose to see that the line of division in every case runs between us and those who depart from the New Testament. We make no charges "of extravagance" against Brother McLean. Why should we? He represents a denomination we do not belong to. The point we make against him is the same argument we make against all other denominations—viz., the denomination he represents is unscriptural and antiscriptural. Brother McLean is no doubt a well-meaning and kind-hearted man. So also are the Methodist bishops. However, "self-sacrificing" is probably not his strongest point, since his salary is about $2,500 a year above expenses. Abler men do harder work and more of it for less money. Still, the denominational organization he represents would be none the less unscriptural and antiscriptural if he worked for nothing and paid his own expenses. We decline to do our work as we please, or to do it at all; our idea is to put in all our time doing God's work as God pleases, and the juiciest piece of fruit in that line is to show that the denomination Brother Pettit belongs to and Brother McLean represents is, like all other denominations, unscriptural and antiscriptural. We are not sectarian at all. We belong to nothing and oppose everything in the way of a religious party or sect which does not include and consist of all Christians. This is the point with which we hit hard the denominational institution variously called "the current reformation," " our movement," " we as a people," " the disciples," " our brethren," etc. It is a religious party which does not include all Christians, but has all the denominational organization and accouterments any other denomination has. It is a religious denomination pure and simple, and as such it is neither better nor worse than any other denomination. They are all chips from the same unscriptural and antiscriptural block. One is as bad as another, if not worse.

NOT A PERNICIOUS MISREPRESENTATION.

The following excerpt appeared in these columns July 15, 1897:

The trouble with the State evangelist of Alabama is that he uses the wrong word to express his idea. It is not co-operation he is driving at, but denominational organization pure and simple. He probably does not know that he is trying to organize a denomination. He doesn't seem to understand the dictionary any better than the New Testament.

To this the State evangelist replies as follows:

F. D. Srygley can sit up cross-legged in the third story of the building occupied by the Gospel Advocate Publishing Company and tell the readers of that paper that I am trying to organize a new denomination in Alabama, and draw a large salary for these pernicious misrepresentations, while his own native Alabamians are dying and going to hell in their sins, not having obeyed the gospel.

The statements that the State evangelist of Alabama represents " denominational organization pure and simple " and " is trying to organize a denomination " in

15

Alabama are not " pernicious misrepresentations " at all, nor any other kind of misrepresentations. He may not know this, but it is nevertheless true. He belongs to the Christian Church, or Disciples of Christ, which is as clearly defined and fully organized a denomination as can be found anywhere. It is a general religious party smaller than the church of the New Testament; it has tests of fellowship and terms of membership which by its own admission are not conditions of salvation, as is evident from the fact that it does not include all Christians or claim that no one will go to heaven who does not belong to it. One can be a Christian while he lives and be saved when he dies without belonging to it at all, or ever so much as hearing of it. The church of the New Testament is entirely a different thing from this Christian Church. That church is a spiritual body, over which Christ is the Head and in which every Christian is a member because he is a Christian. No one can possibly be a Christian and not belong to the New Testament church, for the reason that the same process which makes one a Christian adds him to the church in the New Testament sense. There is no Christian Church in any other than a denominational sense. The same process which makes one a Christian does not add him to the Christian Church, else no one could possibly be a Christian and not belong to it; nor does the process which makes one a Christian add him to any other denomination in Christendom. As the same process which makes one a Christian while he lives and enters him into heaven when he dies does not constitute him a member of the Christian Church, it necessarily follows that the Christian Church has tests of fellowship and terms of membership which are not conditions of salvation. It takes more to add one to the Christian Church than to make him a Christian and save him in heaven. He can be a Christian and go to heaven and not belong to the Christian Church at all or ever hear whether there be any such thing.

The Christian Church which the State evangelist of Alabama belongs to and represents publishes a yearbook, giving the number of its churches, preachers, communicants, schools, colleges, newspapers, books, publishing houses, etc. This yearbook, by the way, claims hundreds of churches and thousands of preachers and communicants that do not belong to it at all or have any more interest in it or sympathy for it than any other denomination. These erroneous and misleading figures ought to be corrected. Similar statistics appear in the United States census reports every decade. These statistical data show that the Christian Church is entirely cut off and clearly distinguished from all other Christians. When thus cut off, it is a sect or party of Christians; and as the world must have some name by which to designate it, the logic of the situation demands the use either of an unscriptural term or a scriptural term in an unscriptural sense to denominate it. When it is thus unscripturally denominated, it is, of course, an unscriptural denomination. There is no scriptural name for it, for the simple reason that the thing itself is not in the Scriptures. An effort to find a scriptural name for an unscriptural thing must always be a dismal failure. Whenever a man finds a thing for which there is no name in the New Testament, he may feel sure the thing itself is not in that book. There is a name in the Bible for everything that is in the Bible. Any man who belongs to anything in the way of a general religious party save the spiritual body over which Christ is the Head and in which every Christian is a member because he is a Christian and as long as he remains a Christian is a partisan or denominationalist; any man who tries to induce Christians, preachers, or churches to go into anything in the way of a religious party which he himself admits does not include and consist of all Christians is trying to organize or build up a religious party or denomination, whether he knows it or not. Anything which a religious party that does not include and consist of all Christians has in the way of organization, save local congregations, for any purpose, is " denominational organization pure and simple," for the reason that it is organization in and of the denomination. To try to form churches, preachers, and Christians into any kind of a general religious organization or body that does not include and consist of all Christians is simply an effort to organize a denomination, whether those who do it so understand and intend or not.

In the way of denominational organization, the Christian Church, which the State evangelist of Alabama belongs to and represents, has State, district, and county organizations all over the country. It also has a foreign society, a home society, a woman's society, a church building society, a society to provide for old preachers, and a society to do work among the colored people. Each of these societies is governed by a board and represented by a secretary or traveling agent, and special days are appointed and particular arrangements are made to take separate collections for each society in all the churches of that denomination every year. State work in Alabama, like State work everywhere else, is little else than an effort to organize preachers, Christians, and churches into this denominational machinery, whether those who engage in it so understand and intend or not. If any other denomination in Christendom has anything in the way of denominational organization which the Christian Church does not have, it is something the leaders in that church have not yet heard of; and they will probably adopt it by unanimous resolution the first general convention that meets after they hear of it. A State evangelist is himself a purely denominational dignitary, whether he knows it or not. There is no such thing as a State evangelist mentioned in the New Testament or found in the spiritual body of Christ, which is the church; nor is there any place at all for a State evangelist anywhere except in a purely denominational organization. All these things in the Christian Church, which the State evangelist of Alabama belongs to and represents, constitute denominational organization pure and simple, as much so and as destitute of New Testament authority as Baptist associations or Methodist conferences. Whether Christians, churches, and preachers will have any part or connection with such organization is simply a question as to whether they will belong to a denomination. Every one must decide that question for himself, of course; but to seriously argue that all these things are·not denominational organization is to display pitiable, if not inexcusable, ignorance of the English language. When Christians, preachers, or churches decide to go into denominational organizations, sensible people understand that they desire to be regarded, recognized, and treated as denominationalists. They are, therefore, accorded a place among sister denominations; and their fellowship is necessarily denominational in its scope, character, and limitations. They are neither better nor worse than any other denomination, for the reason that all denominations and denominational organizations are in violation of the plain teaching of the New Testament and a sin against God. The Christian Church is no better than any other denomination in this respect. They are all cuts from the same bolt. The thing to do is to distintegrate, disband, and abandon them all and put Christianity on the New Testament basis of individual effort and personal consecration in the spiritual body over which Christ is the Head and in which every Christian is a member because he is a Christian.

WHO SHOULD AFFIRM?

Under the general heading, "Who Should Affirm?" the *Gospel Messenger* philosophizes thus:

Some folks seem very anxious to have us affirm that our special plan of coöperative or organized mission work is taught by the sacred writers. In our recent convention of the Disciples in Tennessee, held in this city, one of the brethren spoke at length on this subject. If we represent him correctly, he took the position that if the apostles and early disciples had a special plan of doing evangelistic or missionary work, and if they had revealed it unto us through their sacred writings, we ought to be able to follow the very same plan in doing the same sort of work; and then, if we remember correctly, he showed that they evidently did not have a special plan of doing this work, but that they no doubt experimented until they got the best plan, and adopted this, adjusting it to the peculiar circumstances in each case. He cited Paul's experiment in 2 Cor. 9: 13 as evidence for this. We freely confess that if there is an inflexible plan for doing evangelistic or missionary work through all the ages laid down in the Scriptures, we have failed to find it; and in the honesty of our souls we would thank any one for a specific spark on this subject. And now why not, if some one sees the way, let him or her affirm that the Holy Scriptures do specifically lay down rules for disciples and churches of Christ to follow in the evangelization of the world throughout the ages? If we have represented this brother fairly (and we think we have), we believe he would take the negative, for he is a man who fears no opponent. We do not offer this to get up a discussion, but because many honest people think and say that the Lord's way of doing evangelistic work is as plainly taught as faith, repentance, and baptism for the remission of sins. If it is, we should love for this way to be fraternally and specifically pointed out to us.

The advocates of organized effort are not asked to "affirm that our special plan of coöperative or organized mission work is taught by the sacred writers." Everybody knows they do not believe this, and nobody expects them to affirm what they do not believe. The point on which they are pressed is why they persist in doing something which they and everybody else know is not "taught by the sacred writers." The day of discussion has passed. The only question now is whether people will stand by what everybody knows is "taught by the sacred writers," or persist in doing something nobody believes "the sacred writers" ever taught. State work is "a special plan." There is no "special plan" of any kind "laid down in the Scriptures." What those who oppose State work and every other special plan propose to affirm is this: The fact that no special plan is "laid down in the Scriptures" proves that God intended the work to be done without a special plan. The truth is, this thing called "a special plan" is simply another name for a denominational organization. There is no such organization in the New Testament. The whole issue is: Shall Christians and churches form themselves into a general denominational organization, or shall they conduct all religious work and worship without any general denominational organization? Every denominational organization on earth sustains itself by the same argument the *Messenger* makes for State work. No well-informed Methodist believes there is any such thing as the method of the Methodists laid down in the Scriptures. How, then, does he sustain it? By the same argument exactly which the *Gospel Messenger* parades in support of State work among the Disciples. So also with the denominational organizations of all sorts of Baptists, every kind of Presbyterians, and everything else that has crystallized into a special plan of denominationalism. This is the rock on which they all stumble. They all admit that there is no special plan of denominational organization laid down in the Scriptures, and from this they all erroneously argue that they are authorized to experiment till they find a special plan that suits them and seems best adapted to the purpose. As to what is "the best plan" they honestly differ, as a matter of course; and some stand for "Baptist usage," some for Presbyterian organizations, some for the method of the Methodists, and some for Disciple State work. They are all chips from the same block. They are denominational organizations pure and simple which divide the children of God and foment strife and discord in the spiritual body of Christ. Organized effort among the Disciples is not one whit better or more scriptural than any other denominational institution.

The reference to " Paul's experiment in 2 Cor. 9: 13 " is amusing. If this gauges the level of State work in point of Bible information, there is no better missionary ground this side of Greenland's icy mountains than organized effort in Tennessee. The commonly used version of the New Testament reads: " Whiles by the experiment of this ministration they glorify God for your professed subjection unto the gospel," etc. The State-work argument is based entirely upon the assumption that Paul and other Christians were simply trying an " experiment " in this case to find " the best plan " to do something; whereas the truth is, they were obeying instructions given by inspiration in the matter of sending contributions to relieve suffering among the saints in Judea. The " experiment " was not an experiment at all in the sense State work uses that term in the argument. The Revised Version translates the experiment entirely out of it by rendering the passage thus: " Seeing that through the proving of you by this ministration they glorify God for the obedience of your confession unto the gospel of Christ, and for the liberality of your contribution unto them and unto all." It is not an experiment at all, but an experience, or, rather, a proving of themselves by their conduct in doing what the gospel of Christ required in this matter. The word is rendered " proving," instead of " experiment," in the Revised Version, and in some commentaries it is rendered " experience; " but no matter how it is translated, the context plainly shows it cannot possibly mean what the State-work argument assumes.

WHAT IS A STATE EVANGELIST, ANYWAY?

Now that this State-evangelist business is up for consideration in Tennessee, it might be pertinent to inquire what sort of a thing a State evangelist, or any other kind of evangelist, for that matter, really is, anyhow! To say nothing of the teaching of the Scriptures on this subject just now, I quote from an article by an unknown writer in the *Christian Standard* to this effect:

He must provide for the pastoral care and spiritual training of those whom he leads to Christ, if such provision be not already made. . . . He must set the church in order, as well as call it together. He must provide a shepherd, as well as gather a flock. If the flock be large enough to need all the time of two or more shepherds, then two or more should be provided; but if the one flock be too small to need all the time or be too weak to support one shepherd, then two or more contiguous flocks must be placed under the care of one shepherd. If any one thinks it is certain that the conditions and needs of the churches in Scripture times were such that the scriptural evangelists did ordain two or more elders in every city, it is *far more certain* that the conditions and needs of the churches of the present time are such that it is often an imperative necessity that two or more churches be placed under the care of one shepherd. He [the evangelist] must take the oversight of the overseers whom he may ordain in regard to both their doctrine and their lives, stopping the mouths of some unruly and vain talkers and charging others that they teach only the things that minister to godly edifying, rebuking some before all, that others may fear, and counting others worthy of double honor.

This puts the idea definitely before us. The theory was a little more felicitously described a few years ago

by Brother Munnell, in the *Guide,* when he said, in substance, that the Methodist brethren are nearer the true
New Testament church polity than we, except in the
name of their bosses. They call them "bishops," while
the New Testament calls them "evangelists." I shall
not stop to argue this question now. I have only to
say that if a State evangelist "must take the oversight
of the overseers" in Tennessee and stop "the mouths"
of such men as David Lipscomb and E. G. Sewell, I
don't want the job, unless arrangements can be made
to work it by telephone from an office in Canada or
Mexico!

RUNNING IN A RUT.

A writer in one of my exchanges gives "the ancient
order of things" in some churches a vigorous shaking
up, scores those who are incessantly crying out for
"apostolic order" and "the Lord's plan," and protests
against "running in ruts" on general principles. No
doubt but that there is a vast deal of foolish talk and
unprofitable dogmatizing about "the Lord's plan,"
"apostolic order," the "old paths," and all that sort of
thing; but when I strike a man on whom the effect of
the very sound of such phrases is as the shaking of a red
rag in a bull's face, I conclude that, in his prejudice
against those who, as he thinks, abuse such sayings, he
has about lost all respect for divine revelation. Brethren, keep cool. Don't lead the world to think that you
don't care a cent about the "Lord's plan," "apostolic
order," or "the old paths," just because some one abuses
these terms. "The Lord's plan" is a very good thing

in a religious way, howbeit some people don't seem to know much about it. Don't allow your prejudices against those who oppose your methods of work to drive you into flippant, irreverent, contemptuous, and presumptuous sneering at the "Lord's plan" and "apostolic doctrine." And don't you worry about running in ruts, either. Do you stick to the Scriptures. A rut is a good enough thing for a little wheel like yours to run in, anyhow, if God in the Scriptures so directs. Instead of trying to keep out of ruts, you better read Matt. 15: 14, and look out that you don't run into the ditch.

HIS LIST SUPPLIED.

A State evangelist writes to " a leading paper: "

My list is well supplied with some of the best pastors, evangelists, teachers, etc., we have among us. Churches and colleges should write me.

Within the last few weeks I have seen similar statements in the papers from as many as three State evangelists, and it is safe to say that in every State where we have had such an evangelist for any great length of time his "list is well supplied" with applicants for a job. On such lists there are some good men, but they are in bad company. It is a well-known fact that our State evangelists are handicapped and that our organized mission work is burdened by a lot of deadbeats who are everlastingly on somebody's list waiting for a job. It is growing worse every year. It is even now well-nigh as bad as the civil-service department of government, in proportion to the amount of money to be distributed.

The lamented F. G. Allen spoke earnestly against this evil in the land more than once toward the close of his life. It cannot be denied that what we call "our organized mission work," instead of being what the great and the good among us desire it to be—an earnest, unselfish effort to save souls—is fast degenerating into an unholy zeal to collect money and provide places for the support of professional preachers who are missionaries "for revenue only." I speak earnestly, but not without discrimination. Good men sometimes put their names on these lists, but they are the exceptions and not the rule. In all my denominational exchanges I see no such public parade of lists of the names of place hunters. And yet all denominations have their methods of organized mission work. Why can't our State evangelists learn something by observation, and why can't our preachers and churches· proceed in mission work in a way to show more anxiety for the salvation of souls and less interest in the matter of providing places for preachers who are too utterly destitute of the missionary spirit to attempt any work for the Lord till some man or organization secures them an easy place on a good salary?

MISSIONARY FOR REVENUE ONLY.

Some weeks ago I called attention to the fact that "our organized mission work" is embarrassed by some "professional preachers who are missionaries for revenue only," and suggested that it would not be a bad idea for State evangelists and such like to take more interest in the preaching of the gospel in destitute places and manifest less zeal to collect money and provide places for

" preachers who are too utterly destitute of the missionary spirit to attempt any work for the Lord till some
man or organization secures them an easy place on a
good salary." I was careful to say twice in that short
paragraph that I recognized the fact that there were
some good men engaged in such organized mission work,
and that my remarks were not intended to apply to
them. Ignoring this discrimination and carefully con-
cealing from his readers all evidence that I made such
a distinction, my good brother of the *Christian Courier*
feels called upon in a private letter to denounce my well-
meant suggestions as an " onslaught upon the work in
which some as good men as are in the church are engaged," and all that sort of thing. I am sure the
brother misunderstands me. What I said was not an
" onslaught " at all. I never made an " onslaught " in
my life, and I couldn't play a tune on one if I had it.
What I did state was a *fact,* and not an " onslaught."
I can't play a tune on an " onslaught; " but when I get
my fingers on a *fact,* I can make it fairly *hum.*

The *Courier* makes this reply to what its editor calls
my " onslaught: "

This very earnest speech from Srygley would fall with
heavier weight if we could all see that he exemplified his
preaching by his practice in cutting loose from churches,
papers, real-estate syndicates, etc., and giving the Lord some
missionary work that does not have the smell of revenue
only.

From all this it would seem that the *Courier* expects
to run the concern, with all its faults, on my meanness.
All right. If it can run on that kind of support, I
hereby authorize " the board " to increase its force of
workers indefinitely, and draw on me for the sinews of

war. I have done a great many mean things in my life, but I have never yet put my name on a State evangelist's "list" or applied to a "board" for a job. The editor of the *Courier* is red-headed; I am in a good humor.

THAT "GREAT GENERAL ORGANISM."

I have just read, with much interest, an address on "The Lord's Plan," delivered by my beloved Brother J. H. Roulhac before "The State Missionary Convention, held at Hot Springs, Ark., June 9-11, 1891." It will be remembered that Brother Roulhac delivered a similar address on the same subject before the State Missionary Convention, held at Chattanooga, Tenn., last fall, which was also published and gratuitously circulated by the convention, and favorably commended, without a word of adverse criticism, by several of "our leading papers."

With much of this address I am in happy accord, but there is one fundamental error of grave import in it, if I rightly understand the matter, which ought not to pass unchallenged.

The views of Brother Roulhac or any other man, on this or any other subject, are of small moment one way or another; but the fact that this particular address has been thus indorsed by two State conventions and commended by "leading papers," without a word of adverse criticism, singles it out as a sort of representative document and, therefore, makes it worthy of more than passing notice.

The points in this address which are of special interest to me just now, as well as of deep significance as to the trend of the two State conventions which have in-

dorsed it and the papers which have commended it, are
certain passages which squint strongly in the direction
of "the method of the Methodists." Beginning near
the bottom of the seventeenth page I quote:

> But is it true that the local church is the only organism
> known to the New Testament? I answer, *No*, unless the
> phrase, *local church*, is the exact equivalent of the phrase,
> *body of Christ.*

He then cites several passages of scripture which
speak of the one body, etc., etc., and concludes:

> Now if this is not the whole body in the largest sense,
> including all true, all obedient believers, then I confess my
> inability to understand the force of language; and if this is
> not a definite description of a *perfect organism*, an organ-
> ism that is alive and at work for the Lord, then I would
> not know one if I should see it—yea, a great general organ-
> ism, with each several part coöperating in its work and min-
> istering to its success in building up itself in love, and so
> making increase of the body. Here, then, is a grand organ-
> ism, known to the Scriptures, larger than any local church,
> adapted to a work grander and broader than that which can
> be done effectively by any single congregation.

At page seventeen he says:

> Paul sent preachers to set in order the things wanting in
> the churches and ordain elders in every city, and even the
> elders themselves seem to have been answerable to the
> preachers.

And at the same page, speaking of the question which
arose in the church at Antioch as to whether Gentile
converts should be circumcised, he says:

> That difficulty, we have seen, was not adjusted either by
> the local church at Antioch or Jerusalem, but by a conven-

tion of inspired apostles and the elders and others. But if
the view now held by some, that the local church is the
only organism that can scripturally act, is correct, why
was not this trouble settled by the local church?

At page ten, speaking of this same question, he says:

This difficulty about circumcision was not adjusted by
the church at Antioch nor by the church at Jerusalem, but
by a convention composed of the apostles and elders and
of those sent from Antioch, with, perhaps, some of the party
who were advocating the necessity of circumcising Gentile
converts. So, it seems, the local organized church played
a very small part in this important matter. If the extreme
views of church independency held by some, who regard
the local congregation as the only organ through which divine work of any kind can be carried on, are correct, it
would be exceedingly difficult to account for the fact of this
convention at Jerusalem, or tell why the church at Antioch,
where the trouble arose, did not settle it.

These passages from the address mean, if they mean
anything at all, that there is a general ecclesiastical organization of the whole spiritual body of Christ, and
that in this general ecclesiasticism elders are " answerable to preachers " and conventions have ecclesiastic jurisdiction and disciplinary authority over local congregations. This may shed a few flickering rays of bor-
rowed light upon Brother Growden's enigmatical ex-
clamation in his sermon before the late convention in
this city: " I would to God we had the method of the
Methodists ! " This does look very much like something
of that sort, sure enough.

It is unfortunate that Brother Roulhac made no effort
to clearly define this general ecclesiastical organization
of the whole spiritual body of Christ. For one, I am
curious to know what it takes to constitute it. I should

16

like to know, especially, what official positions and prerogatives are in it, what the general officers are called, how they are placed in their respective offices, what are their qualifications and official duties, to whom they are amenable, and how they are held to the performance of their duties. All these things are clear enough in the Methodist " Discipline " as to the " great general organism " of the Methodist Episcopal Church, South, North, or any other direction. But how is it in the New Testament as to the ecclesiastical " great general organism " of the spiritual body of Christ, which Brother Roulhac is so sure " is known to the Scriptures? " When I began to look for these things in the New Testament, to use Brother Roulhac's words in another part of this address, " I felt like I was groping in chaos, and the further I went, the more chaotic and confusing things appeared, until at last I discovered I was engaged in a vain quest for that which had no existence." The thing is a myth.

It is worthy of note that Brother Roulhac claims but one convention in the New Testament. According to the chronology given in my Bible, the beginning of the church on the day of Pentecost was in the year 33, and the last part of the New Testament was written in the year 96. If we grant all he claims, therefore, the " great general organism " which he thinks is " known in the Scriptures " was successfully operated sixty-three years, with only one convention. " We as a people," I believe, held the first convention in 1849, and since that date " we " have held one general convention every year, and, at the very lowest estimate, probably about twenty State, district, and county conventions every year. This makes, say, about eight hundred and eighty-two conventions, which, according to my arithmetic, would be sufficient to run Brother Roulhac's " great general organism," allowing one convention to each sixty-three years, as he claims for it in the New Testament, fifty-five thousand five hundred and sixty-six years. According to these figures, our next convention ought not to be held till the year 57415, which will probably put it several years after the resurrection! This looks rather gloomy.

But, what is worse still, the convention which Brother Roulhac claims, if all the scholars and commentators I have examined can establish a proposition by their unanimous testimony, had nothing at all to do with this alleged " great general organism." Brother Roulhac's argument seems to proceed entirely upon the *assumption* that the question which arose in the church at Antioch, as to whether Gentile converts should be circumcised, should have been settled either by a local church or a convention. As it was settled by a convention, his conclusion is that we ought to have conventions to settle such questions nowadays. If that same question should be raised in the church at Memphis to-day, for instance, his idea seems to be that the proper course to pursue would be for the corresponding secretary, *alias* State evangelist, to call a convention to settle it. His argument is that the settlement of this question for the church at Antioch by a convention in Jerusalem is a precedent for conventions with ecclesiastic jurisdiction and disciplinary authority over local churches nowadays. His reference to " the extreme views of church independency held by some " clearly implies that the convention which settled this question was such a convention as we ought to have these days to settle troublesome questions for local congregations. It would seem from

this that he gravely argues that this question was settled
by just such a convention as we may have, and ought to
have, in the " great general organism " in these modern
times; and in that case, the only evidence we have that
Gentile converts ought not to be circumcised is the mere
dictum of such a convention as was recently held in
this city! But such conventions are by no means infallible. So, it seems to me, Brother Roulhac ought to
be circumcised a little, anyhow, just to guard against a
possible mistake in the decision of the convention!

But Brother Roulhac will no doubt say the convention
at Jerusalem was not such as we have these days. It
was a convention of inspired apostles, and its decision
is therefore final and infallible. Exactly so. Then
what becomes of his statement that " if the extreme
views of church independency held by some, who regard
the local congregation as the only organ through which
the divine work of any kind can be carried on, are correct, it would be exceedingly difficult to account for the
fact of this convention at Jerusalem, or to tell why the
church at Antioch, where the trouble arose, did not settle
it? "

The exact truth is that this question was not settled
either by a local church or by a convention, such as we
have these days, *but by inspiration.* And this is why it
was not settled by the church in Antioch. It is also
why the convention which did settle it is no precedent
for a convention nowadays in a " great general organism " with ecclesiastic jurisdiction and disciplinary prerogatives over local churches. It is my understanding
that this question was referred to the apostles at Jerusalem " *by an express revelation of the divine will* " and
in order to get the concensus of apostolic inspiration on

the subject, and that, therefore, this convention had nothing at all to do with an ecclesiastical "great general organism." There was, at that time, no other way by which the minds of *all* the apostles could be obtained, for the New Testament had not yet been written. On this point scholars and commentators, so far as I have examined, speak with one voice. I quote, for instance, from Professor McGarvey's "Commentary on Acts:"

If the brethren in Antioch had estimated at its proper value the authority of an inspired apostle, they would have yielded implicitly to Paul's decision without this mission to Jerusalem. But they were as yet too little accustomed to reflection upon the profound mystery of apostolic infallibility to properly accredit it, and their deep prejudice on the subject under discussion was a serious obstacle in the way of clear thought. It is probable that apostolic authority is more highly appreciated now than it was then; yet the prejudices of sect and party are so intense that even now the *dictum* of a living apostle would prove insufficient, in millions of cases, to convince men of their errors. Like the disciples in Antioch, who had the testimony of Paul, men now are not easily satisfied with a single inspired statement upon a point in dispute or with the statements of a single apostle, but demand an accumulation even of divine evidence. It is probable that Paul would have objected to making this appeal to the other apostles, on the ground of its apparent inconsistency with his own claims to inspired authority, had not the proposition been sustained by an express revelation of the divine will. In the second chapter of Galatians, where Mr. Howson very clearly proves that Paul has reference to this journey, he says: "I went up by *revelation* and communicated to them that gospel which I preached among the Gentiles." It was the divine purpose to settle the question, not for the church in Antioch alone, but for all the world and for all time.

Professor McGarvey, who, by the way, is one of those who hold what Brother Roulhac so flippantly calls " extreme views of church independency," does not find it at all " difficult to account for the fact of this convention at Jerusalem, or to tell why the church at Antioch, where the trouble arose, did not settle it." If I rightly catch his meaning, and I think I do, he accounts for the fact of this convention at Jerusalem and tells why the question was not settled by the church at Antioch, on the ground that those who wanted the convention did not estimate " at its proper value the authority of an inspired apostle."

In fact, he clearly states that " if the brethren in Antioch had estimated at its proper value the authority of an inspired apostle, they would have yielded implicitly to Paul's decision " and settled it at Antioch " without this mission to Jerusalem." By the way, several folks account for the fact of conventions these days and tell why efforts are being made to make " elders answerable to preachers " and local congregations subject to the ecclesiastic jurisdiction of conventions in an ecclesiastical " great general organism " on precisely the same ground. And I am not sure but that Professor McGarvey leans somewhat to this view when he says " the prejudices of sect and party are so intense that even now the *dictum* of a living apostle would prove insufficient, in millions of cases, to convince men of their errors."

But enough has been said to dispose of the only convention Brother Roulhac claims to find in the history of his ecclesiastical " great general organism " for sixty-three long years, and a " great general organism " that can be successfully operated for sixty-three years without a convention is not the sort of a "great general organism" we need in our business.

The State evangelist of Mississippi, whatever that may be, says:

We *cannot* preach the gospel into the *ears* of the Mississippians without going at them in a well-fitted-up, independent way. They *will not* hear a man talk who does not make a respectable, well-fed appearance. You can say what you please about the above sentence, but it is true, just the same. Question: How can a man make this kind of appearance without money, and how can a man get the money in Mississippi without coöperation?

It would seem from this that the Mississippians wouldn't pay any attention to a man who had a raiment of camel's hair and a leathern girdle about his loins and whose meat was locusts and wild honey. Nor yet would they listen to a man who would frankly confess that "silver and gold have I none." Much less would they hear a man who would go among them, saying: "The foxes have holes, and the birds of the air have nests; but the Son of man hath not where to lay his head." And as for a man who had been beaten with many stripes, thrust into the inner prison and his feet made fast in the stocks, he probably couldn't find a place to stay all night among "the Mississippians." Ah, no, Brother Stevens, you mistake the feelings of the Mississippians! The love of God shed abroad in our hearts by the Holy Ghost will give us a much better hearing in Mississippi or anywhere else, my brother, than stovepipe hats and claw-hammer coats.

EDUCATION IS GOOD, BUT IT IS NOT EVERY-
THING.

The *Christian Courier* publishes four letters, "just as they were written," to show what folks think of that paper. Three of those letters extravagantly commend the *Courier* and clearly commit their authors to certain questions of church polity which it advocates. Those three are written in faultless English, and their authors seem to be men of scholarly attainments. The fourth one orders the *Courier* discontinued, boldly protests against the editorial policy of the paper, and openly commits its author to certain positions which such men as David Lipscomb advocate. I think this is the third time the *Courier* has done this thing in the last year, and it has also been perpetrated several times by other "leading papers." The point in the thing is to make the impression that the educated folks are all on "our side" and the uneducated folks are all "against us." The assumption is that, because "we" are educated and "you" are not, therefore "you" ought to stand aside and let "us" run the thing. I am not disposed to admit on such flimsy evidence that all the education in the world is on one side of any question, especially when I am on the other side. Any paper in the world could do what the *Courier* has done. Even the GOSPEL ADVO-CATE sometimes gets highly complimentary letters from very good scholars, and occasionally gets "blowed up" by uneducated folks. But even if all the educated folks are on one side, I don't think the rest of us are bound to stand by and see a lot of educated nincompoops run the whole thing to everlasting smash without a word of protest or friendly warning.

There is something ludicrous, to my mind, in such

clod hoppers as Homan and McPherson putting on such lofty airs of feigned learning, anyhow. It has been but a few years since they were in the backwoods wearing patched breeches and "half-hander" socks, just like the rest of us. The ink is hardly dry on their rustic epistles in which they spelled "corn" and "cabbage," with a "k" and "God" with a little "g," like common folks. In fact, their editorials are, like my own, a little shaky in grammar and spelling yet at times. Before they moved to town and started "a leading paper," and bought some new clothes, and got on "the board," they had to borrow meal, buy meat on a credit, drink sassafras tea, and eat poke salad, just like the rest of us. Ah, no, beloved, education will not perish from the earth when Homan, McPherson, and I die! And, besides all this, I sometimes find a common country preacher who says "simmons" and "taters," and yet knows more about the Bible than some town folks who wear Sunday clothes in the middle of the week and say "poturnips."

GOOD CHURCH PRIVILEGES.

Occasionally I get a letter from somebody who wants to move to some place where he can have good church privileges. Ordinarily such letters go on to explain that the writer is literally starving for the bread of life, and longs to get where he can have a good church to attend every Lord's day and so forth. And the worst of it all is that the writers of such letters evidently think that they are good Christians and holy martyrs; but the real truth of the business is that they are, in many cases, only petrified specimens of extinct orthodoxy. In a gen-

eral way, the man who will not worship God anywhere
it may be his lot to live, and cause a flourishing church
to grow up around him, would be but a poor specimen
of Christianity in any church to which he might move.
Speaking of church privileges, any man has all the
church privileges he needs in any place in these United
States. It is a free country; you can worship God anywhere. And wherever you worship God and hold forth
the word of life in patience and sincerity, the church
will grow up around you; and if you haven't enough spiritual life in you to worship God and get some one to
preach the gospel to your neighbors and convert them
and build up a church where you are, it is hardly probable that you would be benefited by better church privileges than you now enjoy, even if you had them.

SEEMS TO BRISTLE UP AND MISUNDER-
STAND ME.

The *Christian Courier* says:

Srygley, of the GOSPEL ADVOCATE, tells us that he concedes
the right of Christians to work through missionary societies, but at the same time he seems to bristle up to a man
and just dare him to exercise his right.

The *Courier* "seems to bristle up" and misunderstand me. I concede to Christians the right, so far as
I am concerned, to work through missionary societies, or
to join the Baptist Church, or the Methodist Church, or
even the thing called "us as a people," if they want to.
Every man must account to God, and not to me, for
the sort of work he does, the thing he does it through,

the church he joins, and what he joins it for. I am not managing the world this year. But I insist that no man *has* to work through a missionary society, or join the Methodist Church, or the Baptist Church, or anything else of that kind in order to be a Christian and be saved. God does not require any man to join any of these things. Any man can obey every command God has ever given without joining any of them. This is admitted by everybody. Hence, when a man " bristles up " to me and tries to get me to turn aside into any of these things, I generally " bristle up " to him some, too, and beg to be excused. Why not?

THE MISSIONARY SOCIETY AGAINST THE CAMPBELL STREET CHURCH.

My friend and brother, J. B. Jones, has appeared in the *Christian Standard* in an article, which Professor McGarvey thinks is, to some extent, in the imperative mood, in which he describes a preacher and a church without naming either, which R. B. Neal recognizes in the *Worker* as Brother M. C. Kurfees and Campbell Street Church, of Louisville, Ky. Brother Jones quotes a private letter, which Neal says Kurfees wrote, and proceeds to comment upon it in a way to show that he is not in harmony with the views of the writer or the policy of the church he represents. It seems that Brother Jones, as State evangelist, wanted to " finangelize " Campbell Street Church—that is, canvass it for some money for State work—and Brother Kurfees wrote him, in substance, that the church had already made its arrangements to do missionary work this year without

troubling the State evangelist to "finangelize" it, and
it would not be necessary for him to come. This is
what caused Brother Jones to write the article for the
Standard in the imperative mood. The only issue between him and Brother Kurfees, as I understand it, is
the naked question as to whether it is the proper thing
for a church to raise its own money, select its own field
for missionary work, choose its own evangelist, send him
out and sustain him, and manage its own business in
general, in mission work as well as in everything else,
without dictation or interference from the State evangelist or the board. When the controversy is stripped
of all irrelevancies, and this naked issue is presented, I
make bold to say Kurfees and Campbell Street Church
are right and the State evangelist of Kentucky is wrong.
That there may be no room for mistaking the nature of
the issue, I note certain facts which Neal states as to
the missionary zeal, activity, and liberality of Campbell
Street Church. (1) It has determined to send its own
preacher, or evangelist—Brother Kurfees—two months
of his time "to preach the gospel in destitute places."
(2) It has determined to raise money enough to sustain
another competent evangelist all of his time, if possible,
"to preach the gospel in destitute places." (3) It has
already taken a collection of one hundred and twenty-
five dollars in cash for this mission work. (4) It has
always supported, with men, women, and money, from
one to two missions of its own in the city of Louisville.
(5) "Considering her numbers and ability, she is doing more mission work than any other congregation,
without exception, in the State of Kentucky." These
facts are vouched for by Brother Neal, who claims
Campbell Street Church as his home congregation, and

as yet not one of them has been questioned by Brother
Jones. It seems as clear as a mathematical demonstration, therefore, that there is no issue between them as
to whether mission work shall be done, and done by
Campbell Street Church. The naked issue is as to
whether that church has a right to manage its own business without dictation or interference from the State
evangelist or the State Board. Brethren, there is but
one answer to such a question. A church is independent, and it has a perfect right to do its own missionary
work and manage its own business if it wants to. And
certainly the State evangelist and the State Board are
the last ones to complain in such a case. The course of
Campbell Street Church only relieves the State evangelist and the board of that much labor and responsi-
bility. It would be a slight gratification of party pride
for the magnificent work and bountiful gifts of Campbell Street Church to pass through the regular channel
and thus swell the report of " State work " at the next
convention, perhaps, but we ought not to give place to
such feelings of partisan ambition for a moment. What
matters it, just so the gospel is preached, sinners are
converted, churches are established, saints are edified,
and souls are saved, whether we so much as have any
State evangelist, State Board, conventions, or big reports? My judgment is that it is best both for the
churches and for mission work for each church to manage its own mission funds and direct its own mission
work, just as Campbell Street Church is doing. I think
every State Board and State evangelist in the land ought
to encourage churches to do this. It certainly does not
require much of a philosopher to see that a church will
take more interest, do more work, and pay more money,

when it feels that the work is its own and that it is individually and solely responsible for it, than when it feels that the work is merely a general one in which it has only an insignificant part. Who does not know, as a business man, that the interested and responsible partners in a small partnership business take more interest in the management and labor harder for the success of the business than the insignificant stockholders in a railroad company take in the management of the great corporation business in which their little shares of stock are but as a few drops in the ocean? But whether State evangelists and State Boards agree with me on this point or not, they certainly will not, on sober reflection, undertake to deny the right of a church to pursue the course of Campbell Street Church in the matter of managing its own business. If the State evangelist of Kentucky is not misunderstood or misrepresented, therefore, he is wrong.

Brother Jones insists that I " usurped the throne of God " and impugned the motives of the State evangelist and the board when I said:

It would be a slight gratification of party pride for the magnificent work and bountiful gifts of Campbell Street to pass through the regular channels and thus swell the report of State work, but we ought not to give place to such feelings of partisan ambition for a moment.

Well, if I usurped the throne of God or impugned Brother Jones' motives in that statement, it was wholly unintentional, and I sincerely beg his forgiveness. And now that the question is up, I would be under lasting obligation if Brother Jones would explain to us himself why he is so very anxious for " the magnificent work and bountiful gifts of Campbell Street to pass through the regular channels and thus swell the report of State work." There is a little point right here which I never have been able to understand and which he has never yet made any effort at all to explain. I spoke of this little fact before, and now I am "again facing" it, but there is not a single ray of light to explain it in all Brother Jones has written on this whole subject. Campbell Street Church simply proposes to pay her money for mission work directly to the man who is doing the work, without troubling either the State evangelist or the board in the matter of raising the money or disbursing the funds. And this is the thing, and the only thing, Brother Jones has to object to, so far as I can see, in this whole business. The man selected to do the mission work has heretofore been employed by the board; he is a good preacher, and he has a good report among all the churches. And yet Brother Jones objects to this. Now, if he can explain his objection without coming any nearer impugning his motives than I did, I should like to see how he does it.

As to what he quotes from the second page of the ADVOCATE of April 15, showing how completely it contradicts what I said in the ADVOCATE of May 6, I have only to say I did not write the language quoted from the second page of the ADVOCATE of April 15 at all.

The brother says State evangelists will not "be taught by men who forget what they have written." That is not the issue in this discussion. The problem now is to find out whether State evangelists will be taught by men who do not forget what Paul and Peter and John and other writers in the New Testament have written. I do not consider that it would be any great loss to the world if I and every other creature on earth should

forget every line I ever wrote; but it does seem to me
that we ought all to keep our remembering apparatus
busy holding a firm grip on what the men who wrote
the Bible have written!

Brother Jones wants to know what evidence I have
that he "is impatient and intolerant of those who cannot see their way clearly to join in such things." It
occurs to me that the whole spirit and tenor of all he
has said and done in this matter is one continuous chain
of evidence of impatience and intolerance of the course
of those who cannot work through his organization. If
he is both patient and tolerant of the way Campbell
Street and others who differ from him are doing their
work, why this discussion? And why did he say in the
Standard: "My conscience will not let me rest till his
church [Campbell Street] is enlisted in the work?"
It occurs to me that a man whose conscience will not
let him rest till "those who cannot see their way clearly
to join in such things" are "enlisted" in them is by
no means a model of patience and tolerance.

According to the exegesis of Brother Jones, Professor
McGarvey was not talking about him at all when he
spoke of the three men who attacked him with "bristles
up" and used the "denunciatory language which has
stirred up the gall of bitterness on this question." F.
M. Green, B. F. Clay, and the editor of the *Christian
Standard* were the three bad men from bitter creek,
Brother Jones thinks, who went at our beloved Brother
McGarvey with "bristles up," and all that sort of thing.
And this is the fulcrum, Brother Jones says, which
"lifts me out of the sphere into which your ready pre-
judgment had given me an unenviable position." In
this I think he misunderstands Professor McGarvey,

but I give him the benefit of the doubt for the present
and let him "lift" himself out for a few moments. It
is painful, however, to see how readily he "lifts" the
other fellows in, while lifting himself out. But, worst
of all, he proceeds at once to "lift" himself into the
same hole again by writing to the *Standard* an enthusiastic indorsement of the very editorial which, according to his own statement, came at our beloved Brother
McGarvey with "bristles up" and used the "denunciatory language which has stirred up the gall of bitterness" on this question. In the very next issue of the
Standard Brother Jones says of this very editorial:
"Your editorial in last week's *Standard*—'*Cannot Stop
Here*'—*hits the nail on the head!*" I don't see that it
was any worse for the *Standard* to write that editorial
against Professor McGarvey's conservative position than
for Brother Jones to thus whoop it up and rub it in!
It is surprising that a man will work so hard to "lift"
himself out of an "unenviable position" and then rush
right into print and "lift" himself in again! I am
curious to know how he will "lift" himself out this
time. The exact truth in the matter seems to be that
the *Standard,* with more dogmatism than discretion,
expressed itself against the conservative position of
Professor McGarvey in a style "somewhat overbearing,
if not tyrannical," as Professor McGarvey himself puts
it, and F. M. Green, J. B. Jones, and B. F. Clay—all
very good fellows, but rather reckless and impulsive
youths—seized the bits in their teeth and undertook to
run over the conservative and level-headed old brother.
The *Christian Courier,* taking its cue from the *Standard,* as usual, fell into line, and the whole herd of them
dashed at Professor McGarvey with "bristles up" in

17

pretty much the same style. The *Standard* was discreet enough to see that it was wise to stop, and now some of "the boys" are trying to "lift" themseves out of the middle of a very bad fix!

But my chief offense seems to be that I expressed the opinion that "State work" rests upon human judgment, and that it will, therefore, die. Well, I may be wrong about this; but if so, I have been misled by the writings of some of the founders and leaders of "State work." For instance, Brother Munnell said in the GOSPEL ADVOCATE of July 11, 1867:

There must always be a society until all the churches engage in the work; then the society will be lost, will die; but it will die like the morning star dies in the brightness of a greater light. This is what we are working for, as Brother McGarvey told you several months ago. The coöperation of a few churches, and only a few individuals in each church, is truly but the starlight to what it would be if every church and every member were at work. To this end we are laboring, and until that day the societies must still work on.

In 1866 Professor McGarvey said, in an article in the *Review:*

I would, therefore, adjust the whole controversy in this way. There are some individuals who are abundantly able to sustain each his missionary in the field, paying him a competent support for his family. Every such man ought to do it, and the agents of missionary societies, as well as all other good men who have the opportunity, ought to urge him to do it. Then there are some individual churches who are abundantly able and ought this day to be sending out missionaries to be sustained by themselves. Wherever such a church is found, it ought to be urged to get about the work at once.

This plan was urged before the Kentucky convention in 1866 by Brother McGarvey and others, and in the published report, or minutes, of that convention, page 11, it is argued that the adoption and encouragement of the plan of work here advocated by Brother McGarvey "would satisfy the scruples of some good brethren who doubt the wisdom of our present method; it would make the society promotive of congregational action in the missionary work instead of being, as some allege, antagonistic to it," and "*would raise a much larger amount of money, and the aggregate of good would be greatly increased.*" This is the language of the board of the Kentucky society, taken from the published report, or minutes, of the convention in 1866, page 11. If Professor McGarvey and other conservative friends of "State work" have ever changed their opinion or modified their position on this point, I am not aware of it. It seems difficult to get Brother Jones to understand that what he and Brother Clay, and Brother Green, and the *Christian Standard,* and the *Christian Courier* propose is a radical departure from all precedents in "State work," as well as a violation of a fundamental principle of New Testament church polity—a departure which Professor McGarvey considers "somewhat overbearing, if not tyrannical."

In 1884, when W. L. Butler was discussing this society question with Thomas Munnell, J. B. Jones wrote against Munnell's defense of the society in these words:

All this machinery imposed from without is faulty. It is better than nothing, but it is not what we want. We are like the Athenians. They felt after God; we are feeling after coöperation. . . . Our pledge system fails largely because it is imposed from without. It has not the life-blood of the local church to keep it warm. It is a chignon. It is a set of false teeth. But such as I have I use. It is better to wear false hair than to be bald. Artificial teeth are better than none. Best of all are nature's teeth, united to the body by its blood, nerves, and bones. . . . You will save us from an impending crisis if you will cover the baldheadedness of the churches by infusing from the heart new life into the diseased scalp. We have heart disease and spiritual consumption.

Brother Munnell was State evangelist and J. B. Jones was just a common sort of a Christian when the above was written. The "pledge system" which Brother Munnell was trying to operate and which Brother Jones said "fails largely because it is imposed from without" is exactly the same system which Brother Jones is now trying to operate. It is the same old baldheaded, snaggled-toothed, heart-diseased spiritual consumptive which masqueraded under a chignon as "State work" in 1884.

From all these quotations it seems clear to me that Professor McGarvey, Thomas Munnell, J. B. Jones, and the Kentucky Christian Missionary Convention have been laboring and praying to bring the churches up to the very work which Campbell Street is now doing for lo these many years.

So far as I am concerned, it is a waste of time for Brother Jones to quote what Campbell said. I have made no issue with Brother Campbell. I don't object to the baldheaded and snaggled-toothed old spiritual consumptives wearing the chignons of State evangelists and the false teeth of "State work," but I am unwilling to see them compel their fair sister on Campbell Street to exchange her glossy tresses and pearly teeth for such needless and unsatisfactory substitutes. Chignons are going out of fashion, anyhow, Brother Jones! I am not complaining at the poor, benighted churches for groping their way through the Egyptian darkness of inactivity and heartless formality by the glimmering star-light of societies, boards, conventions, and State evangelists, but I am unwilling to see them undertake to force their more fortunate sister on Campbell Street to turn aside from "the brightness of a greater light," to walk with them in the mists and confusions of human opinions and experiments.

It would seem from all these quotations that I am not the only man who has been "administering poison to our people," or who is disqualified to teach State evangelists because of a failure to remember what I have written! If I read correctly, Thomas Munnell, J. W. McGarvey, J. B. Jones, and the Kentucky Christian Missionary Convention have been administering broken doses of the same kind of "poison" for the last twenty-five years and more. They, too, have been "simply tearing down, or trying to tear down, the work we are doing in the name of the Lord, and can substitute nothing in its place," except a baldheaded, snaggled-toothed old spiritual consumptive, with heart disease and a chignon!

But the brother insists that I evade the issue. He says: "I have accepted and now hold, as the best things in sight, the prevalent views held by Campbell, Allen, McGarvey, Lipscomb," etc., touching the prerogatives of the elders and the right of self-government in every church. "As the best thing in sight" is either a meaningless phrase or an expression which needs explanation. It sounds just a little like the *Standard's* celebrated remark about the notorious "Smith plan"—viz.: "*We think there is room for improvement in this line.*" I am curious to know what better things "*in this line*"

Brother Jones and the *Standard* think there may be just out of sight.

But if Brother Jones does not propose to override the decision of the elders and of the church, there is no, issue between us, and this discussion may as well close. If he does not propose to make any effort to stir up " strife, contentions, insurrections, and rebellion," I have no further argument against him. When I said he had more than intimated his determination, in an article in the *Standard,* to do what he could in that line, I referred to his enthusiastic indorsement of the " denunciatory language which has stirred up the gall of bitterness," as Professor McGarvey says, on this question. In that article he said the *Standard's* editorial against the conservative position of Professor McGarvey " hits the nail on the head," and declared that " my conscience will not let me rest till his church [Campbell Street] is enlisted in the work." He stated, in substance, that the decision of the elders and the action of the church locked the doors and erected barriers against him, but, nevertheless, he exclaimed: " We rejoice in a liberty that overleaps the barriers." From all this it seemed clear to me that he was overflowing his banks, as we might say, and threatening to completely inundate both the authority of the elders and the independency of the churches.

He continues to air his goodness by saying he has waived his rights in Campbell Street Church in the interest of peace. Waived his rights, indeed! How did he come to have any rights in that church or any other church against the decision of the elders and the policy of the church? If he wants to make an issue at this point, I undertake to say he has no more rights in Campbell Street Church or any other church against the decision of the elders and policy of the church than the humblest Christian in the land. The fact that he is State evangelist gives him absolutely no rights in any church which declines to adopt the plan of work he represents. He has only the rights of an ordinary mortal and an humble disciple of Christ.

He still insists that the issue is a question as to whether the elders of Campbell Street Church, and, in fact, the whole church, did right or wrong touching certain matters concerning the policy of the church. It may be well enough to say on this point, once for all, that it is not the province of a State evangelist to review the decisions of elders or reverse the settled policy of churches. Brother Jones has expressed the opinion that the elders and the church did wrong, and I have expressed the opinion that they did right. That is all either of us has to do with it. Neither Brother Jones nor myself understand the facts. The elders are men of sound judgment, unquestioned piety, and acknowledged Scripture intelligence. They know all the facts, and upon them rests the solemn obligation to take care of the flock over which the Holy Ghost has made them overseers. They have as much sense as either Brother Jones or myself, they are as good men as either of us, they understand the Scriptures as well as either of us, and they know more about the facts in the case than both of us put together. They are probably managing that little matter as wisely, scripturally, and successfully as Brother Jones could do it.

But if he has reconsidered the matter and decided to make no effort to override the policy of the church and the decision of the elders, I shall close this discussion feeling that my feeble efforts to teach him the way of the Lord more perfectly have not been wholly in vain.

Brother Jones gives his last article the title of "Kentucky Coöperative Mission Work." I presume he does this for the sake of euphony. Certainly the title does not indicate the issue between us. I have no objections to coöperative mission work in Kentucky or anywhere else.

I do not understand that Thomas Munnell was opposed to coöperative mission work when he said:

> There must always be a society until all the churches engage in the work; then the society will be lost, will die; but it will die like the morning star dies in the brightness of a greater light. This is what we are working for, as Brother McGarvey told you several months ago.

It has never occurred to me that J. B. Jones was opposed to coöperative mission work when he wrote his now celebrated document about chignons, heart disease, false teeth, and spiritual consumption.

It is not my understanding that J. W. McGarvey was opposed to coöperative mission work when he said:

> There are some individual churches who are abundantly able and ought this day to be sending out missionaries to be sustained by themselves. Wherever such a church is found, it ought to be urged to get about the work at once.

I do not understand that the State Board of Kentucky was opposed to coöperative mission work when it encouraged each church to raise and disburse its own funds in mission work, just as Campbell Street is now doing, and said this course "would satisfy the scruples of some good brethren who doubt the wisdom of our present methods; it would make the society promotive of congregational action in the missionary work instead of being, as some allege, antagonistic to it," and "*would raise a much larger amount of money, and the aggregate of good would be justly increased.*"

Now, if these princes of Kentucky coöperative mission work can write this without opposing coöperative mission work, I don't see why I should be denounced as the chief of sinners for the few desultory remarks I have made along the same line, and accused of "trying to tear down a work which has rescued the island of the sea from cannibalism." If J. W. McGarvey, J. B. Jones, Thomas Munnell, and the State Board of Kentucky can "feel after coöperation" in such passages as I have quoted and yet not be guilty of "fighting a coöperation without which you could have no Bible societies," I don't understand why we should see "a thousand workers in foreign lands robbed of their food and clothing and the whole heathen world put into the uncertain and chaotic hands of a disorderly host, anxious to supplant a successful and known method by an individualism without sanction in scripture and condemned by reason and experience"—all because I fumbled around a little after coöperation, too! I had no idea my scattered remarks were at all calculated to create such widespread and alarming consternation in "foreign lands." Brother Jones ought not to get impatient with me. He should remember that this State-work business is a growth. All I need is time to develop. I am worrying along in the primary lessons of the thing now. Twenty-five years ago Thomas Munnell and others who are now stoutly advocating such a plan as the Methodists have—a plan in which district evangelists correspond to presiding elders and State evangelists to bishops—were no further along than I am to-day, as the quotation I have just given abundantly shows. In fact, I was as far advanced as J. B. Jones in 1884, and but for my failing health, which lost me my place in the class, I would have perhaps been fully his equal now. The whole Methodist Episcopacy is simply a growth, and all other forms of general denominational organization and sectarian ecclesiasticism are developments. Be patient and give me time, my beloved, and I will come out all right. The point I have made from the beginning of this discussion, and the only point of any importance in it, is that every church has a right to manage its own business in cooperative mission work, as well as in everything else, without dictation or interference from State boards or State evangelists. This is all Campbell Street has proposed to do, and I insist that every church has a perfect right to do this.

Whether or not churches have a right to work under boards and State evangelists is not the issue in this discussion. I have made no such issue. The question is whether a church has a right to manage its own business in cooperative mission work and everything else without dictation or interference from State boards and State evangelists. To deny this right is to argue for an authority for ecclesiasticism or general denominational organization, such as the Methodists and Baptists have adopted. As to whether churches can form themselves into such an authoritative ecclesiasticism or general denominational and sectarian organization without ceasing to be churches of Christ is not the issue in this discussion. I have three or four very good ideas on that point, but I have not expressed them in this discussion because they are wholly irrelevant. The point I make now is that a church can be a church of Christ, obeying every command God has given, observe every ordinance God has ever established, and fulfill every requirement of the Scriptures as a church of Christ, without joining itself to any such authoritative ecclesiasticism or general denominational sectarian organization of churches.

I agree with Brother Jones that nothing is settled till it is settled right; but my idea is that a church is about as competent to settle its own business right as a State evangelist. The brother is wrong again, as usual, when he says the Gospel Advocate "assumes the right by the circulation of a petition in the form of a religious paper through" the congregations which "the State Board has enrolled and working peacefully under the cooperative plan" "to review the decision of the eldership and to reverse the settled policy of these congregations." It is my understanding that boards and State evangelists do not allow the congregations which they have enrolled and working under them to read the Gospel Advocate. The truth is, the Gospel Advocate has no more chance to unsettle things in such churches than in Methodist churches.

As I understand the matter, Campbell Street is not opposed to coöperative mission work. By unanimous decision of its elders and cheerful acquiescence of its members, that church determined to do its full part in Kentucky coöperative mission work by supporting one of the men engaged in the work, without troubling either the board or the State evangelist in the matter of raising and disbursing the funds. They support the same man to do the same work, in the same field, whom the board has heretofore supported. When the board sup-

ported this man to do this work in this field, Brother
Jones called it "Kentucky coöperative mission work."
The problem now is to find out what sort of work it is,
if not Kentucky coöperative mission work, when Campbell Street supports the same man to do the same work
in the same field. When Campbell Street sent money to
the State evangelist, and the State evangelist paid it
over to the board, and the board paid it over to Brother
South, who did the preaching, it was called "Kentucky
coöperative mission work." Now, I am curious to know
what sort of work it is when Campbell Street pays the
money directly to Brother South, who does the same
work in the same field, without troubling either the
State Board or the State evangelist in the matter of
raising or disbursing the funds.

And, by the way, I am still trying to find out why
Brother Jones is so very anxious for Campbell Street
Church and other churches to send money to the men
who do the work *by way of the State evangelist and the
State Board.* I have called his attention to this little
point and asked him to explain it before, but it seems
impossible to get him to attempt any explanation "in
this line," as the *Standard* would say. When Brother
Jones was notified of the decision of the elders and the
policy of the church, he rushed into the *Standard* to
lament the "barriers" which the church had thus
erected against him and to give notice that "we rejoice
in a liberty which overleaps the barriers" and to declare
that "my conscience will not let me rest till" this
church is reenlisted in a plan of work which, after long
trial and prayerful consideration, it had decided to abandon. It occurred to me that the brother was leaping
entirely too high for an humble disciple of Christ, and

that the course he proposed to pursue would probably create discord and lead to "envying, strife, and divisions" in the church. So I modestly expressed the opinion "that it is not the province of a State evangelist to review the decisions of elders or reverse the policy of the churches." And for this humble expression of an honest opinion he now denounces me as a pope, and boldly declares that "editorial modesty is dead and buried." He seems to think nothing smaller than a pope has any right to express an opinion touching the province of State evangelists. When an ordinary editor presumes to speak a word concerning the doings of State evangelists, Brother Jones at once concludes that "editorial modesty is dead and buried." Indeed! But I am persuaded that the world in general does not stand in such awe of State evangelists, after all. A man need not be a pope, or even an editorial star, either ascending or descending, to freely express his opinion as to the prerogatives of State evangelists. The humblest disciple in the land has a perfect right to state, with all freedom, at any time, what he conceives to be the scriptural province of State evangelists—that is, if they really have any scriptural province, which, I confess, seems to be an unsettled question. My idea used to be that the province of a State evangelist was to behave himself, mind his own business, let churches and other evangelists alone, collect his salary, and preach the gospel some in destitute places or somewhere else—if he had any time to spare for that work after raising his salary. But "State work" has developed a new and different idea of this whole convention and State-evangelist business. I take the following brief outline of this new theory from an article in the *Christian Standard* of May 16, 1891, which warmly indorses and stoutly defends it:

1. I would have State conventions, as we now have them, of regularly appointed delegates from the congregations, one delegate for each given number of members. This convention should be a republican assembly in the strictest sense. It shall be the highest body in the State.

2. The congregation gives to the State convention the authority to assign to it the amount of money it shall contribute for all missionary, educational, and benevolent works which it determines to undertake.

3. The congregation gives to the State convention the authority to select and locate with it a pastor whenever it is without one, provided it is not able, for any cause, to select one itself within a reasonable time. This the convention may do by its board or State evangelist.

4. The congregation . . . waives the right to employ any man as its pastor . . . who is not commended or approved by the executive board of the State convention.

5. The relation between a church and its pastor is not to be dissolved without the consent of the State executive board, except under circumstances so extraordinary as to demand immediate action.

6. The congregation delegates to the State convention the authority to investigate and settle all troubles which seriously threaten its peace and prosperity. This the convention may do by its board, evangelist, or a committee raised for that purpose.

7. If a congregation has as its pastor a man whose preaching and teaching are unscriptural, and whose influence is consequently pernicious, the State convention shall have the authority to arraign and try him, and, if found guilty as charged, to remove him from the pastorate.

8. There shall be a general convention, composed of delegates appointed by the several State conventions, which shall meet, as now, annually. This convention shall have

the authority to apportion to each State convention the
amount of money to be raised for the general and foreign
missionary work, for educational purposes, church exten-
sion, and all works requiring the expenditure of means.

The work of the presiding elder, with slight modification,
is identical with the work of the New Testament evangelist.

At the ordinary rate of progress in "State work," I
should say it would take Brother Jones at least ten years
to advance from his present position to the theory thus
briefly outlined and warmly advocated by a writer in the
Christian Standard; but as he seems to be an unusually
bright pupil, from the progress he has made since 1884,
he may possibly complete the course, say, in eight years,
if he is not held back too much by such dull pupils as
Professor McGarvey!

Brother Jones says I will not confront the facts.
Well, he ought not to blame me for that. It is not my
fault. I have squarely confronted everything he has
brought forward in this discussion. The brother says:

When brought face to face with a contradiction or misrepresentation, the front-page editor denies that he is the
author of a statement charging me with denouncing Campbell Street as antimissionary and factious.

Yes, I denied being the author of any such statement
before I was brought face to face with it; and if he
had been a little more respectful in his bearing toward
me and a little less confident of his own superiority, he
would have accepted my denial without making an unsuccessful effort to prove that I had forgotten what I
had written. He appealed to me personally "as a
Christian gentleman" to correct the statement I had
made. I told him I had made no such statement, and
in nervous haste and blind self-confidence he undertook

to prove that I did make the statement, notwithstanding my denial, and even sneered at me for forgetting what I had written. He evidently has a very small opinion of either my memory or my honesty, and esteems it a light job for a man of his caliber and official position to show that I am always wrong as to "facts, dates, and persons" concerning anything that may come up in this discussion. The brother should profit by this bit of humiliating experience. David Lipscomb wrote the language Brother Jones objects to. He says he so understood Brother Jones at the time, but accepts his denial, of course, and retracts the statement. I hope this will be satisfactory. And, by the way, this is a good time and place to answer his celebrated argument based on Daniel Webster's speech in the Girard will case. How would it do, for instance, to say the gospel can be preached some in foreign lands and the church can be built up a little in waste places now and then by the method Campbell Street has adopted? I think I could prove this by Brother Jones, especially since he so vigorously objects to being accused of " denouncing Campbell Street as antimissionary." My idea is that a church which is liberal and active in the missionary cause is liable to preach the gospel in foreign lands and build up the church in waste places every now and then, boards or no boards!

Brother Jones thinks I have " violated a code of honor existing between man and man, politician and politician, merchant and merchant, not to say preacher and preacher," in publishing " a private correspondence without permission." I beg his pardon. I did not know the document was private. It was not sent to me by Brother Butler. A copy of what J. B. Jones said in 1884 was sent me by another man, with full permission to publish it if I wished. I published it, but not to save a "trembling cause," as he seems to think. The cause is not trembling; and if it were, anything J. B. Jones said in 1884 or at any other time would not be much of a prop to it. As an authority on spiritual consumption, heart disease, false teeth, and chignons, he is worthy of passing notice; but as a prop for an important principle of New Testament church polity, such as I am defending in this discussion, he is decidedly a limber twig. But I don't see why he should be ashamed of that document. So far as I have heard an expression, it is unanimously considered the best thing that has yet appeared from his pen on this subject. I am inclined to think it will make him more reputation than anything else he has written in this discussion.

The brother says I make the impression upon my readers that he "was not, at the time when this" private letter "was written, working under the board." I think myself that I did him injustice at this point, but it was not intentional. I beg his pardon. I was editing the *Guide* and living in Louisville in 1883-4. When he returned from Florida in 1883, he "entered the work," as he says, but my recollection is that he entered it as financial agent under Thomas Munnell, who was State evangelist. Brother Munnell had a good salary and nothing to do but "set in order the things that are wanting," whatever that may mean. Brother Jones had to rustle around and get up money to run the concern, and I had to help all I could by boosting the thing in the *Guide*. To be sure he was working under the board. The document I published from him, written about that time, sounds exactly like it was written by a man under

18

a board! As I now remember those days, he and I had many long and serious, not to say " sky-blue," conversations about the health of the baldheaded, snaggledtoothed old spiritual consumptive, whose heart disease and chignon were a weariness to the flesh by day and a hideous nightmare by night to us both! But by and by the fashion of chignons changed and the offices of financial agent and State evangelist were combined in Brother Jones, and Brother Munnell was transferred to another conference, as we might say. A little later the pledge system, which Brother Jones says " fails largely because it is imposed from without," was exchanged for the assessment system, which probably is doing no better for the same reason. Now, the pledge system, which, Brother Jones says, was spiritual consumption, heart disease, false teeth, and a chignon, simply permitted each church or individual to give to the board what the giver deemed proper for mission work. The present system, which is commonly called the " assessment system," is for the board to assess each church what it deems proper without consulting the church about it at all, and then send the " finangelist " around to collect it. And Brother Jones thinks I have committed a grave sin in saying the present system is " the same old baldheaded, snaggled-toothed spiritual consumptive which masqueraded under a chignon as State work in 1884." Well, is not that true? Was it not " State work" in 1884? The change from the pledge system to the assessment system did not make a new creature. It was only a change in the style of chignons. And, by the way, it is a new and brilliant idea in the practice of medicine to try to cure heart disease and spiritual consumption by changing the style of a chignon!

My idea is that a much better remedy would be " the love of God shed abroad in our hearts by the Holy Ghost which is given unto us."

Brother Jones says the old system " is as dead to us as the gospel is to the law of Moses." It is my painful duty to inform him that the old system is still in force in " State work " in Texas, Arkansas, Mississippi, Tennessee, Alabama, and several other States. What Brother Jones would term the " gospel dispensation of the assessment system in State work " has not been introduced yet in any of these States. We are still under Moses and suffering from chronic consumption and heart disease in " State work " throughout the South. And, by the way, the Judaizing zealots of " State work " in Tennessee, Alabama, Arkansas, Mississippi, and Texas, it seems to me, open up a wide and inviting field for missionary work to Brother Jones!

The brother makes an unnecessary parade of the fact that Professor McGarvey committed himself, at the Mount Sterling convention in 1886, to the proposition that the matter of raising funds for missionary work be committed to the officers of the various churches, and that " these local and divinely appointed leaders in every good work . . . continue to secure an annual fund for State missions." If I rightly understand matters, Professor McGarvey has been committed to that idea during his whole life as a public man. It is my understanding that Campbell Street is committed to the same idea. In fact, I don't know anybody that is not committed to that idea, except those who propose to " overleap the barriers " of " these divinely appointed leaders." This proposition does not involve the issue between us in this discussion at all. The issue between us is as to whether these " divinely appointed leaders in every gcod work " shall have the privilege of paying the " annual fund for State missions " directly to the man engaged in the work after they have raised it, or must they be compelled, on pain of excommunication, to pay it over to the State evangelist, so that the State evangelist may pay it to the board and the board to the man engaged in the work? I should like to see Brother Jones undertake to get Professor McGarvey to commit himself to this proposition.

The brother grows reckless when he says:

In vain do you appeal to apostolic precedent, when A. Campbell and a host of others agree that methods of work were left to reason and to the adjustment of the church to meet the peculiar emergency of the age, conditions, and country.

It has never been my understanding that what "A. Campbell and a host of others agree " can rightly be ranked above apostolic precedent. But suppose it can; what then? If this question is to be left to reason and the church, why not respect the reason and action of Campbell Street Church? If this thing must be settled by reason, for my part I am unwilling to give the State evangelist of Kentucky a monopoly of the business, or even a controlling interest in it. He will pardon me for saying, in all candor, that, from the showing he has thus far made in this discussion, I am inclined to think the men who are managing Campbell Street Church are not inferior to him in reason, which is sometimes called " sanctified common sense," and they think also they have the mind of the Spirit—a thing which he does not claim to have at all!

But the brother says he is not " going to try to meet

me on this plane," whatever that may mean. I think
myself he is making decidedly a poor showing " on this
plane; " and if he thinks he can do any better on any
other " plane," I heartily agree with him that he ought
to " shift his ground." But no matter what " plane "
he may select, I will cheerfully meet him on it and defend, as best I can in my feeble manner, the right of
every church to manage its own business without dictation or interference from State boards and State evangelists !

HEADQUARTERS OF ORGANIZED MISSION WORK.

I have read with much interest the statistics of
Brother Lipscomb and Brother Myhr touching the ratio
of disciples to population where we have and where we
haven't missionary societies. It occurs to me, in this
connection, that there are a few facts lying around St.
Louis and Cincinnati which might shed some light on
the subject under discussion. It should be noted, first
of all, that Cincinnati is the place where " our first general convention " was held in 1849. It has also been
the headquarters of all our general missionary societies,
both home and foreign, from that date to the present
time, by constitutional requirement. Still further, it is
the place where the Standard Publishing Company does
business, and from which the *Christian Standard* is published, which, according to its own confession, has always been the very life and soul of all of " our missionary societies." St. Louis is the place where the Christian Publishing Company has done business all these
years, and from which the *Christian-Evangelist* is pub-

lished, which, according to its own admission, is the greatest factor in all of "our missionary organizations" to be found in all this broad land. These two cities, therefore, are headquarters—and hindquarters, too, for that matter—of what, for want of a better term, is called "organized mission work." Very well. To speak in round numbers, these two cities, with a population of eight hundred thousand, have only about two thousand disciples, or, say, one to four hundred; while Nashville, with a population of only seventy-five thousand, has three thousand, or one to twenty-five. I heartily second the motion, therefore, to bring the next general convention to Nashville, if for no other reason, in order that those who attend it may have "church privileges" while it is in session. And now that the question of removing some of "our missionary boards" from Cincinnati is being discussed in the *Standard* and the *Evangelist*, I suggest that it would be well to consider this question of "church privileges" as an inducement to bring them all to Nashville. I would go even further and urge the removal of the Standard Publishing Company and *Christian Standard*, the Christian Publishing Company and *Christian-Evangelist*, to Nashville for the same reason, but for the fact that these institutions have been so long without such "means of grace" that they probably do not estimate them very highly, and would not utilize them or profit by them even if they were situated so they could have easy access to them. Moreover, David says they are not in "full fellowship and good standing," anyhow.

PASSING RESOLUTIONS AND ADOPTING REPORTS.

The *Christian-Evangelist* remarked some time ago:

One of the evils under the sun connected with our missionary conventions is the passing of resolutions which there is no serious effort to carry out and the adoption of reports recommending certain things to be done which no one feels under any special obligation to do. It is an easy matter for a convention to resolve that a particular thing should be done, but the *doing* of it involves qualities of a much higher order. Nothing could give greater assurance of the growth of our people in these virtues than a report at one of our annual conventions that all the resolutions and recommendations made at the previous convention had been faithfully carried out. But many of these reports, containing recommendations of great importance, when once adopted, are never called up again, and standing committees often stand idle all the year and construct a hurried report after the convention assembles. These things, it scarcely need be said, are not consistent with the dignity and representative character of our national or State conventions. The truth is, they are demoralizing to a high degree, and tend to bring such bodies into disrepute and to destroy their influence. . . . In the case of a missionary society the failure to carry out good resolutions is probably due to the lack of a general distribution of the sense of obligation among the members of that body. This is seen in the fact that many who vote for and even advocate certain measures in a convention feel under no special obligation to exert themselves to carry them out. This could hardly be the case if there were in the minds of these brethren a proper sense of the obligation which their own action and that of their brethren impose upon them. What avails it to write large reports and recommendations, and to support them with our votes and even with eloquent speeches,

if we make no corresponding effort to *realize* what we recommend to be done and what we resolve should be done?

In these timely words the *Christian-Evangelist* lays
bare a serious defect in what is commonly called "organized effort." Probably the chief reason that conventions engage so extensively in "the passing of resolutions which there is no serious effort to carry out" will
be found in the fact that there is nobody to carry them
out. Conventions themselves are, as a general rule,
composed largely of people whose chief occupation is
"the passing of resolutions" for other folks to carry
out; and as for those who do not go to the conventions
to pass resolutions, they usually have something else to
do besides carry out the resolutions other people pass.
The fact is, the world is beginning to grasp the idea
that every man has resoluting apparatus of his own,
and, since religion is intensely a personal matter, each
one is beginning to feel a sort of individual obligation
to pass and carry out his own resolutions through the
organizations which God has ordained for religious work
and worship. In this state of things, if a man should
pass more resolutions than he can or does carry out himself, the chances are that what he fails to carry out himself will go to protest. The failure of conventions to
carry out the resolutions they pass, therefore, is not
due to "the lack of a general distribution of the sense
of obligation among the members of that body," as the
Christian-Evangelist suggests, so much as it is due to
the fact that there is no sense of obligation in that body
to distribute. The idea that the society will do the work
if "*we*" will pass the resolutions effectually relieves every member of the convention of anything like "the
sense of obligation." The *chief* idea in forming such

conventions is to relieve the individuals who go into them of "the sense of obligation." This is why mankind in all ages of the world has been in favor of such conventions and God opposed to them. Man seeks relief from "the sense of obligation," but God strikes straight at the individual conscience.

THE BITTER PERSECUTIONS TENNESSEE MISSIONARIES ARE SUFFERING.

Now that the *Standard*, and the *Guide*, and the *Courier*, and the *Evangelist*, and a few others have about pumped the fountain of sympathy dry with their lamentations over the bitter persecutions Tennessee missionaries are suffering, it might be well for us all to dry our tears for a moment and, to use the language of the country "squire" when he married his first couple, "come forward and view the remains!" I regret very much to disturb the mourners at this would-be funeral of missionary martyrs, but it is my painful duty as an enterprising journalist to give an extract from a private letter, written by the editor of one of the papers named above, to a "missionary man" in Tennessee before this "cruel war" began. I am not permitted to give the name of the writer or the man to whom the letter was written, neither do I stop to explain how the letter came into my possession. Here is the paragraph I want:

Let me make a little prophecy, and you can file it away for future reference. Unless there is a radical change in the policy and spirit of the GOSPEL ADVOCATE, its subscription list five years hence will be much smaller than now. More allowance has been made for Brother Lipscomb than would have been made for any one else, but there is a considerable element, and a growing one, in Tennessee that is tired of just such things as D. L. is getting off weekly. Mark my words. The majority of the live members of our churches in Tennessee will in less than five years be contributing to our foreign and home missionary societies. The ADVOCATE need not support these societies in order to live. It could oppose them if it were done in a fair way and keep up for a while at least. . . . Every time the ADVOCATE denounces those who contribute through these societies in effect as apostates it makes lifelong enemies to the ADVOCATE and lifelong friends of the societies. The response to an appeal to take Tennessee for organized mission work you will find is going to be prompt and liberal, and those who are working to that end are, to my knowledge, counting largely on the unreasoning opposition of Brother Lipscomb to help the movement.

Seeing this is the private sayings of an editor of a paper which poses as a model of " decent journalism " and all that sort of thing, it may be well enough to point out a few of its constitutional defects. And, to begin with, the man who seeks to build up anything in the way of a religious institution upon the prejudice and passion of folks is, by all odds, a better piece of timber for a decent journalist than a religious teacher. This sentence refers back to that passage in the letter which speaks of the lifelong enemies to itself and friends to the society which the ADVOCATE makes every time it expresses its convictions on this question in its plain, country style. Men who act from prejudice or passion, rather than from conviction, are no great stakes anywhere; and if they fail to do a vast deal of home missionary work of one sort and another right in their own hearts, the devil will give them a hard race and a close call between death and the New Jerusalem. The editor who seeks to carry a point by working upon the prejudices of men in this way ought not to claim a monopoly of " decent journalism."

And so David Lipscomb seems to be the old heathen these papers which are burdening their columns with obituaries of missionary martyrs in Tennessee, so to speak, are after. I have no convictions against a missionary society on its merits; but I gravely doubt the wisdom of sending such missionaries as we now have to preach the gospel to David. I cannot say that I am particularly " stuck " on David myself, especially on those points touching which he does not agree with me, and I would not mind squandering a few sheckles to convert the old cannibal; but I am unwilling to sacrifice our nice, lovely little missionaries in a worse than hopeless effort to save one hardened sinner when other souls just as valuable are hungering for the bread of life at our very doors! To try to convert David with the few missionaries and limited capital we have, is a piece of folly I cannot approve or encourage. Let's try something easier. Suppose we leave David and the GOSPEL ADVOCATE and the "live members of our churches in Tennessee" alone for a time, and "tackle" a few common sinners and "destitute places." Another thing. When we counted "largely on the unreasoning opposition of Brother Lipscomb to help the movement," we "got left," so to speak. We ought rather to have counted on the righteousness of our cause, if it had any, and the help of God. You see, David went square back on us. He has not opposed us much, and what opposition we have been able to get out of the old curmudgeon has not been at all "unreasoning." In fact, it has

been altogether too *reasoning* for our purpose. I know
the papers before mentioned *say* he has done ever so
many ugly things; but those editorials, like the letter
I have quoted, might have been written before we began
the work. You see we depended "largely on the unreasoning opposition of Brother Lipscomb to help the
movement," and of course we have worked that
"racket" for all that was in it. Finally, brethren, such
persecution as we missionary folks are suffering down
here in Tennessee will not run this thing. We must try
some other plan of "sanctified common sense." I know
it has been said that "the blood of the martyr is the
seed of the church," but what little blood missionary
martyrs are putting into this business will not raise
much of a "crap" in Tennessee soil!!

A MISSIONARY SOCIETY NOT REQUIRED.

The *Christian Standard* disclaims any intention to
argue that a missionary society is *required* by the Lord
in the Scriptures when it said such a "society is only
a committee in the church for special work, just as the
deacons, in Acts 6, were a committee for the special
work of looking after the poor." Its position, as I now
understand it, is that "the deacons, in Acts 6, were a
committee" specifically *required* by the Lord, while a
missionary society is a "*voluntary* committee" permitted, but not required, by the New Testament. I
accept this explanation and pass that point with the remark that there were no such committees as missionary
societies among Christians and churches in New Testament times, either voluntary or otherwise. Christians

and churches can obey every command of God, fill the measure of apostolic order in work, worship, government, organization, and everything else, and be saved in heaven in these modern times without such committees as missionary societies. If the *Standard* admits all this, as I now understand it to do, I do not feel inclined to press it further on this point in this connection. The other counts in the *Standard's* reply call for fuller notice.

The original argument to which I objected was that missionary societies are authorized by the teaching of Christ and his apostles, because "Christ, working through his church," has "redeemed the millions of Africa, Asia, and the islands of the seas," and yet all this "grand missionary work which has been done in foreign lands during the present century . . . is almost exclusively the work of missionary societies." Yes, and it is almost exclusively the work of the various denominations, too. If missionary societies are "authorized by the teaching of Christ and his apostles" because they have done all this "grand missionary work," why are not the various religious denominations "authorized," too, and for the same reason? Does the *Standard* seriously think the various religious denominations are authorized by the Scriptures, and that "Christ, working through his church," has done all this denominational business in this country and in foreign lands? It would seem so. At this point it makes this reply:

And do we understand the ADVOCATE to say that he has not? Are not Methodists, Baptists, Presbyterians, Congregationalists, and Episcopalians called *sectarians* because they maintain divisions in the body of Christ? And how can they divide that of which they are not a part? Is it not laid upon them as a reproach that they wear names other than that of Christ? What right have they to wear his name if they are none of his? Have we, for three-quarters of a century, labored for Christian union when there is nothing to unite?

The *Standard* is confused. The question is not whether Methodists, Baptists, Presbyterians, Episcopalians, and Congregationalists are "in the body of Christ," but whether those denominations themselves are "authorized" by the *Scriptures*. Nor is it a question as to whether those who labor through missionary societies are Christians, but whether the missionary societies themselves are "authorized" by the New Testament. Christians are prone to organize, work through, belong to, and build up many things not authorized by the Bible. It is in this way that they "maintain divisions in the body of Christ." Shall we accept what the denominations have done in redeeming "the millions of Africa, Asia, and the islands of the seas" as conclusive evidence that denominations are "authorized" by the Scriptures in the absence of any warrant for them in the New Testament? Or shall we take the same work done by missionary societies as satisfactory proof, without any corroborative evidence from the Bible, that missionary societies are authorized by the Scriptures? The *Standard* seems inclined to answer both of these questions in the affirmative. The ADVOCATE is somewhat disposed to answer both of them negatively. This defines the issue.

I agree with the *Standard* that Methodists, Baptists, Presbyterians, Episcopalians, and Congregationalists— some of them, at any rate—are "in the body of Christ." I further agree with it that they are " called *sectarians* because they maintain divisions in the body of Christ," and I am trying to think of some reason why those who " maintain divisions in the body of Christ " by building up societies which the New Testament does not require should not be called *sectarians* some, too.

The *Standard's* next paragraph runs thus:

> To begin with, it is sheer Romanism that an authorized *work* is invalid without a specially authorized *agent.* . . . The Bible, so far as we know it, knows nothing of authorized and unauthorized churches. People are in Christ or they are out of him. The heathen who have been brought to Christ by the denominations are either in him or they are out of him. If they are in him, they are in him by his authority, since *all* authority in heaven and earth is given unto him. Here is a *definite issue.* Is the Advocate prepared to take it?

And who has said " that an authorized *work* is invalid without a specially authorized agent," pray? Certainly I have never said it, nor do I believe it. But what has all this to do with the question? Nothing. The point before us is whether the work which has been done by missionary societies is of itself sufficient proof that such societies are authorized by the New Testament in the absence of any corroborative evidence in favor of them in the Scriptures. If it is " sheer Romanism " to hold that " an authorized *work* is invalid without a specially authorized *agent,*" what is it to argue that the agent must per consequence be authorized by the Scriptures because the *work* is good? Sheer *Standardism,* eh? And what is that but " sheer Romanism " turned inside out and wrong end up? Paul did not argue that the agent was necessarily authorized because the work was good. He tells us of some who preached Christ " even of envy and strife." He rejoiced that Christ was preached, but he did not argue, as the *Standard* seems inclined to do, that the "envy and strife" were authorized because they did such mission work. If I rightly understand him, he preferred that Christ be preached without "the envy and strife." In truth, he seems to have thought Christ could be more effectively preached in other ways, and to that end he stoutly argued against that particular way of doing it. In like manner we may rejoice when Christ is preached by the Methodist Church and by missionary societies, no matter if it is done "even of envy and strife," as is frequently the case; but we need not conclude with the *Standard* that the Methodist Church and missionary societies, with their usual accompaniments of "envy and strife," are, therefore, authorized by the Scriptures, and hence not to be opposed. There is probably "a more excellent way."

The *Standard* grows reckless when it says "the Bible, so far as we know it, knows nothing of authorized and unauthorized churches." Perhaps the *Standard* does not "know it" very far. How about "the church of God, which he hath purchased with his own blood?" (Acts 20: 28.) And how about the church which "Christ also loved, . . . and gave himself for it; . . . that he might present it to himself a glorious church, not having spot, or wrinkle, or any such thing; but that it should be holy and without blemish?" (Eph. 5: 25-27.) It is the understanding at this office that churches of that kind are "authorized." Such churches, however, did not have any missionary societies in them as committees "for special work." This may explain why the *Standard* has never discovered that the Bible knows anything about them. As missionary societies seem to be the *Standard's* favorite hobby, it perhaps lost interest in the Bible, and quit reading it when it found that it could get no information or encouragement in its favorite line of work from that book. Folks usually find the Bible rather dull reading when they are laboring to build up things which the Scriptures do not require.

I agree with the *Standard* that the "heathen who have been brought to Christ by the denominations are either in him or they are out of him." There is scarcely room for a difference of opinion here. I also agree with it that "if they are in him, they are in him by his authority." But what has all this to do with the question? Nothing. The question is not whether "the heathen who have been brought to Christ by the denominations are" in him or out of him, but whether they are in anything else where they "hadn't ought to be"—the denominations and missionary societies, for instance. Nor is it a question as to whether those who are in him are in him by his authority, but whether those who are in other things where they "hadn't ought to be"—the denominations and missionary societies, for instance— are in those things by his authority. "Here is a *definite issue*. Is the" *Standard* "prepared to take it?"

The brother must be hard pressed for the authority of Christ to be in and work through denominations and missionary societies, when he claims it on the broad ground that "*all* authority in heaven and earth is given unto him." The argument here is, if I rightly understand it, that as folks can't get into the work through denominations and missionary societies without authority from some source, and as "*all* authority in heaven and earth is given unto" Christ, the very fact that peo-

19

ple get into such things at all is sufficient evidence that
they are "authorized by the teaching of Christ and his
apostles." That argument is certainly broad enough
to cover the case, but the *thickness* of the thing—or,
rather, the *thinness* of it—is the point I make against it.
I can conceive that it might be possible for a saloon
keeper to preach the gospel, bring a sinner to Christ, and
actually induct souls into Christ, as far as human agen-
cies can do such a thing. To put it even stronger, I
am reliably informed that such things were actually
done many years ago. In such a case the *Standard's*
argument would prove that the liquor traffic is authorized by Christ as conclusively as it proves that denominations and missionary societies are authorized. And
yet it would not rank high as an argument in a prohibition canvass.

Reverting to the point passed in the first paragraph
of this article, I must now remind the *Standard* that a
missionary society is not "a committee in the church
for special work," as it would have us believe, if the
New Testament is to be accepted as authority on church
polity. According to that book, there is no *organization* larger than a local congregation in the way of a
church. Where there is no organization, there are no
committees, of course. Missionary societies are not in
local congregations. They are wholly outside of each,
and common to all local congregations. Besides, the
Standard is fully committed to the position that it is
not necessary for folks to be members of the church at
all in order to be acceptable workers in missionary societies. Just how work done through a missionary society by folks who are not members of the church can
be fairly counted by the *Standard* as "the work of the

church through the society" is by no means clear. If the editor of the *Standard* cannot explain this, perhaps the artist of that journal might make it plain by a few original illustrations.

In so far as a missionary society is religiously inclined at all, it would perhaps be much nearer the truth to say it is a committee in the *denomination*. To get at the very root of the thing, therefore, I gravely doubt the scripturalness of all denominational federations of churches. In the New Testament, when the church is not limited by a geographical term, it includes all Christians, and is not an organization. Any church or brotherhood not limited by a geographical term these days, which does not include all Christians without organization, is a denomination. The real issue, therefore, is whether "we as a people" shall form a denominational federation of churches for missionary work or anything else and constitute another denomination. If that question is answered negatively, missionary societies and several other things will soon fall into "innocuous desuetude;" but if it is answered affirmatively, the demand for missionary societies, general boards, and other denominational machinery will continue firm, if it does not slightly increase. We must form a denomination before there is any room for such societies, boards, *et cetera*. Just at this point I feel disposed to borrow the *Standard's* words to say, "have we for three-quarters of a century labored for Christian union" without learning that we cannot compass it by building up another denomination? The shortest and only scriptural route to Christian union is to abolish all denominational federations of churches and leave each Christian free to study his own Bible and each church complete in itself and wholly independent of all other churches in all matters of work, worship, organization, government, discipline, *et cetera.* That is the kind of Christian union they had in New Testament times, and I am disposed to try it a while by way of experiment nowadays.

THOSE BAD AND ABANDONED WOMEN.

The secular papers have been burdened for several days with the details of a great sensational scandal in Nashville. Dr. Harris, a prominent preacher and editor of the *Cumberland Presbyterian,* has been involved in a lawsuit with some "bad and abandoned women," and the public has taken the usual interest in the facts brought out in the case. It is not my purpose or province to pass judgment as to the guilt or innocence of the parties to the suit, but the case has revealed a state of public sentiment on which it seems eminently proper to make a few remarks.

The visit of a prominent preacher to a noted house of prostitution is the central fact of consuming interest to the public. That this is a fact is not denied by any one. The preacher explains it by stating that as he was taking a stroll in the evening, as was his custom, two women engaged him in conversation in the vicinity of the house in question, snatched his hat from his head and ran into the house with it. Discovering what manner of women they were, he followed them into the house to get his hat. He feared they would identify it and publicly parade it as evidence that he had visited the house for improper purposes. They refused to restore him the hat except on condition that he would pay them

a hundred dollars. This he agreed to do, to prevent
any publicity, and promised to return the next night,
pay the money, and get the hat. The next night he
returned and paid them the hundred dollars, as per
agreement, but still they refused to give up the hat.
This is the preacher's statement of the case. The women
tell an entirely different story about it all. Finally the
case got into the courts, and then into the papers, and
all Nashville and the whole country have been in a broil
over it. I shall assume that the facts in the case are
just as the preacher states them. On this state of facts
it seems pertinent to ask why a preacher of the gospel
should feel willing to pay a hundred dollars of his hard-
earned money to rescue his old hat from the possession
of these vile sinners. Is there anything in the life or
teaching of Christ to justify such prodigality in the use
of money to save a preacher's old clothes from contact
with iniquity? Is there any scriptural excuse for such
reckless extravagance? Would it not have been in-
finitely better to sell the old hat for its legitimate value
and give it to the poor? Evidently it was not the in-
trinsic value of the hat that caused the brother to part
so readily with a cool hundred dollars of his hard-
earned cash. It was the fear of what the people might
say It would never do to give the immaculate nabob
society here in Nashville grounds to suppose that even
a preacher's old hat had been companying with such
publicans and sinners. And yet some men who stand
high in such society in this town visit those houses of
prostitution oftener than they go to prayer meeting.

The facts in this case show that the people understand
that the devil holds an absolute monopoly in certain
quarters, and that church people dare not enter those

strongholds of iniquity. Not a single ray of gospel
light, nor a scintillation of the salutary principles of the
Christian religion can penetrate those dark regions of
debauchery. Any evidence that a preacher of the gospel
has crossed this devil's dead line is seized upon as proof
strong as holy writ that he has denied his Lord, com-
promised his dignity, and surrendered himself to the
devil to be led captive at his will. Here in the very
midst of a city of preachers and churches the devil has
fortified himself, and from this citadel of iniquity he
defies the armies of Israel and openly despoils the people. From this stronghold of sin, this devil's den of
debauchery, the satellites of hell stalk forth in the glare
of open day to wreck the lives and damn the souls of our
brothers and sisters. And the churches are making but
little effort to dislodge the enemy of souls from this
devil's headquarters. Organized religion has simply re-
treated to the more respectable and less sinful parts of
the city, erected fine houses, bought costly organs, hired
stilted pastors, and gone into the winter quarters of
heartless, formal, routine worship. Brethren, I protest
that this is not right. If there are any people on this
earth who need preaching, and plenty of it, they are the
habitants of these haunts of vice? Why not turn a flood
of gospel light upon these dark dens of sin and deviltry?
Why not disinfect these foul sinks of hell by scattering
Christianity, the salt of the earth, bountifully over the
putrid carcasses and rotting garbage of moral depravity
which they contain? Why not ventilate and fumigate
these loathsome chambers of wickedness with the pure
breathings of the Holy Spirit? Why not turn the river
of life into these foul and disease-breeding devil's closets
and clean them out? No wonder the people of Nash-

ville are sin sick. The sanitary condition of the city, religiously speaking, is well calculated to breed all manner of moral and spiritual diseases. We talk about controlling these infamous people and places " by the strong arm of the law." We might as well undertake to fight yellow fever with gatling guns. We need to try the strong power of the gospel on them. And instead of lifting up our holy hands with pharisaic astonishment that even a preacher's hat should be found in such places, we should be weeping over our sins of omission that immortal souls are left there to go down to everlasting destruction without God and without hope. It is high time for Christian workers in every city to get down to earnest, prayerful efforts to save souls in the very lowest, most sinful classes of society. Christianity began among such classes, and it has never succeeded very well on higher planes to the neglect of such classes. If the brother who has been so unfortunate as to lose his hat in this lair of the devil will throw away his stilted, holier-than-thou, clerical dignity and inaugurate an earnest crusade against the devil in this stronghold, his misfortune may yet prove a blessing to the city, the whole country, the church, and generations yet unborn. And if those who are gaping in open-eyed astonishment at a preacher's hat in a sinful place and bewailing the smirch upon the preacher's character as a reflection on the cause of Christianity will wade into this sink of shame and preach the gospel in earnest, they may yet save many precious souls, and, peradventure, save the hat !

In the progress of this case one of the " bad and abandoned women " was asked whether she ever went to church. She answered :

"No; the religious people in Nashville will not allow my sort to come into their churches."

And yet we sing:

> While the lamp holds out to burn,
> The vilest sinner may return.

Well, perhaps so—if he should happen to be a *man!* But what is this city of churches and preachers doing to save "bad and abandoned women?" What church will throw open its doors and invite these wretched sinners to come and hear the gospel? What preachers or other Christians will go out into the highways and compel them by loving persuasion to come and enjoy the gospel feast? One hundred dollars to save a preacher's old hat from these wretched haunts of vice is good, but an earnest effort to save souls from these cesspools of iniquity would be better. Do not these ruined women need the gospel? Is anybody preaching to them? Does not Jesus love them? Did he not die for them? I am glad to say something has been done for them by the good Christians of Nashville. Some noble, consecrated women have for years been conducting a home mission for these sin-cursed daughters of our common Father. A few noble preachers have defied public sentiment and preached the gospel among these unfortunate sinners. All honor to these blessed people of God for this. But the churches of Nashville have not yet done their whole duty along this line. Indeed, the *churches* of Nashville have not done anything at all. The work that has been done has been simply the individual efforts of a few noble souls.

But we are told that these "bad and abandoned women" cannot be saved. It is argued that they are too far lost to all sense of shame or self-respect to be reached by the gospel. It is sufficient reply to all this to say the Bible teaches that Christ came to call not the righteous, but *sinners,* to repentance. If language means anything at all, the Bible teaches clearly that such characters can be saved. In view of all the Scriptures teach on this point, I am frank to say that if there is no power in Christianity to save a "bad and abandoned woman," the whole thing is a humbug and a delusion. But "bad and abandoned women" have been saved right here in Nashville. And how many of them do we read about in the Bible who were saved? Who was it that received the first messengers sent by the people of God into the promised land, protected them from the violence of a mob in Jericho, sent them out secretly another way, and so saved her soul and immortalized her name by her *faith?* A "bad and abandoned woman." Who believed John, the forerunner sent to prepare the way of the Lord, when the holy church folks declined to hear him? The publicans and "bad and abandoned women." Who listened to the preaching of Jesus at Jacob's well, believed to the saving of her soul, rushed back to her native town, and by her zeal brought the whole village out to hear him? A "bad and abandoned woman." Who heard the loving voice of the Lord in accents tenderly sweet say: "Neither do I condemn thee: go, and sin no more?" A "bad and abandoned woman." Who was it the Lord tenderly loved, and out of whom he cast seven devils? A "bad and abandoned woman." Who stood with the Lord's few steadfast friends in the world's darkest midnight hour, hovering around the cross on which the Prince of Glory died, surrounded by foes and deserted

by friends? A "bad and abandoned woman." Who
was among the faithful few to visit first the tomb in
which the Savior slept and on the resurrection morn first
to greet the risen Lord and proclaim to a sorrowing
world the tidings of great joy? A "bad and abandoned
woman." How strangely does all this contrast with the
case in hand! A preacher takes a leisurely evening
stroll, dressed in immaculate linen, kid gloves, plug hat,
and clerical garments—fat, sleek, self-satisfied, and far-
ing sumptuously every day. He comes near to the place
where scores of wretched women are literally caged
by the devil. Does he lift up his voice and preach the
gospel of our salvation to those sinful women? Of
course not. He dare not attempt such a thing. Public
opinion will not permit it. Why should organized religion try to convert such characters? What could they
do to build up the church or support the ministry if they
were converted? The preacher is hurrying by these
lost souls with his spotless robes of clerical holiness
drawn close about him, when—O, horrors!—they get his
hat. What would nabob society in Nashville say of a
preacher if they knew his old hat had been among these
wretched sinners? The good brother spends a hundred
dollars secretly trying to fish his old beaver out of that
sin-polluted place. This is his statement of the facts.
It was all well enough to save the hat, of course, but
ought not some effort be made to loose those women
whom Satan has bound lo these many years, and save
them, too? They are somebody's sisters. Ah, brethren, in one sense they are everybody's sisters. There
was a time when they could carry their sorrows and
troubles to loving mothers, and weep, and pray, and
laugh, and love in purity and innocence under the sa-

cred roof of the old family home. Somewhere there are loving, breaking hearts yearning for them now, and many a grief-stricken home would be filled with joy and gladness at the news of their salvation. There would be joy with the angels in heaven if one of these poor sinners should turn away from her life of shame and purify her soul in obeying the truth. And can it be possible that these poor sinners never sigh for the rest which none but Jesus can give? Do they never feel weary and heavy laden? Is there no way to lead them gently and lovingly out of the miseries of their loathsome lives into the peace and joys of righteousness and true holiness? Do they never think of mother, sisters, father, brothers, the dear old home, and the innocence and pleasures of their childhood? Do they never think of the old family burying ground, with its sacred memories and its quiet solemnity? Do they never long for a loving word, a tender caress, or a mother's kiss? Do they never think of death or long for heaven? Have they no pains, fevers, sorrows, or cares which make them feel the need of friends and of Jesus? Ah, brethren, it cannot be that all longings for a better life are dead in them! If they can only be made to understand how dearly Jesus loves them, how anxiously angels long to see them repent, and how tenderly all true Christians would share their sorrows, comfort their hearts, and lead them away from these devil's dens of misery and ruin, surely they will repent and be saved.

"Go ye into all the world and preach the gospel to every creature. He that believeth and is baptized shall be saved; but he that believeth not shall be damned." "Come unto me, all ye that labor and are heavy laden, and I will give you rest. Take my yoke upon you, and learn of me; for I am meek and lowly in heart; and ye shall find rest unto your souls. For my yoke is easy and my burden is light." "For the Son of man is come to seek and to save that which is lost." "They that be whole need not a physician, but they that be sick." These texts of scripture certainly recognize no line beyond which we are not required to preach the gospel.

I have no *plans* to suggest, no *policy* to dictate. If only the Spirit of the Master can touch and quicken the hearts of the disciples, I believe—yea, I *know*—the gospel of the grace of God will be carried freely to those who now sit in regions of darkness without God and without hope within a stone's throw of our churches.

THE DEVIL IN THE CHURCHES.

In commenting on Sam Jones in Nashville last week, I took occasion to say the church population of Nashville did not back up the gifted evangelist from Georgia very heartily on some points. In fact, I intimated that the thing which Sam Jones called the "church population of Nashville" is no better than it ought to be, anyhow, and frankly expressed the opinion that a vast deal of it is a humbug so far as piety, or even morality, is concerned. Some of my remarks were copied into the *Evening Herald,* of this city, and attributed to David Lipscomb. This created quite a stir in certain quarters, and, for a time, it looked like we would have a sure enough "tempest in a teapot." Some of my own dear brethren seemed particularly worried for fear I would "damage the cause" or "injure our meeting," and insisted on inserting the following modifying paragraph in the next issue of the *Herald:*

To the Herald:

You published in yesterday's *Herald* an article, purporting to be from Brother David Lipscomb, the reading of which would indicate that it is an official attack by the Christian church upon Sam Jones, which is not true. The church did not authorize the article, neither do I believe it would indorse all of it. Furthermore, the Christian church has no official organ.   J. C. MARTIN.

I was inclined to think when I wrote the article that the church would not indorse all of it—that is, a *part* of the church. There was an uncomplimentary allusion to the race track, and a statement that some church members in Nashville under certain circumstances would get "too drunk to carry a torchlight in a Democratic procession," which I was afraid would not be *unanimously* indorsed by the church. And if the GOSPEL ADVOCATE had been the *official* organ of the church, it might not have touched those things up. I have never had anything to do with official organs. The fact is, I have never learned to play a tune on one yet. Neither have I ever asked the church to "authorize" any article I feel it my duty to publish. I have made no attack on Sam Jones. I honestly differ from him in some things; and if the church will not "authorize" me to modestly express my opinion about as public a man as Sam Jones, I think Sam himself will grant me that small privilege. Is it the sin unpardonable to criticise Sam Jones? "On what meat doth this our Cæsar feed, that he hath grown so great?" My only criticism on him was a modest expression of an opinion that he would accomplish more good by keeping out of politics and devoting himself entirely to the preaching of the gospel. This criticism, if indeed it be lawful to call it a " criticism," applied to every preacher in the world, as well as to Sam Jones. Sam may differ with me about this, and I may be wrong, but it is my honest conviction modestly expressed. In all this I protest that I have made no " *attack* " on Sam Jones.

The line of my attack is against the devil in the churches in Nashville; and if those few brethren of mine will not allow the " Christian church " to " authorize " me to make an " official attack," then I will make the best fight I can on my own hook, so help me God. Let it be understood, then, that this fight is a little personal matter between me and the devil. Those few brethren of mine will keep the " Christian church " at a safe distance till the " tussel " is over. If I should get the best of the fight, they may let the " Christian church " " authorize " me to be " an official organ; " who knows? But if the devil should clean me up, it is only my business. And if these little personal difficulties between me and spiritual wickedness in high places in Nashville are liable to " damage the cause " or " injure the meeting," it would not be a bad idea to close the meeting and send " the cause " to the country for its health. If the devil and I both stay in this town, there is going to be trouble sure. We never have been able to get on peaceably since I joined the church.

Notwithstanding the points of difference between me and Sam Jones, I like him. He is, in many respects, a man after my own heart. He made a brave fight against some evils in Nashville which sadly need correcting. Church members are notoriously connected with some things Sam Jones justly criticised, and along this line he was not heartily supported by the churches. The fact is, some church folks in Nashville are afraid to go squarely at certain public sins, for fear they will "damage the cause" or "injure the meeting." Everybody in Nashville knows, if he knows anything at all, that the celebrated Nashville races are largely owned, operated, and patronized by members of churches. The public records of our courts give abundant evidence of gross immorality, corruption, and fraud, the very name of which is too bad to mention in these columns, in some of the most prominent, widely known, and influential lay members of churches in the city. Alluding to the statement in my last week's article that some church members under certain circumstances will get "too drunk to carry a torchlight in a Democratic procession," those few brethren of mine who are taking care of the "Christian church" admit that they know a goodly number of that sort themselves. If there is a church in Nashville that has no member that is notoriously guilty of unscriptural conduct, let it speak, for it "have I offended." But, brethren, I am frank to say that I feel no particular interest in the welfare of any "cause," or the success of any "meeting," that can be damaged by a plain, straightforward rebuke of these things. But I am told it will damage the cause of prohibition to expose these things just now. I am accused of being in league with whisky men. Ah, brethren, in one sense I am in league with a few whisky men, I confess. God bless you, we all belong to the same church! But do we hope to carry prohibition by covering up such iniquities in the churches? Suppose we should carry prohibition and close all the saloons, what then? How are we going to run the churches on the present basis with-

out saloons? Where would the brethren get the need-
ful? I don't believe there is a church in Nashville
that could be run twenty-four hours, with its present
membership, without whisky. I have been a prohibi-
tionist many years myself. I have voted for prohibition
on all parts of the ground. I am beginning to think,
however, it would be well to take a little broader view
of this question. Why not make a bold dash for prohibition in the churches as well as in politics while we are
about it?

I have heard preachers denounce and abuse politicians
and public officers for corruption, fraud, and cowardice
till it is becoming monotonous. What I want to hear
now, by way of varying the monotony, is the opinion of
politicians and public officers as to the cowardice of
preachers. We are told by clerical politicians that the
political parties are afraid to avow themselves against
immorality in politics, lest they damage the party and
defeat the nominee. We are told that even public officers wink at violations of the law and neglect to prose-
cute those who trample the laws of the country under
their feet, lest they defeat themselves for another term
of office. Doubtless this is all true. But what of the
preachers? What do they more than others? Are not
churches sometimes afraid to show themselves against
ungodliness in religion, lest they " damage the cause "
and " injure the meeting? " Do preachers always enforce the laws of their own churches against ungodly
members who boldly and openly trample the sacred
principles of religion under their impious feet? Have
preachers proved themselves fearless and faithful in the
matter of enforcing the laws of their own churches
against rich and influential members? In one word,

are the laws which govern churches enforced by preachers any better than our public officers enforce the laws which govern the State? And if preachers have not the backbone to enforce the laws of their own churches, what assurance have we that they would enforce the laws of the State if they should be elected to public office? If a preacher will wink at open violations of the laws of his own church in those who are rich and influential for fear of losing his pastorate in the next election, what assurance have we that he would not pass by the offenses of rich and influential politicians, if he were a public officer, for fear of losing the nomination in the next convention?

Is it more important to enforce the laws of Tennessee in politics than to enforce the laws of God in the church? Nay, verily. I am not sure but that a godless, world-loving, time-serving, popularity-seeking, and sin-concealing church will do as much deviltry in a community as a saloon. The fact is, such church is little more than the gilded antechamber and ornamental screens behind which the deviltry of saloons, gambling dens, and houses of prostitution is carried on. Such a church corrupts the right way of the Lord, makes a mock of religion, puts Christ to an open shame, and neutralizes the power of the gospel to save sinners. Our boys all know that a saloon is a bad place. They are taught to shun it as they would shun a deadly thing. But a church poses as a model of virtue and morality. It draws all men unto it. And once a boy sees the hypocrisy and ungodliness of such a church, he feels encouraged and emboldened to enter into all kinds of sin and debauchery. I have worked and prayed and voted for prohibition these many years. I expect to continue

20

along that line. I would rejoice to see the day when the abominable traffic in intoxicating liquors is ended. But that day will never come till we have a better state of things in the churches and religious homes in this country. And while we are laboring to close up the saloons, I give my voice to clean out and convert or else close up the ungodly and time-serving churches all over the land. And when I suggested that if preachers would benefit the cause of law and order, morality and prohibition, they should let up on politics long enough to overhaul the moral running gear of their own church members, "at my first answer no man stood with me, but all men forsook me"—save David Lipscomb and a few others, God bless them! The public was hastily informed that "the Christian church did not authorize the article," and that it would not indorse it. All men were notified that I was not an "official organ," anyhow. "I pray God that it may not be laid to their charge." I am a poor and unworthy servant of the living God—a sort of homeless orphan in a strange land, as it were. I wandered out from Arkansas but a few months ago, and I may have to return soon with the discouragement of defeat in a "tussel" with the devil shadowing my heart, but by the help of God I will fight it out on this line. Put me down as a volunteer for life or during the war.

For myself, I don't care whether those few brethren of mine "authorize" the "Christian church" to "indorse" me on these questions or not. I am so clearly in the right that I don't feel the need of any indorsement. But while these dear brethren are monopolizing and arbitrarily dictating the indorsing business for the whole church, it occurs to me that it would not be a bad idea for them to see if they can find anybody who will "indorse" that part of the "Christian church" which they represent on the basis they put it.

"YOURS OUTRAGED."

Some time ago a statement appeared in the *Louisville Daily Commercial* concerning the First Christian Church, of Paducah, Ky., to the effect that:

A ladies' society gave a series of entertainments for the purpose of raising a church fund; and as the congregation comprises many wealthy people, they were highly successful. When the time came to put the money to practical uses, a difference of opinion developed, one faction being in favor of expending it on church repairs and the other for a church organ. The church-repair party was headed by Elder J. C. Tully, a minister who is at present without a charge, but couples itinerant preaching with a real-estate and insurance business for a living. The organ faction was led by the Rev. L. H. Stine, the church's stated pastor. The war has been carried on with great bitterness. The organ faction, being in the majority, succeeded in carrying their point, and purchased a three-thousand-dollar organ, besides hiring an organist to play it at a salary of six hundred dollars a year. The result has been to split the church in two, and dissensions and discord reign supreme. At one of the Sunday-morning meetings a short time since a disgraceful altercation took place between Elder Stine and Elder Tully, during which Tully is alleged to have approached Stine in a threatening manner with an open knife. The influence of the church membership was powerful enough to silence the local press, but they could not silence the grand jury, as at its session just closed Tully was indicted for disturbing public worship. It is one of the bitterest church wrangles that was ever inaugurated, and the fact that two Christian ministers are the leaders of the opposing forces renders it intensely interesting, and the rest of the Christian community look on with holy horror.

This extract from the *Louisville Daily Commercial* was published on the first page of the GOSPEL ADVOCATE, with a few words of comment, and soon afterwards the following letter was received at this office, written from Fulton, Ky.:

My attention has just been called to a slanderous article on your first page of last issue. You, of course, are ready to prove the truth and establish the facts, or you would not defile the pages of the GOSPEL ADVOCATE with that of which you know nothing as to its truth. You will have a chance to air your knowledge, as it is my intention when I return home to place your paper in the hands of my attorney, with instructions to give you a case at law on your hands, and we will see what you know.

Yours outraged,   J. C. TULLY.

I have no disposition to do Brother Tully or any one else the slightest injustice, but I think I understand the situation, and I do not yet consider my comment on the extract from the *Commercial* at all premature or impertinent. The statement went unchallenged in the *Commercial*, greatly to the disgrace of religion and humiliation of the brethren, and it was sent to me by a preacher of well-known discretion and church-wide reputation, who lives in Kentucky, with the suggestion that it ought to receive some attention. It occurs to me that, instead of flippantly referring the matter to "my attorney," Brother Tully ought to give some explanation of how such damaging reports got into the daily papers. And while I am waiting to hear from "my attorney,"

I take occasion to remark that the spirit and tone of the brother's letter would not indicate, to my mind, that he is a bright and shining illustration of the doctrine of Him who said: "Resist not evil; but whosoever shall smite thee on thy right cheek, turn to him the other also. And if any man will sue thee at law, and take away thy coat, let him have thy cloak also. . . . Love your enemies, bless them that curse you, do good to them that hate you, and pray for them which despitefully use you and persecute you." If I wanted to gather together a congregation of folks who would give the world an illustration of this doctrine in their daily lives, it seems to me that I would not care to take into the number very many such people as "yours outraged" seems to be, judging from the spirit and tone of his letter. A very little of such spirit as this letter expresses, when mixed up with a three-thousand-dollar organ and a six-hundred-dollar organist, will soon cause trouble in an average city church.

A QUESTION OF DIAGNOSIS AND PRESCRIPTION.

Another secular paper in Kentucky has published a sensational account of the troubles in the church at Paducah, and still another paper in Ohio has copied this new version of the fracas. I notice also an account of it in a Texas paper, and still further information has reached me from trustworthy private sources as to the lamentable condition of affairs in that congregation. Up to the present writing I have heard nothing from "my attorney," and I shall probably not have an op-

portunity to " air " my knowledge in " a case at law,"
after all.   The letter from " yours outraged " may have
been designed to make the impression that the reports
were false and slanderous without committing even the
writer of the letter to a straightforward denial of the
facts.   How many other papers have published and
commented upon the unpleasant affair I do not know,
but it is safe to say the matter is no longer a secret
with the reading public.   All this furnishes material for
reflection and more business for " my attorney " and
" yours outraged."   It may as well be remarked that
many people, even at this distance, have known for a
long time an unscriptural state of affairs existed in that
church; but so long as it was a merely local and somewhat private and personal matter, it was not deemed
the province of a public religious journalist to advert to
it.   Now that it has become a topic of public comment
and general notoriety, however, it seems pertinent to
descant upon the scriptural and unscriptural principles
involved in it.   After a three-thousand-dollar organ had
been bought and a six-hundred-dollar-a-year organist
had been employed, and after the church had been " split
in two," and " dissensions and discord reigned supreme,"
according to the latest version of the case, as published
in a secular paper, " the row culminated in an altercation in church between the two preachers, when Tully
is alleged to have drawn his knife and threatened to go
for the intestines of Stine."   This is the case as I understand it.   The issue between Tully and Stine is not
whether the organ should be used in the worship.   If I
rightly understand them, they both favor the use of the
organ.   Nor do " dissensions and discord reign supreme " in the church on account of any difference

among the members as to whether the organ should be used. The church has used an organ regularly for years; and if I am not misinformed, even other musical instruments besides the organ have been used at one time and another as a sort of band in that church, "to draw a crowd and build up the cause." Indeed, they seem to have tried about everything to build up the church, except, possibly, a good supply of what the Methodist brethren would call "heartfelt religion," and I dare say they would have tried that a few times by way of experiment if they could have bought it and hired somebody to operate it on reasonable terms. That church seems to be very enterprising, and liberal almost to a fault in the use of money collected by "a series of entertainments," in the matter of pushing various schemes "to draw a crowd and build up the cause." The naked issue in this case is whether certain money which "a ladies' society" has collected by "a series of entertainments" shall be used to repair the church or pay for the new organ. Stripped of all irrelevancies, the whole matter seems to resolve itself into a simple question as to who shall have his way and carry his point in the case. As between Tully, who is in favor of repairing the church, and Stine, who favors the purchase of the organ, my sympathies are decidedly with Tully in the fracas. If there is one thing in the wide world which the case, on its very face, does show, it is that the church ought to be repaired. In truth, I am ready to go even further than Tully and say boldly that instead of "repairing the church," we ought to have a new one out of the whole cloth. And if there is anything which these warring preachers, in their present state of feelings, do not need, it is an organ. Feeling as they do just now, it may well be doubted whether they could play a tune on an organ if they had one. Possibly this explains why they have agreed to pay a man six hundred dollars a year to play on it for them. These belligerent preachers seem to be somewhat like the man who, according to Shakespeare, " hath no music in his soul." What we ought to do, first of all, therefore, is strive to bring about a more harmonious tone in these two discordant notes in the sacred harp, as we might say. And to this end, I am disposed to think myself that the internal apparatus of both preachers ought to be overhauled; but Tully's diagnosis is clearly at fault in locating the trouble in the *intestines,* and his remedy is even worse than his diagnosis. The real seat of the malignity is unquestionably in the *heart,* and a surgical operation would only weaken the patient without the slightest prospect of arresting the disease. " The love of God shed abroad in our hearts by the Holy Ghost which is given unto us " is a specific for all such maladies, and no other remedy contains " the potency and the promise " of relief. Nothing can be done, therefore, till Tully puts up his knife, and I shall steadily press this point, not because I think Stine is at all likely to receive any bodily injuries from him, but that there is danger that he may hurt himself or cut some of his friends in his wild career. " They that take the sword shall perish with the sword." Moreover, he is but wasting precious time and aggravating the disease with a remedy as inefficient as Godfrey's Cordial for original sin. The Scriptures clearly require him to love Brother Stine, no matter how Stine has treated him and no matter whether he can agree with him or not, and he will find it just as easy to love him *en masse,* as it were, as by sections after he has cut him all to giblets.

This fracas is all the more to be deplored because both preachers are bright and shining specimens of progressive methods in church work and luminous advocates of sweet-spirited journalism in religion. Moreover, they are both missionary men of the most pronounced type, and all their influence is freely given to arouse a missionary spirit in the churches. It is gravely to be feared, therefore, that their animus may spread abroad even to heathen nations, and in that case the last state of those benighted races might be as bad as these belligerent preachers. Now if Tully and Stine and the churches they influence were do-nothing, antiorgan, antimissionary, and antieverything-else sort of people, this difficulty would be a matter of small moment one way or the other. In such a case it might well be left to its inevitable fate to " die out like the old Hardshell Baptists." But under all the circumstances I make bold to say: " Beloved, these things ought not so to be." The public should be apprised of the nature and extent of this spiritual malady; and if nothing can be done to arrest the contagion in that locality, those who have any regard for the spiritual health of other regions should promptly and rigidly quarantine against it. And, after all, if this unpleasant affair shall serve to turn the public mind and heart away from human weakness and folly to the strength and wisdom of God, it will not be without good to the world. The proneness of folks to measure " themselves by themselves " and compare " themselves among themselves " is only evil continually, and anything which tends to shake the confidence of the public mind in human plans and parties in religion and turn the individual heart to the appointments and ordinances of the Lord as revealed in the Holy Scriptures should be hailed as a public blessing, even though it come in the guise of a humiliating church wrangle or a disgraceful altercation between two preachers in the house of God. Those who drink the waters of life from polluted streams after they have meandered through the cesspools of man's iniquity, can never enjoy vigorous spiritual health, anyhow, and anything which stirs up the filth of human depravity so as to drive the world to the refreshing fountain of free grace and divine perfection in Christ Jesus, as revealed in the Holy Scriptures, is a rich blessing to the world. Therefore we exhort: "Fret not thyself because of evil doers." "Trust in the Lord, and do good; so shalt thou dwell in the land, and verily thou shalt be fed."

INDEX.

Printed in the United States
1182600003B/58-135